THE ETHNIC-RELIGIOUS IDENTITY
of the ETHIOPIAN IN ACTS 8:26–40

THE ETHNIC-RELIGIOUS IDENTITY
of the ETHIOPIAN IN ACTS 8:26–40

Echoic Allusion, Culture, and Narrative

Jongmun Jung

WIPF & STOCK · Eugene, Oregon

THE ETHNIC-RELIGIOUS IDENTITY OF THE ETHIOPIAN IN ACTS 8:26–40
Echoic Allusion, Culture, and Narrative

Copyright © 2024 Jongmun Jung. All rights reserved. Except for brief quotations in critical publications or reviews, no part of this book may be reproduced in any manner without prior written permission from the publisher. Write: Permissions, Wipf and Stock Publishers, 199 W. 8th Ave., Suite 3, Eugene, OR 97401.

Wipf & Stock
An Imprint of Wipf and Stock Publishers
199 W. 8th Ave., Suite 3
Eugene, OR 97401

www.wipfandstock.com

PAPERBACK ISBN: 979-8-3852-1462-4
HARDCOVER ISBN: 979-8-3852-1463-1
EBOOK ISBN: 979-8-3852-1464-8

VERSION NUMBER 052324

Scripture quotations are from The ESV® Bible (The Holy Bible, English Standard Version®), © 2001 by Crossway, a publishing ministry of Good News Publishers. Used by permission. All rights reserved.

IN MY LOVE

Dong Kyun JUNG

&

Kyhi Ja KIM

Contents

Abbreviations | ix
Introduction | xv

CHAPTER 1
Scholarly Studies of the Ethiopian | 1

CHAPTER 2
Methods of the Study | 20

CHAPTER 3
Textual Tradition of the Assembly of the Lord | 37

CHAPTER 4
Cultural Background of the Ethiopian | 100

CHAPTER 5
Literary Approach to the Ethiopian | 129

Conclusion | 162

Bibliography | 167

Abbreviations

AB	Anchor Bible
Ag. Ap.	*Against Apion*, by Josephus
AGJU	Arbeiten zur Geschichte des antiken Judentums und des Urchristentums
AMS	Artscroll Mishnah Series: A Rabbinic Commentary to the Six Orders of the Mishnah
ANAKN	*Ancient Nubia: African Kingdoms on the Nile*. Edited by Marjorie M. Fisher, Peter Lacovara, Salima Ikram, and Sue D'Auria. With photographs by Chester Higgins Jr. Cairo: The American University in Cairo Press, 2012.
Ann.	*Annales*, by Tacitus
Ant.	*Jewish Antiquities*, by Josephus
AOAT	Alter Orient und Altes Testament
ApOTC	Apollos Old Testament Commentary
AYBRL	Anchor Yale Bible Reference Library
BAFCS	The Book of Acts in Its First Century Setting
BBR	*Bulletin for Biblical Research*
BCAW	Blackwell Companions to the Ancient World
BDAG	Danker, Frederick W., Walter Bauer, William F. Arndt, and F. Wilbur Gingrich. *Greek-English Lexicon of the New Testament and Other Early Christian Literature*. 3rd ed. Chicago: University of Chicago Press, 2000
BDB	Brown, Francis, S. R. Driver, and Charles A. Briggs. *A Hebrew and English Lexicon of the Old Testament: With an Appendix containing the Biblical Aramaic*. Oxford: Clarendon, 1906

BECNT	Baker Exegetical Commentary on the New Testament	
Bell. civ.	*Bella civilia*, Appian	
BHS5	*Biblia Hebraica Stuttgartensia*. Edited by Karl Elliger and Wilhelm Rudolph. Revised by Adrian Schenker. 5th ed. Stuttgart: Deutsche Bibelgesellschaft, 1997	
Bib	*Biblica*	
BibInt	*Biblical Interpretation*	
BibInt	Biblical Interpretation Series	
BNP	*Brill's New Pauly: Encyclopaedia of the Ancient World*. Edited by Hubert Cancik. 22 vols. Leiden: Brill, 2002–2011	
b. Šabb.	Babylonian Talmud Šabbat	
BSac	*Bibliotheca Sacra*	
b. Yebam.	Babylonian Talmud Yebamot	
BZAW	Beihefte zur Zeitschrift für die alttestamentliche Wissenschaft	
CCS.OT	Communicator's Commentary Series Old Testament	
CFTL	Clark's Foreign Theological Library	
Cher.	*On the Cherubim*, by Philo	
Claud.	*Divus Claudius*, by Suetonius	
ConcC	Concordia Commentary	
CRINT	Compendia Rerum Iudaicarum ad Novum Testamentum	
Cyr.	*Cyropaedia*, Xenophon	
Det.	*That the Worse Attacks the Better*, by Philo	
Deus	*That God Is Unchangeable*, by Philo	
DJG	*Dictionary of Jesus and the Gospels*. Edited by Joel B. Green, Jeannine K. Brown, and Nicholas Perrin. 2nd ed. Downers Grove, IL: InterVarsity, 2013	
DLNT	*Dictionary of the Later New Testament and its Developments*. Edited by R. P. Martin and P. H. Davids. Downers Grove, IL: InterVarsity, 1997	
DOTP	*Dictionary of the Old Testament: Pentateuch*. Edited by T. Desmond Alexander and David W. Baker. Downers Grove, IL: InterVarsity, 2003	
EBC	*The Expositor's Bible Commentary*	

Ebr.	*On Drunkenness*, by Philo
ECC	Eerdmans Critical Commentary
EDNT	*Exegetical Dictionary of the New Testament*. Edited by Horst Balz and Gerhard Schneider. ET. 3 vols. Grand Rapids: Eerdmans, 1990–1993
EEC	Evangelical Exegetical Commentary
EncJud	*Encyclopedia Judaica*. Edited by Fred Skolnik and Michael Berenbaum. 2nd ed. 22 vols. Detroit: Macmillan Reference USA, 2007
Exp	*The Expositor*
FAT	Forschungen zum Alten Testament
Flac.	*Pro Flacco*, by Cicero
Flacc.	*Against Flaccus*, by Philo
GELS	*A Greek-English Lexicon of the Septuagint*. Takamitsu Muraoka. Leuven: Peeters, 2009
Geogr.	*Geography*, by Strabo
Haer.	*Against Heresies*, by Irenaeus
HALOT	*The Hebrew and Aramaic Lexion of the Old Testament*. Ludwid Koehler, Walter Baumgartner, and Johann J. Stamm. Translated and edited under the supervisions of Mervyn E. J. Richardson. 4 vols. Leiden: Brill, 1994–1999.
HBM	Hebrew Bible Monographs
HCOT	Historical Commentary on the Old Testament
Her.	*Who Is the Heir?*, by Philo
Hist.	*Histories*, by Herodotus
hist. Alex.	*History of Alexander*, by Curtius
Hist. eccl.	*Ecclesiastical History*, by Eusebius
HNTC	Holman New Testament Commentary
HOTE	Handbooks for Old Testament Exegesis
HTR	*Harvard Theological Review*
ICC	International Critical Commentary
Ios.	*On the Life of Joseph*, by Philo

ISBL	Indiana Studies in Biblical Literature	
ITC	International Theological Commentary	
J.W.	*Jewish War*, by Josephus	
JAAC	*Journal of Aesthetics and Art Criticism*	
JBL	*Journal of Biblical Literature*	
JSJ	*Journal for the Study of Judaism*	
JSJSup	Supplements to the Journal for the Study of Judaism	
JSNT	*Journal for the Study of New Testament*	
JSNTSup	Journal for the Study of the New Testament Supplement Series	
JSOTSup	Journal for the Study of the Old Testament Supplement Series	
JSS	*Journal of Semitic Studies*	
KEK	Kritisch-exegetischer Kommentar über das Neue Testament	
LCL	Loeb Classical Library	
Leg.	*Allegorical Interpretation*, by Philo	
Legat.	*On the Embassy to Gaius*, by Philo	
LHBOTS	Library of Hebrew Bible/Old Testament Studies	
Life	*The Life*, by Josephus	
LLS	Lightfoot Legacy Set	
LNTS	The Library of New Testament Studies	
LXX	*Septuaginta*. Edited by Alfred Rahlfs. Revised by Robert Hanhart. Rev. ed. Stuttgart: Deutsche Bibelgesellschaft, 2006	
MBI	Methods in Biblical Interpretation	
Migr.	*On the Migration of Abraham*, by Philo	
MT	Masoretic Text	
Mut.	*On the Change of Names*, by Philo	
m. Nid.	Mishnah Niddah	
m. Yebam.	Mishnah Yebamot	
NAC	New American Commentary	
NETS	*A New English Translation of the Septuagint*. Edited by Albert Pietersma and Benjamin G. Wright. New York: Oxford University Press, 2007	

NICOT	New International Commentary on the Old Testament
NIDOTTE	*New International Dictionary of Old Testament Theology and Exegesis*. Edited by Willem A. VanGemeren. 5 vols. Grand Rapids: Zondervan, 1997
NOAA	*The New Oxford Annotated Apocrypha: New Revised Standard Version*. Edited by Michael D. Coogan. 4th ed. New York: Oxford University Press, 2010
NSBT	New Studies in Biblical Theology
NSVS	Nelson's Super Value Series
NTC	New Testament Commentary
NTD	Das Neue Testament Deutsch
NTE	New Testament for Everyone
NTL	New Testament Library
NTS	*New Testament Studies*
OBS	Oxford Bible Series
ÖBS	Österreichische biblische Studien
Od.	*Odyssey*, by Homer
OQR	Oxford Quick Reference
OTL	Old Testament Library
OTM	Oxford Theological Monographs
OTP	*Old Testament Pseudepigrapha*. Edited by James H. Charlesworth. 2 vols. New York: Doubleday, 1983, 1985
PACS	Philo of Alexandria Commentary Series
PBM	Paternoster Biblical Monographs
PFES	Publications of the Finnish Exegetical Society
PNTC	Pillar New Testament Commentary
QE	*Questions and Answers on Exodus*, by Philo
RB	*Revue Biblique*
REC	Reformed Expository Commentary
RevQ	*Revue de Qumran*
SBGP	Stuttgarter Beiträge zur Geschichte und Politik
SBL	Society of Biblical Literature

SJ	Studia Judaica
SJLA	Studies in Judaism in Late Antiquity
SNTSMS	Society for New Testament Studies Monograph Series
Somn.	*On Dreams*, by Philo
SP	Sacra Pagina
Spec.	*On the Special Laws*, by Philo
SS	Studia Samaritana
TANZ	Texte und Arbeiten zum neutestamentlichen Zeitalter
TDNT	*Theological Dictionary of the New Testament*. Edited by Gerhard Kittel and Gerhard Friedrich. Translated by Geoffrey W. Bromiley. 10 vols. Grand Rapids: Eerdmans, 1964–1976
TDOT	*Theological Dictionary of the Old Testament*. Edited by G. Johannes Botterweck and Helmer Ringgren. Translated by John T. Willis et al. 8 vols. Grand Rapids: Eerdmans, 1974–2006
TJ	*Trinity Journal*
TOTC	Tyndale Old Testament Commentaries
TTC	Teach the Text Commentary
TS	*Theological Studies*
TynBul	*Tyndale Bulletin*
Virt.	*On the Virtues*, by Philo
VT	*Vetus Testamentum*
WBC	Word Biblical Commentary
WUNT	Wissenschaftliche Untersuchungen zum Neuen Testament
y. Yebam.	Jerusalem Talmud Yebamot
ZECNT	Zondervan Exegetical Commentary on the New Testament
ZNW	*Zeitschrift für die neutestamentliche Wissenschaft und die Kunde der älteren Kirche*

Introduction

ACTS 8:26–40 IS THE episode of the Ethiopian. Philip, one of the seven chosen to care for the Hellenist Christians in the Jerusalem church, approached the Ethiopian and evangelized him. Luke introduces the Ethiopian as (1) an Ethiopian, (2) a eunuch, (3) an official, (4) a pilgrim, and (5) as reading the Isaiah scroll. Among others, his origin from Ethiopia and his attachment to the temple in Jerusalem cause scholarly interest in his ethnic and religious identity. Scholars propose one of three options for this topic: this man is (1) a God-fearing uncircumcised gentile, (2) a gentile who converted to Judaism through circumcision, or (3) an African of Jewish descent.

To continue this scholarly discussion, five questions must be answered: (1) Is it legitimate to use the Deut 23:1 stipulation as a criterion to conclude that the Ethiopian in Acts 8:26–40 was an uncircumcised gentile? (2) Is Luke using so-called strategic ambiguity as a technique to make the Ethiopian appear to be distinct from Cornelius in Acts 10, although he is not so in terms of ethnicity and religion? (3) Is there room for the Ethiopian, as a eunuch, to be more closely related to the Samaritans (Acts 8:9–25) in accordance with the social entities of "foreigners" and "eunuchs" in Isa 56:1–8? (4) As an individual episode, in what ways is it meaningful? (5) How does it contribute to Luke's narrative development in the geographic, ethnic, and religious expansion of the gospel?

These are the areas to be studied in this work. The goal is to prove that the Ethiopian in Acts 8:26–40 is an African of Jewish descent who is affiliated to God's covenant people but excluded from the cultic setting of the temple, as the Ethiopian episode fits well into Luke's gradual narrative development in regard to the geographic, ethnic, and religious progression of the gospel in Acts.

One of the challenges in this scholarly discussion is how to define ethnicity. Anthropologically, this subject matter is ambiguous, often confused

xvi Introduction

with race.[1] This thesis uses David G. Horrell's definition of ethnicity: "the default term we use for discussing the kind of constructed group identity that is built on beliefs about the range of issues," such as "kinship, ancestry, homeland, culture, language, and so on."[2] His view is inclined toward the presupposition that religion is part of ethnicity, thus emphasizing their interrelatedness.[3] Although this aspect cannot be neglected, it is clear that Luke distinguishes between ethnic Jewishness and religious Judaism, as shown in Acts 2:11 ("Jews and proselytes"), 6:5 ("Nicolaus, a proselyte of Antioch"), and 13:16 ("men of Israel and you who fear God"). This distinction helps gain a better understanding of the Ethiopian.

With a focus on the Ethiopian's ethnicity and religion, this section introduces different views proposed by scholars. It begins with a brief introduction of six monographs.

---

1. Horrell, *Ethnicity and Inclusion*, 82. According to Horrell, race is related to "physical or biological characteristics." It is an outsider's point of view, "especially if these attribute particular moral qualities to a group on the basis of physiognomy or ancestry."
2. Horrell, *Ethnicity and Inclusion*, 82.
3. Horrell, *Ethnicity and Inclusion*, 83–89.

Chapter 1

Scholarly Studies of the Ethiopian

Lawrence, "The History of the Interpretation of Acts 8:26–40"

William Frank Lawrence Jr. focuses on the Ethiopian's desire to get baptized (8:27) and studies how the church fathers used the Ethiopian's baptism to defend their views about what baptism should be like. Lawrence states:

> The eunuch was often used [by the Church Fathers] as a model: (1) to encourage the unbaptized to be baptized quickly and thus put an end to the problem of Christian table fellowship with the unbaptized (Pseudo-Clement); (2) to prove that hasty baptism is permissible for those with correct faith, under abnormal circumstances, such as religious persecution (Cyprian); (3) to combat the practice of reducing the time of preparation and instruction for baptism (Augustine); (4) to convince the recalcitrant uninstructed to accept human instruction in hermeneutics (Augustine).[1]

In other words, the church fathers interpreted the Ethiopian's baptism as (1) "exceptional" (i.e., not to be followed) or (2) exemplary (i.e., a model to be followed) so that Christians should not delay their baptism.[2]

Concerning the Ethiopian's ethnic and religious background, Lawrence focuses on three points found in Acts 8:27. First, he understands the term "Ethiopian" as racial, and thus he assumes that the Ethiopian was a

---
1. Lawrence, "History of the Interpretation," 24.
2. Lawrence, "History of the Interpretation," 6.

black African.³ Second, the word "eunuch" for the Ethiopian leads him to view that the Ethiopian was a castrated eunuch. This condition negates the possibility that the Ethiopian was circumcised, so he could not be a proselyte (i.e., a circumcised gentile convert to Judaism).⁴ For this view, Lawrence uses Deut 23:1, which is the stipulation of prohibition of such a person from being admitted to the assembly of the Lord. Third, the Ethiopian's pilgrimage to Jerusalem ("to worship") shows his deep attachment to Judaism.⁵

Also, Lawrence looks at the Ethiopian's ethnic and religious background from the perspective of Luke's narrative development. He states, "There can be little doubt that for Luke the conversion of the Ethiopian eunuch shows that the Christian mission has moved beyond the conversion of Jews and Samaritans."⁶ Luke's positioning of the Ethiopian in the narrative after Jews and Samaritans leads Lawrence to argue that the Ethiopian, ethno-religiously, lies "between Jews and Samaritans, on the one side, and Gentiles, on the other side."⁷

As seen, Lawrence regards Deut 23:1 as critical in determining the Ethiopian's ethno-religious identity. Yet the nature of this verse—how it was applied in Judaism—needs clarification. Also, Luke's use of the word "Ethiopian" does not necessarily point to the Ethiopian's ethnicity. This possibility leads our study to be more focused on the diaspora Jews in the Greco-Roman world.

Martin, "The Function of Acts 8:26–40"

Clarice Jannette Martin's view about the Ethiopian's ethnicity is based on her study of how Ethiopians and the land of Ethiopia were perceived in the Greco-Roman world. For this, she refers to Homer, Herodotus, Polybius, and Strabo. Concerning the word "Ethiopian," Martin argues that the Greco-Roman world understood it as "the most common generic word denoting a Negroid type."⁸ Also, the ancient Ethiopians were active in their

---

3. Lawrence, "History of the Interpretation," 56.

4. Lawrence, "History of the Interpretation," 57. The notion that a castrated male is not circumcised is most likely because of the assumption that the practice of castration is related to his penis.

5. Lawrence, "History of the Interpretation," 57.

6. Lawrence, "History of the Interpretation," 57.

7. Lawrence, "History of the Interpretation," 57.

8. Martin, "Function of Acts," 86. Frank M. Snowden also states, "The skin of the Ethiopian was black, in fact blacker, it was noted, than that of any other people." Snowden, *Blacks in Antiquity*, 2.

international relations with the Egyptians and the Romans, so they were not an isolated people.[9] Assuming that Luke had this common understanding, Martin argues that Luke had in view the Ethiopian as such—a black African man. Also, Martin suggests that the Greco-Roman world often described the land of Ethiopia as the end of the earth.[10] However, Martin does not identify the phrase "the end of the earth" in Acts 1:8 as the land of Ethiopia, as she states:

> The results of our investigation thus far have shown that, principally, ἐσχάτου τῆς γῆς was used metaphorically to define the geographical limits of the world. This sense of geographical extremity is also apparent in classical literature in instances where ἔσχατος is used in conjunction with words that express a particular geographical proximity.[11]

Martin's point is that the Greco-Roman world often described Ethiopia as the end of the earth, yet this does not necessarily mean that Luke's use of "the end of the earth" in Acts 1:8 should be regarded as Ethiopia.[12]

From a missional perspective, Martin sees the Ethiopian's conversion to Christianity as the symbol of the mandate's (Acts 1:8c "the end of the earth") fulfillment, at least in the dimension of its initial activation.[13] The function of the Ethiopian's conversion in narrative is to foreshadow "both the inauguration of the Gentile mission, and the geographical and cultural scope of the Christian mission in general."[14] From a literary point of view, Martin understands "foreshadowing" as a literary device used by Luke to give "a clue or hint of future action, more or less definite, but stripped of exact details."[15] That is, through the Ethiopian episode, Luke intends to foreshadow a near future event (i.e., Cornelius as the gentile Christian) and a far future event (i.e., the Ethiopian's mission in the land of Ethiopia).

---

9. Martin, "Function of Acts," 92–93.

10. Homer, *Odyssey*, 1.23 "the farthermost of men" (ἔσχατοι ἀνδρῶν), 1:4–5. Herodotus, *Hist*. 3.115 "the most distant parts of the world in Asia and Libya" (ἔν τε τῇ Ἀσίῃ ἐσχατιαί εἰσι καὶ ἐν τῇ Λιβύῃ). Herodotus, *Herodotus*, 140–41. Strabo, *Geogr.* 2.5.15 "the most remote people south of the territory of Carthage" (τῶν περὶ Καρχηδόνα τόπων ὕστατοι). Strabo, *Geography of Strabo*, 460–61.

11. Martin, "Function of Acts," 80.

12. Cf. Acts 13:47.

13. Martin, "Function of Acts," 123.

14. Martin, "Function of Acts," 123.

15. Martin, "Function of Acts 8:26–40," 132. Martin introduces George Eckel Duckworth's suggestion of how a writer would utilize "foreshadowing" to develop "suspense of anticipation" (135–37). Duckworth, *Foreshadowing and Suspense in the Epics of Homer, Apollonius, and Vergil*, 37–98.

Martin's research of Ethiopia and the Ethiopians is helpful in gaining a broad picture of how the Greco-Roman world understood them. However, as she noted, Luke's use of the phrase "the end of the earth" (Acts 1:8c) might not be a referent to Ethiopia. This awareness makes it appropriate to reexamine Luke's use of the word "Ethiopian." Also, for the issue of how to synthesize the Ethiopian episode and the Cornelius episode, she emphasizes the former as what foreshadows the latter. However, the Ethiopian episode itself could be meaningful in terms of Luke's gradual narrative development.

Stachow, "'Do You Understand What You Are Reading?' (Acts 8:30)"

Mary Ann Stachow focuses on how Luke and his original audience would perceive Ethiopia. Her scope of research is on the Septuagint, Greco-Roman literature, and Second Temple Jewish literature. Her purpose is to "establish the milieu in which Luke's narrative of this particular conversion was told."[16] Her work is helpful in that it illumines the Ethiopian in Acts 8, in particular, in light of the historical relations that existed between the Israelites and the Ethiopians in the Jewish context. For this, Stachow refers to the Septuagint. The Septuagint shows five categories of perception about Ethiopia and Ethiopians: (1) depicted as positive, or at least neutral; (2) symbolic for a faraway land; (3) famous for warriors; (4) as mercenaries, ambassadors, and court officials in Israel; and (5) as a people who will one day come to worship the God of Israel on Zion.[17] Also, she suggests that Greco-Roman literature portrays the Ethiopians as pious, often in connection with Greek mythology.[18]

Concerning the Ethiopian's ethnic and religious background, Stachow argues that the Ethiopian in Acts 8 cannot be Jewish.[19] She offers two reasons, among others. First, Philo of Alexandria does not indicate the presence of the Jews in Ethiopia, even when he describes the diaspora Jews in Egypt and its surrounding regions.[20] Second, there has been no archaeological evidence of the Jewish communities in Ethiopia. Hence, Stachow views the Ethiopian in Acts 8 as "a Gentile from a far-off people renowned for their piety."[21]

16. Stachow, "'Do You Understand What You Are Reading?,'" 16.
17. Stachow, "'Do You Understand What You Are Reading?,'" 80.
18. Stachow, "'Do You Understand What You Are Reading?,'" 210.
19. Stachow, "'Do You Understand What You Are Reading?,'" 249.
20. Stachow, "'Do You Understand What You Are Reading?,'" 207.
21. Stachow, "'Do You Understand What You Are Reading?,'" 252.

Also, Stachow suggests that Luke's use of the word "eunuch" for the Ethiopian has in view the ancient practice of castration, so the Ethiopian was a castrated eunuch. For Stachow, this aspect reflects Luke's broad eschatological picture of inclusiveness—a picture identified in Isa 56:1–8 and Wis 3:24.[22]

Based on Stachow's work, there are a few things to be further studied. First, the Old Testament portrays Ethiopia (i.e., Cush) chiefly (1) as the non-Israelites who would come to Jerusalem to worship Yahweh and (2) the exiled Israelites who would return to Jerusalem. Both of them are related to Israel's eschatological restoration. Notable is Isa 11:11, in which "Cush" (i.e., Ethiopia) is one of the nations in which the Israelites are present.[23] Second, just as Stachow notes, the diaspora Jews were in the land of Egypt. The fact that Ethiopia is geographically located south of Egypt makes it necessary to study the Jews in Egypt and their possible interaction with the Ethiopians—particularly, the Jews in Elephantine, which was the southern border of Egypt neighboring with Ethiopia.

Carson, "Do You Understand What You Are Reading?"

Cottrel R. Carson illumines the Ethiopian episode from two contrasting perspectives. First, he asserts that the Ethiopian was treated as "a social and cultural alien."[24] This is due to his castrated condition, being called a eunuch, as well as his racial identity as a black African. These factors caused him to be alienated in society and even excluded from being accepted into the community of God's people. This is how Luke views the Ethiopian, as the most marginalized. Second, Carson views the church in Acts as all-inclusive, accepting even the marginalized or unaccepted into their community. Concerning this contrast, Carson states:

> I recognize that the Ethiopian eunuch is a marginal character in relation to the dominant culture in which the Acts narrative takes place, but I also recognize that his marginalization to the worldview forwarded in Acts. I understand the Ethiopian eunuch's status of alienation to be a starting point for inquiry into

---

22. Stachow, "'Do You Understand What You Are Reading?,'" 243–45.

23. The LXX translates the Hebrew word כּוּשׁ (Cush), which appears twenty-five times in the MT, as Αἰθιοπία (Ethiopia) or Αἰθίοψ (Ethiopian) except Gen 10:6 and 1 Chr 1:8 (Χους).

24. Carson, "Do You Understand What You Are Reading?," 9.

the type of worldview that Luke promotes in his portrayal of the events of the early Church.[25]

The purpose of Luke's presentation of the Ethiopian is to show "the transformation of the world, [which] entailed the emergence of a radical type of community, in which social and cultural constructs that prevented the inclusion of a radically different person, such as the Ethiopian eunuch, would be left out."[26]

Carson understands the Ethiopian's accepted state in the church as the fulfillment of Acts 1:8c ("the end of earth").[27] That is, he sees this mandate by nature as ethnic. This understanding is a little distinct from the view among scholars that Acts 1:8 is the geographic expansion of the gospel and the Ethiopian's conversion is an initial fulfillment of the end-of-the-earth mandate. By the Ethiopian's conversion to Christ and acceptance into the church, the ethnic division of Jews and gentiles is now obliterated.[28]

Carson raises doubts about Luke's portrayal that Cornelius was the first gentile baptized convert. He assumes that Philip most probably evangelized gentiles after his outreach to the Samaritans and the Ethiopian.[29] Carson's note here indicates that Luke intentionally did not include Philip's possible gentile mission into his text until the Cornelius episode. Carson makes no further discussion as to what lies behind Luke's omission. Hence, this area needs to be further discussed.

Burke, Queering the Ethiopian Eunuch

One of the main areas that Sean D. Burke addresses in his monograph is the word "eunuch" and the ancient practice of castration. The Greco-Roman audience of Acts would have understood it as "a reference to a castrated male."[30] Burke's exhaustive study of the castration practice leads him to identify three characteristics about it: (1) foreignness, (2) pre-puberty males, and (3) removal of testicles.[31]

---

25. Carson, "Do You Understand What You Are Reading?," 56.
26. Carson, "Do You Understand What You Are Reading?," 148.
27. Carson, "Do You Understand What You Are Reading?," 79–80.
28. Carson, "Do You Understand What You Are Reading?," 80.
29. Carson, "Do You Understand What You Are Reading?," 155.
30. Burke, *Queering the Ethiopian Eunuch*, 33.
31. Basically, these three characteristics will be used to understand the Ethiopian in the cultural setting of the castration system in the ancient world. This will be presented in chapter 4.

First, castration was imposed on foreign slaves.[32] Second, the practice's subjects were mostly young male children before they entered puberty rather than adult males. Third, castration involved a removal of the child's testicles but not his penis.[33] Those children were captured as prisoners of war and exiled to other nations. The removal of their testicles was intended to remove their reproductive capabilities, making them incapable of having their own families or descendants. This feature made those young eunuchs appealing to royal families, guaranteeing their absolute loyalty.[34]

Basically, Burke argues that the Ethiopian, as a physical eunuch, is a particularly ambiguous individual in terms of his gender and religious status in Judaism. He states, "The ambiguities in the character of the Ethiopian eunuch in Acts 8:26–40 may be read as functioning rhetorically to deconstruct identity categories."[35] Luke's purpose in introducing the Ethiopian is to deconstruct the binary system in society, like "male and female" or "Jew and gentile," and to introduce a new entity into that system. Burke's basis for this argument is the view of *queering*.[36]

Burke's work involves an extensive study of the ancient practice of castration. It can be used as a vehicle to help illuminate the Ethiopian with respect to that ancient practice. However, Burke's use of a social-rhetorical method is confined to "ambiguities," as he calls them, about the Ethiopian. Burke understands those ambiguities as features that Luke used for his rhetorical purpose of introducing a new social entity into the binary system of society. Most probably, however, Luke assumed that his audience would share certain cultural elements with him, so he did not put them into his text. Yet to modern-day readers, they appear to be ambiguous. In this regard, a cultural gap in narrative is not a means of the author's rhetorical purpose of ambiguities, as Burke implies. Rather, it is an area for modern-day readers to fill in through background studies.

---

32. Burke, *Queering the Ethiopian Eunuch*, 102.
33. Burke, *Queering the Ethiopian Eunuch*, 97.
34. Burke, *Queering the Ethiopian Eunuch*, 101–2.
35. Burke, *Queering the Ethiopian Eunuch*, 64–65.
36. Burke, *Queering the Ethiopian Eunuch*, 42. Burke uses the term *queering*, thereby defining it as "the utilization of multiple strategies in order to deconstruct and to denaturalize the dominant social constructions of identity that underlie any and all binary oppositions between 'the normal' and 'the abnormal.'"

Rhamie, "Whiteness, Conviviality and Agency"

Gifford Charles Alphaeus Rhamie asks the following rhetorical questions: "Why is the Ethiopian eunuch not Jewish? Why cannot the Ethiopian eunuch be imaged as a full-fledged Jew?"[37] According to Rhamie, the link between the Ethiopian and his gentile identity has been dominant in New Testament scholarship because of our racial reasoning that the term "Ethiopian" should be interpreted to mean that he is a black African. As Rhamie points out this bias, he states:

> However, once the data is processed, other epistemological conjunctures will be theorised for a plausible diasporic "Jewish" conception through the Acts 8:26–40 literary signatures of "diasporic pilgrimage" and "the politics of representation." Consequently, the literary location of the Ethiopian eunuch's story in Acts will be seen to inform his socio-political and theological meaning for Acts as a whole and help provide a key to understanding the literary development of missions in Acts.[38]

First of all, Rhamie studies how the church fathers understood the Ethiopian's ethnicity. For instance, Irenaeus (*Haer.* 4.23.2) sees him as having "a Jewish ethnoreligious identity," Eusebius (*Hist. eccl.* 2.1.13) views him as possessing "a Graeco-Gentile ethnoreligious identity," and Jerome and Augustine are ambivalent about the matter.[39] Another approach to Rhamie's study of the Ethiopian's ethnicity concerns Luke's situated historical, political, and cultural world. Luke is "a postcolonial, cosmopolitan theologian who had a broad perspective of what the diasporic, ethnoreligious landscape of first century Judaism was."[40] Rhamie assumes that Luke has knowledge about Jewish settlements in the diaspora, and according to this knowledge, Luke introduces the Ethiopian into his text, assuming that he might be ethnically Jewish.

Third, Rhamie looks at the Ethiopian episode from a narrative-progression perspective. He states, "Hence, in this 'narrative turn' the Ethiopian eunuch, though himself foreshadowing the 'end of the earth' (1.8), represented 'fringe,' distant or diasporic Jews. This is the last group to be canvassed before launching a missional outreach to Hellenised gentiles, beginning with a friend of the Jews, Cornelius (10.22)."[41] That is, the Ethio-

---

37. Rhamie, "Whiteness, Conviviality and Agency," 115.
38. Rhamie, "Whiteness, Conviviality and Agency," 26–27.
39. Rhamie, "Whiteness, Conviviality and Agency," 139.
40. Rhamie, "Whiteness, Conviviality and Agency," 188.
41. Rhamie, "Whiteness, Conviviality and Agency," 213.

pian is a Jew in the diaspora, and Luke's inclusion of the Ethiopian episode "strategically and symbolically completes the canvassing of the diasporic Jews."[42]

There are three significant benefits of Rhamie's monograph. These benefits could also be used as the basis for further study. First, Rhamie approaches the Ethiopian's ethnic issue from an authorial point of view. That is, Luke had knowledge about Jews scattered throughout the Greco-Roman world. This would lead him to have a broad perspective of ethnic Jewishness. This point of view is identified in Luke's use of in-detail categorization of Jews (ex., Jews, Judeans, Hebrews, and Hellenists, diaspora Jews).

Second, concerning the mandate of Acts 1:8, Rhamie points out the gap between God's initiative and the Jerusalem church's lagging behind that initiative. The mandate was intended to include all ethnicities, not just geographies. However, the Jerusalem church, which is represented by Peter, "constantly lags behind the divine initiative."[43] This argument helps draw the narrative progression of Acts from geographical and ethnical perspectives. From a literary approach, this issue can be dealt with further. Luke's characterization about Peter as such is evident, in particular, with regard to the inclusion of gentiles as God's eschatological people. What effect does this create in Luke's narrative development in Acts? This area needs to be discussed.

Third, Rhamie interprets the Ethiopian account as follows: "Luke, before moving onto the mission to the Gentiles proper (as foreshadowed in the conversion of Paul in Acts 9), wished to deal with the mission of all things Jewish, even Jewish by distant, diasporic kinship."[44] That is, the Ethiopian is the final frontier in the broad scope of Jewishness. This recognition needs a further study of how the Ethiopian can be identified as such. Given the fact that the Ethiopian visited Jerusalem to worship, most probably in the temple, how a eunuch like the Ethiopian was perceived among Jews in their cultic system of the temple is an important criterion to evaluate the Ethiopian's marginalized nature.

In spite of all of these benefits, one thing should be mentioned about Rhamie's work. Rhamie often uses the term "ethnoreligious" to suggest that in the ancient world, ethnicity is identified with religion. By contrast, it is notable that Luke tends to regard ethnicity and religion as separate features when he describes characters in narrative. For instance, Luke uses multiple designations to introduce individuals and groups—ethnically and

---

42. Rhamie, "Whiteness, Conviviality and Agency," 219.
43. Rhamie, "Whiteness, Conviviality and Agency," 215.
44. Rhamie, "Whiteness, Conviviality and Agency," 213.

religiously from a Jewish point of view—such as Jews and gentiles, Hebrews and Hellenists, proselytes, and God-fearers, circumcised and uncircumcised, foreigners, and Greeks and so on. Hence, it seems better to approach the Ethiopian account from two perspectives—his ethnic background and his religious affiliation with Judaism.

Other Scholarly Discussions on the Ethiopian Episode

This section will further discuss scholarly opinions about the Ethiopian episode with a focus on three textual elements: (1) "eunuch," (2) "Ethiopia(n)," and (3) "to worship." It will investigate how scholars apply these elements to their interpretation of the Ethiopian account, with particular regard to his ethnic and religious background.

Eunuch

Scholars focus on the Greek word εὐνοῦχος ("eunuch"), which Luke uses to address the Ethiopian (8:27, 34, 36, 38, 39). It is commonly suggested that the Ethiopian's castrated state is what lies behind this addressing.[45] Built

---

45. Keener, *Acts*, 1568; Kern, "Paul's Conversion and Luke's Portrayal," 65; Pervo, *Acts*, 224. Also, J. B. Lightfoot sees the Ethiopian as a eunuch with "a physical defect." Lightfoot, *Acts of the Apostles*, 146–47; Peterson, *Acts of the Apostles*, 291; Schnabel, *Acts*, 422; Garland, *Acts*, 89–90; Holladay, *Acts*, 189. N. T. Wright states, "It is very unlikely, virtually impossible, that he [the Ethiopian] would himself have been Jewish; and, being a eunuch, he could not have been a proselyte to Judaism. He was thus an outsider, forever to remain so within the Jewish system." Wright, *Acts for Everyone*, 133. Polhill, *Acts*, 223–24; Gangel, *Acts*, 126; Longenecker, *Luke-Acts*, 845; Bauer, *Book of Acts as Story*, 139. According to *TDNT*, the ancient practice of castration is "fundamentally alien" to the Greeks, indicating its origin to the Oriental culture. The term "eunuch" in the LXX is often used for "high military and political officials; it does not have to imply emasculation." Schneider, "εὐνοῦχος, εὐνουχίζω," in *TDNT*, 2:765–68. Luke uses the term "eunuch" five times in this account (8:27, 34, 36, 38, 39). Each time, he uses the voice of his adopted narrator to designate the Ethiopian. On the surface, it appears to be a title for the Ethiopian. However, it cannot be rejected that Luke is using the title to implicate the ancient custom of castration embedded in that title. First, Luke uses the term "court official" (δυνάστης) in relation to the Ethiopian's job for his queen. If the "eunuch" is only a job title, then it is redundant to have the following term, "court official." Eunuch is an addressing title, and yet it usually denotes its embedded meaning of the person's castrated condition behind the title. Second, Luke's citation of Isa 53:7b–8a also points to this condition (Acts 8:32–33). The question "Who can describe his generation?" (Isa 53:8a) in Luke's cited text is most likely a lament for the death of a man who does not have his children. Third, Isaiah's illustration of a eunuch as "a dry tree" (56:3) is also related to the infertile nature of a eunuch. Kuecker argues that this feature in the Isaiah text draws attention from the Ethiopian, leading him to ask the

upon this understanding, the scholarly discussion of the Ethiopian account continues in three areas. First, the Ethiopian's castrated condition makes it implausible to regard him as circumcised. In other words, this view relates his castrated state to his lack of circumcision. Second, the Ethiopian's castrated eunuch functions to recall the stipulation of "the assembly of the Lord" in Deut 23:1 ("No one whose testicles are crushed or whose male organ is cut off shall enter the assembly of the Lord"). Based on this stipulation, scholars assume that the Ethiopian was prohibited from admission into the temple. Third, scholars connect the "eunuch" in the text to Isa 56:1–8, where "foreigners" and "eunuchs" are depicted as vulnerable to exclusion.

Craig S. Keener sees the Ethiopian as "a God-fearing African official who is not yet a full proselyte."[46] Keener's basis for this view is that the Ethiopian "was not able to become a full convert by virtue of his being a eunuch (Deut 23:1)."[47] Keener also suggests that Luke's mention of proselytes prior to this episode (Acts 2:11; 6:5) indicates the Ethiopian's God-fearing status in Judaism (i.e., uncircumcised); according to him, the Ethiopian, if he is a proselyte, "does not advance very much the depiction of the promised universal mission."[48]

Who is the first uncircumcised gentile Christian, according to Luke's portrayal? Luke specifies Cornelius as the first one (Acts 10:28; 11:3, 18; 15:7–9). Keener's view about the Ethiopian appears to be in conflict with this portrayal by Luke. Concerning this issue, Keener states, "[T]his official's conversion [the Ethiopian's conversion] is a private event unknown or relatively unknown to the church in Jerusalem, in contrast to the later matter [Cornelius' conversion], which was debated by the Jerusalem church."[49] Keener investigates the Ethiopian from a socio-cultural perspective while considering a narrative progression of the mandate in Acts 1:8.

This opinion (i.e., the Ethiopian as a God-fearing uncircumcised gentile) calls into question how to handle the account of Cornelius in light of the gospel's ethnic progression to the gentiles (Acts 10). According to Ernst Haenchen, "Luke cannot and did not say that the eunuch was a Gentile; otherwise Philip would have forestalled Peter, the legitimate founder of the Gentile mission! For that reason Luke leaves the eunuch's status in a doubtful light."[50] In line with this point of view, Hans Conzelmann states:

---

referent of the Isaiah servant. Kuecker, *Spirit and the "Other,"* 166–67.

46. Keener, *Acts 3:1–14:28*, 1545.
47. Keener, *Acts 3:1–14:28*, 1566.
48. Keener, *Acts 3:1–14:28*, 1567.
49. Keener, *Acts 3:1–14:28*, 1566.
50. Haenchen, *Acts of the Apostles*, 314.

> The story [the Ethiopian episode] was apparently told in Hellenistic circles as the first conversion of a Gentile (cf. Ps 68[67]:32). The story thus rivals the account of Cornelius's conversion in chapters 10–11. Luke has placed the story here so that it now functions as a prelude to Cornelius's conversion. It is a self-contained episode and does not presuppose 8:4–25.[51]

F. F. Bruce deals with this issue from a source-critical approach.[52] For the matter of who was the first gentile convert, Luke was exposed to two different sources, the Hellenistic source and the Jewish source.[53] The Hellenistic source testified to the Ethiopian as the first gentile Christian, whereas the Jewish source testified to Cornelius as the first gentile Christian.[54] It appears that Haenchen, Conzelmann, Bruce, and Keener—among others—attribute the episode of the Ethiopian to the Hellenistic circle of the church through a source-critical approach. From a redaction-critical perspective, they also emphasize Luke's collating and harmonizing redactional composition of the Ethiopian and Cornelius accounts.

The Ethiopian as a God-fearing uncircumcised gentile is implied by his castrated condition, which, in turn, negates his full affiliation with Judaism and prohibits his admission into the temple, even "past the Court of the Gentiles."[55] It seems that scholars in favor of this view tend to directly relate the Ethiopian's castrated condition to his uncircumcision and gentile ethnicity. The present thesis, however, raises a few critical questions about this view. Is it legitimate to use the Deut 23:1 stipulation as a criterion for the conclusion that the Ethiopian was an uncircumcised gentile? Can the stipulation be applied not just to gentiles but also to Jews? Does the physical castration condition negate the possible condition of circumcision? A discussion of these areas will be included in this work. But for now, it has

---

51. Conzelmann, *Acts of the Apostles*, 67.

52. Bruce, "Philip and the Ethiopian," 378. Concerning the source-critical nature of the Ethiopian account, Bruce states, "This episode is isolated in the narrative of Acts in the sense that it is unconnected with anything that precedes or follows it. It is not woven into the fabric of the on-going narrative: if it were removed, there would be nothing to indicate that anything of the kind had ever stood there (Acts 8:26–40)."

53. C. K. Barrett suggests that Luke obtained the accounts of Philip's outreach to the Samaritans and his continual evangelism to the Ethiopian from Philip himself; in Acts 21:8, it is shown that Luke had a contact with Philip. Barrett, *Critical and Exegetical Commentary*, 51.

54. Bruce, "Philip and the Ethiopian," 377.

55. Keener, *Acts 3:1–14:28*, 1567. According to Keener, "[T]he guardians of temple Judaism, following the letter of the Torah, could not have admitted him [the Ethiopian] past the Court of the Gentiles. And as noted below, interested Gentiles often visited the temple but could not proceed even to the Court of Women."

been noted that the term "eunuch" in the text—and its ritual and cultic implications in relation to circumcision and temple worship—leads to the conclusion that the Ethiopian was an uncircumcised gentile.

Ethiopia(n)

Scholars focus on the Greek word Αἰθίοψ ("Ethiopian"). It implies two things about the Ethiopian: (1) geographic origin and (2) skin color. First, it refers to the Ethiopian's geographic origin from the land of Ethiopia (i.e., the Meroë Kingdom), located to the south of Egypt.[56] The textual element "Ethiopia" or "Ethiopian" also draws attention to the mandate of Jesus in Acts 1:8. According to the sequence of the geographical locales mentioned in this mandate, "Samaria" precedes "the end of the earth." Philip's outreach to the Samaritans (8:4–25) leads to the assumption that Philip's evangelism to the Ethiopian is a fulfillment of the Acts 1:8c mandate.

Martin Hengel states, "As a result of the expulsion of the 'Hellenists' from Jerusalem, the gospel was passed on to Samaria and finally, in the figure of the Ethiopian on his way home, reached 'the ends of the earth.'"[57] Hengel sees the Ethiopian episode as the fulfillment of God's promise to gentiles (Ps 68:32; Zeph 3:10; Luke 11:31). In line with this opinion, Ben Witherington refers to the Greco-Roman world's understanding of Ethiopia as the end of the earth, and states:

> We are entitled, then, to suspect that Luke the historian has decided to portray in miniature a foreshadowing of the fulfillment of the rest of Jesus' mandate (Acts 1:8) in Acts 8, for here we find stories both about a mission in Samaria and (with the eunuch) in Judea, but also in the case of the eunuch a mission that potentially would reach the ends of the earth, as the eunuch went on his way back to Ethiopia.[58]

Witherington also argues that "Luke, like Ephorus and other ancient Hellenistic historians, seems to have followed a procedure of arranging his data κατα γενος, by which is meant both by geographical region and therefore also by ethnic group."[59] If based on his view about the κατα γενος arrangement, which indicates the association of geographic region and ethnic

---

56. Meroë was the capital of the kingdom, located in the middle between the Fifth Cataract and the Sixth Cataract in the Nile. The Meroë Kingdom governed the land south of Egypt from 590 BC to AD 350.

57. Hengel, *Acts and the History of Earliest Christianity*, 80.

58. Witherington, *Acts of the Apostles*, 290.

59. Witherington, *Acts of the Apostles*, 290. See also 34.

group, the Ethiopian's conversion "on the road to Gaza"—within the land of Judea—could point to the Ethiopian's ethnic relatedness to Jewishness.

However, Witherington stresses the Ethiopian's origin from Ethiopia, regarding him as a non-Jewish black man.[60] This presentation does not reflect the locale of Philip's evangelism to the Ethiopian and the fact that "Philip's witness is geographically within Judea."[61] In this respect, Gerd Lüdemann suggests that the phrase "from Jerusalem to Gaza" (Acts 8:26) "fits Luke's concept of mission."[62] What is essential, as reflected in the episode, is Philip's evangelism, although the Ethiopian's mission in the land of Ethiopian is not unimaginable.[63] As a record of witnessing to the risen Christ, Acts emphasizes Christ's witnesses, for instance, Peter and John, Stephen, Philip, and Paul. Luke seems to be developing his narrative along with these characters and their witnessing.[64]

Second, the term "Ethiopian" brings about the assumption that for the original audience of Luke's work, the Ethiopian was perceived as a black man. R. C. H. Lenski states, "He was an Ethiopian, a black man! Αἰθίοψ, from αἴθω, 'to burn,' and ὤψ, 'countenance,' points to race and nationality and not merely to residence. Thus, the idea of his being a Jew who had risen to great power in Ethiopia is at once excluded."[65] Scholars often refer to Frank M. Snowden's argument: "Ethiopians were the yardstick by which antiquity measured colored peoples. The skin of the Ethiopian was black, in fact, blacker, it was noted, than that of any other people. Indians were dark or black but not all of them to the same extent as Ethiopians."[66] It is notable

---

60. Witherington, *Acts of the Apostles*, 295.

61. Talbert, *Reading Acts*, 74. Talbert sees the Ethiopian as a God-fearing gentile (76).

62. Lüdemann, *Early Christianity*, 102. Concerning the role of Philip, Simon Kistemaker states, "As a Greek-speaking Jew from the dispersion, he [Philip] has a distinct role in the expanding ministry of the Church. And as a Jew from the dispersion, he bridges the gap between the Jew and the non-Jew." Kistemaker, *Exposition of the Acts of the Apostles*, 310.

63. Luke's use of the Greek word ὁδός is notable in the Gospel and Acts. Luke seems to be using it as a major motif in narrative. Octavian Baban suggests that the on-the-road setting is "a common, prominent features" of the Emmaus road encounter (Luke 24:13–35), Philip's evangelism of the Ethiopian on the Gaza road (Acts 8:26–40), and Saul's encounter with the risen Christ on the Damascus road (Acts 9:1–31). Baban, *On the Road Encounters in Luke-Acts*, 1–2.

64. This study of the Ethiopian will investigate the locale of Philip's evangelism to the Ethiopian ("on the road to Gaza") and its implications.

65. Lenski, *Interpretation of the Acts of the Apostles*, 337.

66. Snowden, *Blacks in Antiquity*, 2.

that biblical scholars, like Lenski, use a racial concept to interpret what Luke had in view when he referred to the Ethiopian as "Ethiopian."

The linkage of the term "Ethiopian" to blackness, however, should be reconsidered, given how Luke uses terms like "Ethiopian" in Acts. Just as Horatio B. Hackett suggests, the term "Ethiopian" refers to "the country where he [the Ethiopian] resided, or to his extraction."[67] Another factor for this discussion is that blackness was not uniform in the Greco-Roman world; there were so-called racial mixtures, just as evidenced in Acts (e.g., Timothy; Acts 16:1). According to Jewish material, such as Philo, Jewish settlements were in the region of Egypt and perhaps even in Ethiopia.[68] It is known that there was a Jewish settlement in Elephantine, which was on the southern border of Egypt with Ethiopia. This study will thus scrutinize Luke's use of terms like "Ethiopian," in particular, when he introduces characters in the narrative of Acts. Also, an investigation of Jewish settlements in the land of Egypt, particularly in Elephantine, will help illumine the Ethiopian in Acts in light of the cultural dynamics of that time.

Worship in Jerusalem

The third textual element on which scholars focus is the Ethiopian's pilgrimage to Jerusalem to worship in the temple (8:27), along with his reading of the Isaiah scroll (v. 30) and his determination to get baptized (v. 37). All of these elements implicate that the Ethiopian had a deep sense of affiliation with Judaism. This aspect of the Ethiopian—his religious life—makes it insufficient to regard him as a gentile like Cornelius in Acts 10.

Darrell L. Bock, as he emphasizes the Ethiopian's attachment to Judaism, states, "In sum, we cannot be sure of his [the Ethiopian] exact status, but it is quite likely that he has been significantly touched by Judaism, since he is reading Isaiah and coming from Jerusalem. As such, he would not be seen as a pure Gentile."[69] Luke T. Johnson, while seeing the Ethiopian as a physical eunuch, also stresses the Ethiopian's piety and refers to him as "one of the righteous from among every nation, whom God is calling to the

---

67. Hackett, *Commentary on the Original Text*, 154.

68. The island Elephantine is in the land of Egypt. It had Jews on it. It is the closest location to the land of Ethiopia. Lenski, while referring to papyri, suggests that there was "a Jewish military colony that was at first under Pharaonic, then under Persian, later under Ptolomaic, and finally under Roman jurisdiction." Lenski, *Acts*, 339.

69. Bock, *Acts*, 338. Le Cornu and Shulam also stress the Ethiopian's religious devotion, revealed in his pilgrimage and reading the Isaiah scroll. Le Cornu and Shulam, *Commentary on the Jewish Roots of Acts*, 1:415.

restored people."⁷⁰ In spite of possibly being restricted from entering the temple in Jerusalem, the Ethiopian travelled such a long journey to worship God. This characteristic is well-attested in the text.

Scholars propose the idea of locating the Ethiopian in between Jew and gentile—both ethnically and religiously. F. Scott Spencer states, "Ethnically, he [the Ethiopian] appears to occupy some border position between Jew and Gentile."⁷¹ Provided that the term "eunuch" in the account refers to a castrated male, Simon J. Kistemaker refers to him as "a half-convert to Judaism," just like "the Samaritans, who were in between the Jew and the Gentile."⁷² Jacob Jervell, who basically views Luke's use of the term "eunuch" not as his castrated condition, states, "Eine Erzählung aber über die Bekehrung eines Proselyten fehlt, und eben die gibt uns Lukas hier."⁷³

Alan J. Thompson addresses the Ethiopian as "an outcast," now being included under the rule of the Davidic king. For Thompson, Luke introduces all of the entities of Israel, including even the exiles (2:16–17) and the Samaritans (8:5–25), as God's people under the exalted Davidic king. Concerning the Ethiopian, Thompson states, "The remainder of Acts 8 continues this emphasis on the fulfillment of God's saving promises. In view now are the promises to include outcasts among the people of God."⁷⁴ The pan-Israel idea, according to Thompson, includes the Samaritans but not the Ethiopian.

In contrast to Thompson's view, James D. G. Dunn puts the Samaritans and the Ethiopian in parallel vis-à-vis the setting of cultic worship in the Jerusalem temple in that they are both excluded. Dunn states:

> Like the Samaritans he [the Ethiopian] represents a half-way house between a movement still completely within Judaism, in the first five chapters, and the later mission of Paul to the Gentiles. As the Samaritans were an offshoot from an earlier phase, before the religion of Israel became 'Judaism' proper, so an Ethiopian who went up to Jerusalem to worship (8:27) represented those members of other nationalities who attached themselves to Israel out of admiration for the character of its religion and

---

70. Johnson, *Acts of the Apostles*, 160.

71. Spencer, *Journeying through Acts*, 101–102.

72. Kistemaker, *Acts*, 312.

73. Jervell, *Apostelgeschichte*, 271. Jervell views that the term "eunuch" does not refer to his castrated condition; this fact, according to Jervell, is clarified by Luke's further description of the Ethiopian as "official." For Jervell, the Ethiopian was either a diaspora Jew or proselyte; but the fact that Luke dealt with the diaspora Jews in Acts 2 makes it less likely for him to see that the Ethiopian was a diaspora Jew.

74. Thompson, *Acts of the Risen Lord Jesus*, 116.

who were received sympathetically by Judaism. But as with the Samaritans, who had broken with Israel over the centralization of cultic worship in Jerusalem, so the Ethiopian eunuch represented those close to Israel, but still disadvantaged in relation to its central symbol, the Temple.[75]

Dunn interprets the Ethiopian episode in relation to the setting of the Jerusalem temple. Just as the Samaritans were not part of the cultic system in Jerusalem, so also the Ethiopian was excluded. Dunn's suggested idea is meaningful in that putting the Samaritans and the Ethiopian in parallel calls our attention to Isa 56:1–8, where the social entities of people who were possibly excluded from cultic worship were "foreigners" and "eunuchs."

The question to be answered is, Did Luke have those entities in Isa 56 in mind when introducing the Samaritans and the Ethiopian as part of Philip's ministry in Acts? Given the cited text of Isa 53:7–8 (Acts 8:32–33), it is generally assumed that Luke implicated Isa 56:1–8, although this is not textually explicit in Acts 8. Yet Luke's juxtaposition of the Samaritans and the Ethiopian would prove that it was not an implication but an explication in accordance with Luke's narrative framework.

Unlike Dunn, who sees the Ethiopian as a God-fearing uncircumcised gentile, Joseph A. Fitzmyer regards him as "a Jew, or possibly a Jewish proselyte."[76] Yet, just as Dunn does, Fitzmyer illuminates the Ethiopian account from the narrative flow of Acts. The gentile mission starts with the conversion of Cornelius (Acts 10) after Paul's call (9:15–16); this narrative frame leads him to see the Ethiopian as a Jew. He also suggests a possible link between "eunuch" (Isa 56:3–4) and the Ethiopian's pilgrimage (Acts 8:27). Given that the Ethiopian was reading the Isaiah scroll, Luke understands the Ethiopian as "a diaspora Jew" from "a far-off country," for the image of the Ethiopian's pilgrimage recalls Isa 56:3–4.[77] This aspect parallels

---

75. Dunn, *Acts of the Apostles*, 113–14.

76. Fitzmyer, *Acts of the Apostles*, 410. Shepherd states, "Luke does not clearly state that the Ethiopian is Jewish (Ethiopia would normally be considered Gentile territory), but this is implied by the context—the story of Cornelius is plainly given first place in the account of the Gentile mission." Shepherd, *Narrative Function of the Holy Spirit*, 184–85. Lüdemann suggests that the phrase "to worship" (8:27) implies the Ethiopian as "a Jew or at least a proselyte coming from the diaspora." Lüdemann, *Acts of the Apostles*, 122. Curt Niccum states, "This definition disqualifies the eunuch as a representative of 'the end of the earth,' for Luke depicts the eunuch as a Jew. His story is set amid Samaritans, Saul, Aeneas, Tabitha, and the tanner, all 'Jews' of questionable status. Also, for Luke, Cornelius is the first Gentile convert (15:7, 14)." Niccum, "One Ethiopian Eunuch Is Not the End of the World," 2:890.

77. Fitzmyer, *Acts of the Apostles*, 410.

the general understanding that Luke has Isa 42–66 in mind as a framework for developing the entire narrative of Acts.[78]

Summary

There are several characteristics identified in the scholarship of the Ethiopian account with regard to his ethnic and religious identity. First, the assumption is notable that the Ethiopian's castrated condition, inferred from Luke's addressing of him by "eunuch," points to his uncircumcised state. Deuteronomy 23:1 is also used as a means to support this assumption. This thesis, however, raises doubts about this identification of castration with uncircumcision and its application of Deut 23:1 to gentiles alone. This awareness leads to the need of how Deut 23:1 is used in its textual tradition and how a male's castration most probably occurred in the ancient practice of castration.

Another characteristic in the scholarship of the Ethiopian is its attempt to understand the Ethiopian account in light of Isa 56:1–8, which deals with the inclusion of "eunuchs," along with "foreigners," in the cultic setting. Generally, scholars agree that Luke recontextualizes the Isaiah text in his presentation of the Samaritans and the Ethiopian. To continue this scholarly discussion, this thesis will focus on how Luke implicitly uses the Isaiah text—and its principles—to reveal (1) his polemical intent by his presentation of the Samaritans and the Ethiopian and (2) his emphasis on their inclusion in Christ's eschatological temple.

Third, the Acts 1:8c mandate ("to the end of the earth") is often utilized as the ground for the view that the Ethiopian's conversion is an initial fulfillment of the gentile mission. This understanding has three assumptions. First, the Ethiopian is an ethnic gentile. Second, Ethiopia is a faraway land, something like "the end of the earth." Third, in Acts 8, the account of the Ethiopian appears right after that of the Samaritans; this leads to the view that the Acts 1:8c mandate, which follows "Samaria," is connected to the Ethiopian's conversion.

To determine if these assumptions are valid, this thesis will deal with two areas, among others. First, it will investigate the cultural dynamics of the diaspora Jews with a focus on their geopolitical situatedness and their pilgrimage to Jerusalem. This investigation will increase the probability that the Ethiopian was ethnically connected to Jewishness. Second, it will

---

78. Pao, *Acts and the Isaianic New Exodus*, 10. Pao states, "The narrative of Acts should primarily be read within the hermeneutical framework of the Isaianic New Exodus."

investigate Luke's narrative development in terms of the gospel's progression, which is characteristic of three trajectories (i.e., geographic, ethnic, and religious). This will help locate the position of the Ethiopian in each of the trajectories. As a result, it will be clarified how the Ethiopian's account, as an individual episode, contributes to Luke's overall theological working in Acts, while at the same time it is clearly distinct from the account of Cornelius.

Chapter 2

Methods of the Study

FOR AN INVESTIGATION OF the Ethiopian in terms of his ethnic and religious identity, this study will employ three methods: (1) echoic allusion, (2) cultural gaps in narrative, and (3) narrative criticism. The first method is related to this thesis's examination of Deut 23:1–4 in Jewish literature. In particular, Isa 56:1–8, to which Acts 8 alludes, implicates a rejection of the original meaning of the Deuteronomy text in pursuit of "justice and righteousness" (Isa 56:1), a theme emphasized in the Gospel of Luke and Acts. The second method is part of this study's historical reconstruction of the Ethiopian with a focus on his castrated condition and his pilgrimage to Jerusalem. Research into these areas will concern cultural background, which will help to illuminate the Ethiopian. The third method is used to locate the Ethiopian in the progression of narrative, which draws three trajectories (i.e., geographic, ethnic, and religious). This study uses the Gospel of Luke's prologue (Luke 1:1–4) as the basis for its rationale for this method.

Echoic Allusion

The text of Deut 23:1–4 (MT 23:2–5) often appears in Jewish literature. This fact indicates that this text has its own tradition, being used in different contexts. Scholars like Michael Fishbane and Gary E. Schnittjer have studied its textual tradition. According to their study, its implicit occurrence in Isa 56:1–8 is unique.

Schnittjer states, "The striking lyrical pronouncement at the opening of the last major unit of Isaiah is widely regarded as making an extended allusion to the law of the assembly in Deut 23:1–7 [2–8], though verbal parallels are few."[1] According to Schnittjer, there is a textual interrelatedness between the two passages, which he calls "allusion." He relates "eunuchs" and "foreigners" (Isa 56:1–7) to "the person with a damaged male organ" and "Ammonites and Moabites" (Deut 23:1–4).[2]

Fishbane also states:

> Trito-Isaiah, it will be recalled, forecast a time when all Israelites would serve as priests (Isa. 61:6), and when even foreigners would serve in the shrine (56:6–7, 60:7, 66:18–21)—including those whose genitalia were maimed, in apparent flagrant violation of priestly (cf. Lev. 21:16–23) and non-priestly law (cf. Deut. 23:2). Indeed, such allowances are so revolutionary and so contradictory to ancient practice that they can hardly have been justified by exegetical means alone. Proof for this lies in the fact that these various innovations—particularly those stated in Isa. 56:1–7—are presented as new divine teachings, remarkably transforming the ancient Pentateuchal revelations and regulations.[3]

In terms of textual meaning, Isa 56:1–7 is antithetical to Deut 23:1–4. Deut 23:1–4 is the stipulation that excludes the four entities of people from the assembly of the Lord: (1) the emasculated male, (2) the child of a forbidden union, (3) the Ammonite, and (4) the Moabite. In contrast, Isa 56:1–7 is an oracle about admitting the two entities of people into the temple: (1) the foreigner and (2) the eunuch. Conceptually, the foreigner and the eunuch in the Isaiah text can be understood as the Ammonite, the Moabite, and the emasculated male in the Deuteronomy text.

In terms of form, their textual interrelatedness is an allusion. In terms of function, their relationship is antithetical. To gain a better understanding of what the Isaiah text implicates, this study introduces "allusion" on the basis of *relevance theory*, a pragmatic linguistic theory proposed by Deirdre Wilson and Dan Sperber, along with the works of David R. Klingler, Cooper Smith, and Young-Sam Won. It will be suggested that Isaiah's use of Deut 23 in the form of allusion is (1) to reject the idea of exclusivism in it and (2) to promote a better ideal to the audience.

---

1. Schnittjer, *Old Testament Use of Old Testament*, 247.
2. Schnittjer, *Old Testament Use of Old Testament*, 247.
3. Michael Fishbane, *Biblical Interpretation in Ancient Israel*, 128.

Allusion: Elusive

In biblical studies, the term "allusion" is frequent, along with its related terms like "allude" and "allusive."[4] Allusion is "an indirect or passing reference to some event, person, place, or artistic work, the nature and relevance of which is not explained by the writer but relies on the reader's familiarity with what is thus mentioned."[5] In terms of textual relation, allusion occurs between two texts; one text alludes to another. Also, allusion is an indirect mode of reference, so it is not easily recognizable. For further discussion, this section will examine allusion from three perspectives: (1) authorial, (2) formal and functional, and (3) ironical, polemical, and rhetorical.

Allusion: Authorial

There is a debate concerning who is in charge of allusion. Joseph Pucci argues that "(1) the allusion exploits the constructed, arbitrary quality of literary reading, drawing specifically on the power of the reader to configure meaning in relation to his desires, as (2) the power of the author to intend meaning and the power of language to mean in a set, stable, referential field evanesces."[6] Pucci sees allusion as what is occurring inside the realm of the reader.

However, as Cooper Smith points out, allusion is part of human communication, which presupposes "a presumed intention."[7] For Robert Alter, allusion is "a conscious literary device."[8] Robert B. Chisholm sees allusion as a conscious attempt by a narrator "in order to draw a thematic and/or theological correlation between events."[9] David R. Klingler states, "Literary allusions are literary devices utilized by an author whereby literary signals or markers are placed into a developing textual meaning in order to activate meaning in the evoked text."[10] It appears that it is the reader's job to iden-

---

4. Won, *Remembering the Covenants in Song*, 45–77.

5. Baldick, *Oxford Dictionary of Literary Terms*, 9–10. As seen, Baldick stresses the role of a reader, rather than that of an author.

6. Pucci, *Full-Knowing Reader*, 28.

7. Smith, *Allusive and Elusive*, 51–52.

8. Alter, *World of Biblical Literature*, 110.

9. Chisholm, *Interpreting the Historical Books*, 81.

10. Klingler, *Validity in the Identification and Interpretation*, 38. However, David M. Gunn and Danna N. Fewell emphasize the role of the reader for allusion: "Allusions can foreshadow; they can help the reader fill gaps in terms of character motivation, for example, or of social expectation. Allusions reflect the larger text or context of literary expression and give the reader a sense of both the commonality and the uniqueness of

tify an allusion in the text, but it is the author who initiates it. The reader's role, although it can be extended outside the realm of the text, should be within the narrative world of the text. In this respect, William Irwin defines, "An author must intend this indirect reference, and it must be in principle possible that the intended audience could detect it."[11]

Textual Signal of Allusion: Formal and Functional

An allusion occurs between two texts. The source text is alluded to in a new text. How is it that one can be certain that the latter alludes to the former? Scholars agree that there is a *formal* piece of evidence in the alluding text (i.e., textual signal). Smith calls it "a reference with *implicit correlation* with a source."[12] According to Smith, it is "only between limited textual units"[13] and "only correlated—not duplicated—so the similarity is sufficient to evoke the source without extended repetition."[14] That is, a word or phrase can activate a whole text. The textual signal of allusion is a little piece, but it provokes an echo to the alluded text.

Does this textual signal work as a sufficient factor for the formation of allusion? Smith regards the "contextual interplay" between the two texts as another prerequisite for the formation of allusion. A word or phrase could appear in another text at random; in this case, it is not a signal for allusion. In this regard, Smith's recognition of "contextual interplay" is significant. He states that "when using an allusion, the alluding agent intends the audience to import certain contextual associations from the source in order to fully appreciate the alluding work."[15]

As an illustration, the slogan "Black Lives Matter" itself is controversial, perhaps because of its implication of narrowness in terms of application. In this context, the slogan "All Lives Matter" has appeared. Each of the slogans has its own context, but the latter was born in the context of the former.

---

the work in question." Gunn and Fewell, *Narrative in the Hebrew Bible*, 163.

11. Irwin, "What Is an Allusion?," 293.

12. Smith, *Allusive and Elusive*, 37.

13. Smith, *Allusive and Elusive*, 38. Concerning the issue of a textual marker for allusion between the two texts, Alter lists its possible entities, such as "phrasing, motif, or narrative situation." Alter, *World of Biblical Literature*, 111. Klingler refers to the textual marker as "allusive" and states that its function is "to direct the reader to the appropriate text containing the allusion." Klingler, *Validity*, 80. Irwin regards allusion as "a reference that is indirect in the sense that it calls for associations that go beyond mere substitution of a referent." Irwin, "What Is an Allusion?," 293.

14. Smith, *Allusive and Elusive*, 38.

15. Smith, *Allusive and Elusive*, 40.

As apparent in this illustration, the latter slogan alludes to the former; the words "Lives" and "Matter" are a formal signal, and their contextual interrelatedness is an indicator for allusion.

Imagine an international student has arrived in the United States. He has no knowledge about social issues like the "Black Lives Matter" movement. In the United States, he has heard the slogan "All Lives Matter." He understands the meaning of the slogan, but with no contextual understanding of how that slogan was born, his understanding about the slogan is limited in comparison to that of local people. For this un-allusive case, Smith states:

> If the allusion to a source text is missed, this does not necessarily render the entire alluding text incomprehensible. Thus, recognizing an allusion is necessary for *complete* meaning but is not necessary for *sufficient* meaning. This is because allusions complement the meaning of the alluding text along a pre-existent trajectory; they do not constitute the meaning of the alluding text in its entirety. Therefore, missing an allusion does not alter the pre-existent trajectory of meaning, it simply does not refine and augment this non-allusive meaning.[16]

It is noted that the textual signal of allusion can evoke the original context of the alluded text and make it echoic in the context of the alluding text. This concept parallels what Wilson and Sperber have proposed concerning relevance theory. First, according to this theory, human communication has an ostensive-inferential nature. Its suggested maxim is that human cognition "tends to be geared to the maximisation of relevance" in the correlation of the two variables "cognitive effects" and "processing effort" where (1) "the greater the cognitive effects, the greater the relevance" and (2) "the smaller the effort needed to achieve those effects, the greater the relevance."[17] In view of relevance theory, a textual signal of allusion is the result of the author's intentional choice to create the maximal degree of relevance to his audience; it potentially has a great impact on them while demanding less effort from them.

What is the function of the textual signal of allusion in relation to the new context of the alluding text? According to relevance theory, three possible effects could occur.[18] First, the textual signal (i.e., a new piece of information) strengthens an existing assumption. Second, it contradicts and eliminates an existing assumption. Third, it combines with an existing assumption to yield contextual implications. In other words, the author's

---

16. Smith, *Allusive and Elusive*, 58.
17. Wilson and Sperber, *Meaning and Relevance*, 200.
18. Wilson and Sperber, *Meaning and Relevance*, 200.

choice of a textual signal for allusion aims to have an influence on the cognitive environment of his audience, which has an existing assumption. Isaiah 56:1–8 contains the Hebrew terms "foreigner" (בֶּן־הַנֵּכָר) and "eunuch" (סָרִיס). Isaiah's use of the terms recalls the text of Deut 23:1–8 and evokes its context as well as its cultic implications. How does this allusion signal, along with its evoked context, work in the new context of Isa 56:1–8? This issue will be dealt with in chapter 3.

Echoic Allusion: Ironical, Polemical, and Rhetorical

One text alludes to another. For the formation of allusion, there is a formal allusion of a text and a functional interaction with that text's context. The author's use of the alluded text in his own text by the means of allusion is meant to enrich the contextual meaning of his text. In fact, both of the texts have their own contextual meanings. The issue is how to define the relation between these contextual meanings. Klingler lists five different possibilities in this regard: (1) equal to, (2) greater than, (3) less than, (4) similar to, and (5) not equal to (i.e., ironic opposite).[19] This section will focus on the last possible relation. Does the author use the alluded text in his own text to enrich his point of view, even if his intended contextual meaning appears to be antithetical to the meaning of the alluded text in its own context? If so, then what is his basis for this antithetical implication?

Wilson and Sperber see that "an ironical utterance" contains an "echoic interpretation" of that utterance, and they propose that "verbal irony invariably involves the implicit expression of an attitude" and that "the relevance of an ironical utterance invariably depends at least in part, on the information it conveys about the speaker's attitude to the opinion echoed."[20] This attitude is that of "the rejecting or disapproving kind"; that is, the speaker "dissociates herself from the opinion echoed and indicates that she does not hold it herself."[21] For the formation of an ironical utterance, Wilson and Sperber propose three conditions: (1) "the utterance is echoic"; (2) "the source of the opinion echoed" is identifiable; and (3) "the speaker's attitude to the opinion echoed is one of rejection or dissociation."[22]

This thesis mentioned previously, as an illustration, the slogans "Black Lives Matter" and "All Lives Matter." In view of Wilson and Sperber's idea about an ironical utterance, the slogan "All Lives Matter" is echoic of the

19. Klingler, *Validity*, 81.
20. Sperber and Wilson, *Relevance*, 239.
21. Sperber and Wilson, *Relevance*, 239.
22. Sperber and Wilson, *Relevance*, 240.

slogan "Black Lives Matter." Also, it contains an attitude concerning the opinion echoed, implicitly pointing out the original slogan's limited nuance. Similarly, Isa 56:1–8 contains "foreigner" and "eunuch," which are the textual signal for an allusion to Deut 23:1–8. As noted above, the role of the textual signal is to evoke the contextual meaning of the alluded text and make it echoic in relation to the new context of Isaiah. Based on this idea of echoic utterance and its ironical function, Isaiah's use of the terms "foreigner" and "eunuch" reflects his attitude regarding the echoed concept that surrounds the terms in the original context of Deut 23:1–8. That is, Isaiah's allusion is interpreted as polemical to the idea of exclusion embedded in the Deuteronomy stipulation.

It has been noted: (1) the alluding text evokes the original context of the alluded text (i.e., evocative, or echoic); (2) the meaning of the alluding text can be antithetical to that of the alluded text (i.e., ironical); and (3) the alluding text reflects the alluding agent's attitude toward the idea that the alluded text retains (i.e., polemical). If so, what is the basis for the agent's polemical attitude? It is assumed that the alluding agent has in mind an ideal superior to that of the echoed idea. The two slogans "Black Lives Matter" and "All Lives Matter" have been used as an illustration in this study. The latter occurs in the context of the former. With this contextual interaction, the latter contains a polemic to the idea that the former retains. At the same time, the ultimate purpose of the slogan "All Lives Matter" is to emphasize that all lives are important, the ideal that the slogan "All Lives Matter" retains. With this aspect in view, the slogan "All Lives Matter" is rhetorical in that its users intend to communicate that ideal to their audience.

Young-Sam Won's distinction between references and allusions based on his study of Ps 105 is significant. According to Won, the psalmist uses "literary references" to the Abrahamic covenant (i.e., the land promise; 105:8–11, 42) and "allusions" to the Mosaic covenant (105:7, 8, and 45). The psalmist's use of "references" to the Abrahamic covenant is intended "[to] construct the historical and conceptual framework for his argument," whereas his use of "allusions" to the Mosaic covenant is "to undergird a vital subtext that culminates in the main point of the psalmist's argument."[23] The context in which the psalmist, along with his audience, is situated is Yahweh's fulfillment of "the land promise" for Israel. In this historical context, the psalmist, by the means of allusion, communicates the need of his audience to be faithful to the Mosaic covenant, just as evidenced in Ps 105:45 ("that they might keep his statutes and observe his laws").[24] Hence,

---

23. Won, *Remembering the Covenants in Song*, 87.
24. Won, *Remembering the Covenants in Song*, 137.

the psalmist uses "references" to indicate a historical context and "allusions" to indicate a rhetorical context. In other words, the alluding agent uses an allusion as his rhetorical purpose of communicating his message (i.e., ideal) to his audience and exhorting them to live according to that ideal.

Isaiah 56 begins with "justice" and "righteousness" (56:1), as Yahweh's commanding demand for his eschatological people. With this demand in view, Isaiah's echoic allusion to Deut 23 does not remain just as polemical to the idea of exclusion in it. The allusion also projects Isaiah's rhetorical message to his audience; in the case of Isa 56:1–8, it is the audience's practice of "justice" and "righteousness." Hence, a textual signal of allusion is implicit in form but provocative in function; it can recall the context of the alluded text and make it echoic in relation to the new context of its alluding text. It also implicates the allusion agent's attitude toward the idea echoed; in the case of irony, it rejects the idea but does so because of the agent's rhetorical message of ideal to his audience.

Rationale for Echoic Allusion in Isa 56:1–8

The echoic-allusion method is beneficial for this thesis because it provides a better understanding of Deut 23:1–8 as the textual and contextual basis for Isa 56:1–8. The Isaiah text itself does not fully reveal a conceptual or thematical picture about its historical context. However, using the echoic-allusion method helps the exegete gain a dynamic picture of the Isaiah text's historical context within the boundary of the literary context without depending on other sources (e.g., Neh 13:1–3) and their historical contexts. In that regard, Won's statement is meaningful: "[T]his type of approach to intertextuality [i.e., allusion] affords scholars a kind of freedom in the exploration of themes and concepts that are not 'found' in the text when read through a historical-grammatical lens."[25] In particular, Isaiah's use of "foreigner" and "eunuch," although it is a non-literary allusion, helps the exegete explore the possible historical context of Isa 56:1–8.

Cultural Gap in Narrative

Luke's two-volume work is a compilation of multiple individual episodes. Each begins with Luke's presentation of a setting. This setting contains pieces of information which appear to be cultural in essence. For instance, Luke provides three main pieces of information as a literary setting for the

---

25. Won, *Remembering the Covenants in Song*, 65.

Ethiopian episode in Acts 8: (1) the nation of ancient Ethiopia, (2) the ancient practice of castration, and (3) the custom of pilgrimage to Jerusalem (v. 27). Built upon this setting, Luke projects his rhetorical or theological point of view for his original audience. In other words, a literary setting, which is characteristic of culture, can be such a significant vehicle through which the original audience gains an understanding of Luke's ultimate intent.

The problem, however, is that those pieces of information in the setting are not textually explicit or self-evident. As a result, this lack of textual clarity often appears as ambiguity to modern readers, thus creating a gap in their understanding of the text, let alone the author's rhetorical or theological point of view. To provide a theoretical rationale for cultural studies, I will investigate (1) how cultural gaps in narrative occur, (2) what assumptions lie behind them, and (3) how those gaps function in accordance with the author's rhetoric. I will conclude that cultural gaps in narrative are not necessarily a rhetorical device that the author utilizes to create ambiguity.

What Is Cultural Gap?

G. B. Caird suggests that there are "at least four types of setting," which are "verbal, situational, traditional and cultural."[26] Caird defines cultural setting as "the cultural background to which he [the author] and his readers belonged."[27] He argues that this cultural information, although its role is potentially significant in implicating the meaning of a text, is often missing in the text.[28] Meir Sternberg sees that this kind of gap in narrative occurs in relation to "basic assumptions or general canons of probability derived from 'everyday life' and prevalent cultural conventions."[29]

Based on this view of a cultural gap, it can work in three ways. First, a cultural gap (i.e., unfamiliar) for modern readers was most probably a cultural norm—shared as common (i.e., familiar) between the author and the original audience. Second, to gain a better understanding of the author's presented narrative, the modern readers should join the cognitive world of the author and the original audience. Third, from the author's rhetorical aspect embedded in narrative, the cultural gap (i.e., the cultural norm) can be what the author uses to introduce the original audience to what is

26. Caird, *Language and Imagery*, 50.
27. Caird, *Language and Imagery*, 52.
28. Caird, *Language and Imagery*, 49. Caird states, "The first and weightiest rule of speech is that context determines meaning." He regards the cultural context of a text as significant in our gaining the meaning of the text.
29. Sternberg, *Poetics of Biblical Narrative*, 189.

superior or even conflicts with that cultural norm. That is, the cultural norm is a vehicle for the author's argumentation.

Assumptions of Cultural Gap

What is a possible assumption behind the occurrence of the cultural gap in narrative? How is it possible that the author fails to put those pieces of information into his text? What lies beneath this omission? These questions can be discussed from pragmatical, authorial, and rhetorical perspectives.

First, pragmatically relevant is that the cultural gap in narrative occurs because of the common cognitive environment that existed between the author and his original audience. Joseph D. Fantin states, "When an author produces a text, there are many aspects of the context shared by both the author and the original readers. These do not need to be made explicit."[30] With this aspect in view, it is assumed that Luke (i.e., the author of the Gospel and Acts) and Theophilus (i.e., the original reader; Luke 1:3; Acts 1:1), along with the Christians of the first-century Greco-Roman world, participated in their common shared culture.

Second, one can infer that the author did not include the shared cultural entities and their conceptions in his text because he assumed that his original audience had a knowledge of them to a certain extent. This aspect excludes the notion that the cultural gap in narrative itself is a means of the author's rhetoric. Rather, it provides a common ground for the author to get his original audience's attention and interact with them.

Third, it is often suggested that the author creates such a gap in narrative and in doing so attempted to make his characters or plots appear to be unclear or ambiguous; hence, the author's omission retains a rhetorical implication. For instance, Burke is in favor of the view that "although there were clear and certain answers to these questions in the world behind the text, the author himself introduced ambiguities into the text in order to serve some particular rhetorical purpose."[31] However, given the assumption that those cultural gaps occurred because of the common shared cognitive environment and the author's assumption that those cultural elements are under the awareness of his original audience, the cultural gap in narrative cannot be regarded as a part of the author's creation for his rhetoric. What appears to be ambiguous to modern-day readers does not necessarily mean that such features were ambiguous to the original audience, nor that the

---

30. Fantin, "Background Studies," 168.
31. Burke, *Queering the Ethiopian Eunuch*, 15.

original audience understood those ambiguous elements as part of the author's rhetoric.

In fact, it is often suggested that Luke did not include details about the Ethiopian in his account in order to make the character appear to be ambiguous to his original audience. Burke, noting five ambiguities about the Ethiopian in Acts 8:26–40, argues that Luke's purpose here is to deconstruct the binary system of male and female and create another one for a new entity.[32] However, Luke's failure to include all of the details about the Ethiopian was not the result of his intention to utilize the omission as a rhetorical device; instead, as noted, Luke's omission was most likely due to his assumption that his original audience had a sense of cultural awareness of the shared cognitive environment. Thus, what is perceived by modern readers as a cultural gap is not to be interpreted as the author's rhetorical device.

Cultural Gap for the Author's Rhetoric

What is the role of this unstated common information in the entire process of the author's argument? Given that the author intends to communicate his point of view to his audience, the cultural gap itself is not a rhetorical tool but a vehicle by which the author leads his original audience to the realm of his argumentation. Wolfgang Iser, suggesting a correlation between what is familiar and what is unfamiliar in the act of recreation, states:

> This process [the dynamic process of recreation] is steered by two main structural components within the text: first, a repertoire of familiar literary patterns and recurrent literary themes, together with allusions to familiar social and historical contexts; second, techniques or strategies used to set the familiar against the unfamiliar.[33]

Iser also identifies the role of "narrative techniques" as creating "links between things we find difficult to connect, so that we are forced to reconsider data we at first held to be perfectly straightforward."[34] Based on Iser's point of view, the cultural gap in narrative is like what is familiar to the original audience; and the author's usage of narrative techniques is a vehicle

---

32. Burke, *Queering the Ethiopian Eunuch*, 135. Burke lists five ambiguities about the Ethiopian (Acts 8:26–40): class, race, gender, religion, and sexuality. He argues that Luke "chose to tell a story about a eunuch, whose very status as a eunuch introduced ambiguity into any and all possible identifications."

33. Iser, *Implied Reader*, 288.

34. Iser, *Implied Reader*, 288–89.

to project what is familiar in order to present his configuration of a new narrative world—that is, what is unfamiliar.

Luke's introduction of the Ethiopian appears to be ambiguous to modern readers—his castrated eunuch status, his pilgrimage to Jerusalem, his nature of worship in the temple, his ethnic identity, and so on. To the modern readership, all these elements can be regarded as cultural gaps. On the other hand, to Luke's original audience, who shared culture with Luke, most presumably did not see those elements as cultural gaps to be filled in. Yet, from the perspective of Luke's entire narrative presentation, all of these cultural elements would be utilized as a vehicle to shed light on what is unfamiliar to the original audience—Christ's work and the Ethiopian's new status as fully included one in God's eschatological people. As an effort to fill in those cultural gaps in the account of the Ethiopian, I will introduce the ancient practice of castration, the diaspora Jews in Elephantine, and the Jewish pilgrimage. This will help gain a better picture of the Ethiopian as an individual, as well as what Luke intended to achieve through the episode.

Narrative Criticism

The account of the Ethiopian has the form of a narrative, thus requiring a careful study of the components in that narrative. In addition, this account is one of the multiple individual episodes that appear in the entire narrative of Luke and Acts. This fact requires an investigation of the episode from a narrative point of view. Concerning the Ethiopian episode, what is the role that Luke had in mind in his progression of the entire narrative? Why is it so significant? How did Luke actualize it? For an investigation of these factors, a narrative-critical approach would be appropriate.[35] I will present a brief introduction of narrative criticism, its characteristics, and its appropriateness based on the Gospel of Luke's prologue (Luke 1:1–4).

What is Narrative Criticism?

According to Jeannine Brown, narrative criticism is "a method of interpreting biblical narratives that attends to their literary qualities and, specifically,

---

35. Scholars affirm that new criticism in the 1940s and 1950s influenced the birth of narrative criticism in biblical scholarship. Resseguie states, "Despite the extreme position of the New Critics (i.e., bracketing the author and the reader from consideration), their emphasis upon the autonomous unity of the text remains immensely influential upon narrative criticism." Resseguie, *Narrative Criticism of the New Testament*, 23. Brown, "Narrative Criticism," 619; Bauer, *Book of Acts as Story*, 12.

to their narrative or storied shape."[36] For their tools, its critics employ rhetorical features such as "plot, sequencing, pacing, point of view, characterization and irony."[37] In other words, narrative criticism is a method by which to study an entire picture of narrative and to understand an individual episode from the perspective of this picture; so, its tools are chiefly related to how the author drew that picture.

A text is born from its author's intent to communicate to his audience in a situated context. The factors recognized here for an investigation of literature are, among others, the author, the text, the audience, and the context. In the world of biblical scholarship, narrative criticism was born in the history of biblical hermeneutics. Prior to its birth, biblical scholars attempted to investigate the world behind the text, asking how the complete form of the text—in particular, each of the Gospels—came into being (source criticism and form criticism). Redaction criticism focuses on "the evangelists' particular theological interests by analyzing changes made to their source material."[38] It also created the rationale for the birth of narrative criticism in two ways. First, its critic turned attention from individual accounts within the text to the completed form of the text. According to Brown, the redaction critic's interest in the final form of each Gospel was "a hallmark of narrative criticism."[39]

Second, the redaction critic's assumption contributed to redirecting biblical scholars to the author and his role in the composition of his narrative. N. T. Wright states, "The Redaction-critics work from the assumption that the Evangelists have a very definite point of view, in the light of which they have rewritten the entire story of Jesus, reworking the traditions they received with more or less sovereign freedom in order to fit in with their own theological stance and *Tendenz*."[40] So, it is generally affirmed among biblical scholars that redaction criticism paved the road for the rise of narrative criticism.

Characteristics of Narrative Criticism

As noted above, the narrative critic focuses on the final form of narrative and the author's role in the process of its composition. Presumably, the author investigated sources that could be useful to him, decided which contents to

36. Brown, "Narrative Criticism," 619.
37. Brown, "Narrative Criticism," 619.
38. Brown, "Narrative Criticism," 619.
39. Brown, "Narrative Criticism," 620.
40. Neill and Wright, *Interpretation of the New Testament*, 283–84.

include in the text, and arranged them in a given sequence. On the surface level, this is the process that the author took to compose the final form of his narrative. But there must be another level beneath this process. How did the author shape the entire narrative? What principles did he use in arranging individual events? What is the purpose (or purposes) that the author intended to achieve through this form of configuration? The level beneath the surface level is what the narrative critic is attempting to investigate.

Seymour Chatman's distinction between "story" and "discourse" is helpful for understanding the author's narrative composition on those two levels. Chatman states:

> Each narrative has two parts: a story (*histoire*), the content or chain of events (actions, happenings), plus what may be called the existents (characters, items of setting); and a discourse (*discours*), that is, the expression, the means by which the content is communicated. In simple terms, the story is the *what* in a narrative that is depicted, discourse the *how*.[41]

Chatman's definition of "story" is related to elements objectively revealed in the author's composition process; so, it is characteristic of the author's objective realm (i.e., the surface level). On the other hand, "discourse" is about how the author communicates his intent through those objective elements; so, it belongs to the author's subjective realm, related to his intentionality (i.e., the level beneath the surface level).

With this distinction in view, there are a few questions to be answered.[42] In fact, events are interconnected to form a narrative. What principle does the author use? It appears that a progression in narrative is made with respect to time (i.e., temporal trajectory). Yet this progression is not always a norm. Given the fact that "events in narratives are radically correlative, enchaining, entailing," their arranged sequence "is not simply linear but causative."[43] That is, the principle of cause and effect (i.e., causation) functions as a connecting knot between events. A narrative appears to be

---

41. Chatman, *Story and Discourse*, 19.

42. The whole discussion in this section is related to plot. Chatman states, "The events in a story are turned into a plot by its discourse, the modus of presentation." Chatman, *Story and Discourse*, 43. According to Resseguie, "[U]nderstanding of plot is important to determine structure, unity, and direction of a narrative. It is the designing principle that contributes to our understanding of the meaning of a narrative. More concretely, the plot is the sequence of events or incidents that make up a narrative." Resseguie, *Narrative Criticism*, 197.

43. Chatman, *Story and Discourse*, 45. Joel B. Green states, "Narratives are constructed through a reversal of cause-effect relations. Knowing how things turned out, narrators go back in time, in search of causes." Green, "Narrative Criticism," 82.

flowing along the progression of time, but in reality, it is developed by the principle of causation.

With the temporal and causational aspects in view, Joel B. Green states, "Narrative locates events in a temporal frame characterized by cause-and-effect relations."[44] This fact provides a few suggestions or ideas for the present investigation of narrative. First, it would somehow offer room for possible changes or inconsistencies to occur in narrative, particularly with regard to the temporal aspect. Also, when a temporal inconsistency is identified, this could mean that the author made an artificial adjustment or modification to that temporal flow for the effectiveness of the causational aspect.

Second, there are numerous events in a narrative. Does the author value all of them equally? If not, then how does he signify the value of each event? Chatman distinguishes between major events and minor events, stating, "Narrative events have not only a logic of connection, but a logic of *hierarchy*. Some are more important than others. In the classical narrative, only major events are part of the chain or armature of contingency. Minor events have a different structure."[45] Concerning major events, Chatman states, "Kernels [major events] are narrative moments that give rise to cruxes in the direction taken by events. They are nodes or hinges in the structure, branching points which force a movement into one of two (or more) possible paths."[46] When it comes to 'minor events', he states, "A minor plot event—a *satellite*—is not crucial in this sense. It can be deleted without disturbing the logic of the plot, though its omission will, of course, impoverish the narrative aesthetically. Satellites entail no choice, but are solely the workings-out of the choices made at the kernel."[47]

Based on Chatman's distinction between "major" and "minor" events, there are a few things to be noted. First, the degree of valuation of each event is intimately related to the author's ultimate purpose that he intends to accomplish through the entire narrative. Second, the role of the major events lies in proceeding with the entire narrative according to the author's destination for the narrative. That is, the author leads his narrative development through major events, which guide the path of the narrative. So, a major event functions as a driving force of narrative progression. Third, minor events can be understood in light of their connected major events. In other words, rather than having their own distinctive voices, minor events help major events and their role of moving the entire narrative forward.

44. Green, "Narrative Criticism," 93.
45. Chatman, *Story and Discourse*, 53.
46. Chatman, *Story and Discourse*, 53.
47. Chatman, *Story and Discourse*, 54.

What else would the author consider in his act of proceeding with the narrative? Resseguie states, "Almost all plots involve some clash of actions, ideas, points of views, desires, values, or norms."[48] This aspect of narrative is another thread continually appearing in the narrative. Darrell L. Bock also states, "They [biblical books] discuss events which involve God's interaction with humanity. But they do so with themes, characters, an unfolding story line, and conflict."[49] The author regards "conflict" as a reality in his progressing the narrative. Given the assumption that the author has in mind the ultimate resolution of that conflict on the horizon, in the process of his narrative development, the author would concentrate on the cause of the conflict, along with its escalation in the process, and the description of the characters involved in the conflict.

Luke's narrative development in Acts is most likely based on Acts 1:8. Its geographic nature in terms of the gospel's expansion is evident. At the same time, as the narrative progresses, it is identified that Luke might also have in view the ethnic expansion of the gospel. Furthermore, Luke's narrative development introduces the gospel's expansion in conflict with Judaism—in particular, the temple and the Mosaic law. This is because of Christ's work and its theological implications.

In the prologue of the Gospel (Luke 1:1–4), Luke introduces his work, most likely both the Gospel and Acts, as narrative. According to Robert C. Tannehill, the term διήγησις ("narrative") refers to "a longer narrative composed of a number of events."[50] This indicates Luke's role as compiling the entire narrative which consists of multiple episodes. How did Luke compile those episodes? He did it by arranging them "in order" (καθεξῆς). Just as Tannehill suggests, the term "in order" does not guarantee "an objective chronology."[51] It could refer to "in sequence in time, space, or logic."[52] Finally, Luke indicates that by doing so, he intended to increase assurance to his audience. That is, his orderly arrangement of those episodes would serve to fulfill that "assurance" goal. Considering Luke's role, method, and purpose, as is revealed in the prologue of the Gospel, makes it essential to investigate the Ethiopian episode's position in the procession of the gospel's expansion—geography, ethnicity, and religion.

---

48. Resseguie, *Narrative Criticism*, 201.

49. Blaising and Bock, *Progressive Dispensationalism*, 86.

50. Tannehill, *Narrative Unity of Luke-Acts*, 10. As for the "a single event," according to Tannehill, the Greek word διήγημα is used.

51. Tannehill, *Narrative Unity of Luke-Acts*, 1:11. Parsons, *Luke*, 45.

52. BDAG, 490.

Summary

To continue the scholarly conversation of the Ethiopian's ethnic and religious background, three methods were introduced by which to illumine the Ethiopian episode: (1) echoic allusion, (2) cultural gap in narrative, and (3) narrative criticism.

The first method, echoic allusion, is based on relevance theory. One text alludes to another text. An allusion between them would use an allusion signal, thus causing their contextual interaction. This signal is provocative enough to retrieve the original context of the alluded text and bring it to the new context that is occurring in the alluding text. The effect of this allusion is to enrich the meaning of the alluding text. Yet the contextual meaning of the alluded text can be antithetical to that of the alluding text. This method would be helpful in understanding a text of which historical background is not clear. It will be applied to the terms "foreigner" and "eunuch" in Isa 56:1–8.

Second, the Ethiopian episode has multiple cultural elements. These elements belong to the cognitive world shared in common between Luke and his original audience. However, the author's rhetorical purpose is to invite his original audience to a new cognitive world, which to a certain extent is distinct from their established shared thought world. To modern readers, those cultural elements in narrative come as unfamiliar cultural gaps. This chapter has suggested the significance of filling in those cultural gaps—in terms of getting into the shared cognitive world between the author and the original audience, as well as gaining an understanding of the new cognitive world that the author's rhetoric is depicting.

Lastly, narrative criticism has been introduced, as well as its usefulness in positioning the Ethiopian episode in Luke's narrative progression of the gospel's expansion—geographic, ethnic, and religious. All three methods presented would be a means of continuing the scholarly conversation of the Ethiopian by further developing what was discussed or presenting what was undiscussed.

The next chapter will explore the textual tradition of Deut 23:1–8 to understand how this text is used in Jewish literature. In particular, its use of an echoic allusion in interpreting Isa 56:1–8 would lead to gaining an eschatological picture of inclusiveness for the ethnically foreign and ritually incomplete—those who are already in God's covenant but are excluded from the cultic system of the temple. This aspect is conceptually embedded in Luke's introduction of the Samaritan (Luke 17:15–19) and the Ethiopian (Acts 8:26–40).

Chapter 3

Textual Tradition of the Assembly of the Lord

SOME BIBLICAL SCHOLARS VIEW the Ethiopian (Acts 8:26–40) as a God-fearing uncircumcised gentile. Their basis for this point of view is Deut 23:1 (MT 23:2 *BHS5*), which prohibits the admission of a castrated male (i.e., eunuch) to the assembly of the Lord. Is it legitimate to use the Deut 23:1 stipulation as a criterion for that view? With this question in view, I will explore the textual traditions of Deut 23:1–8 in the Old Testament, the Dead Sea Scrolls, Josephus, Philo, and rabbinic literature.

I will investigate three areas of research in each of the textual citations or conceptual indications of Deut 23:1–8: (1) the setting of the stipulation's usage, (2) the covenantal status of the ritually unclean or incomplete and the ethnically foreign, and (3) their cultic position in the setting of the temple. This research brings up the following questions: What is the usage of the Deut 23:1 stipulation in history? What is the setting of its usage? Is it ritual or ethnic? Is it communal or cultic? What does it presuppose about the status of God's covenant people? Does it implicate their exclusion? All these questions examine the rationale for using Deut 23:1–8. This study will pay particular attention to Isa 56:1–8. Its overall message challenges the exclusive characteristic of Deut 23:1–8 as it introduces the two groups, "foreigner" and "eunuch," from eschatological, ethical, polemical, and all-inclusive perspectives. These perspectives are conceptually embedded in Luke's presentation of the Samaritans (Acts 8:9–25) and the Ethiopian (8:26–40) regarding the cultic system of the temple.

Circumcision for Inclusion or Exclusion of Ethnic Others

Deuteronomy 23:1–8 is the stipulation of the assembly of the Lord. This stipulation prohibits the six entities of people groups from being admitted to the assembly of the Lord: (1) an emasculated man, (2) a child of a forbidden union, (3) an Ammonite, (4) a Moabite, (5) an Edomite, and (6) an Egyptian.[1] To understand the nature of this stipulation, it is crucial to gain a perspective of how this stipulation works in relation to the covenant rite of circumcision.

The rite of circumcision is the fundamental basis for distinguishing the Israelites' ethnic identity and covenant relationship with Yahweh. It is their identity marker, distinguishing the Israelites from ethnic others.[2] The rite of circumcision also functions as the means of including ethnic others among them, particularly in their cultic setting. Thus, the rite of circumcision has the characteristic of openness to ethnic others. This section will analyze Gen 17:9–14 and Exod 12:43–49 and argue that the covenant rite of circumcision is an essential criterion for categorizing the ethnic non-Israelites into the two groups (i.e., excluded and included) in the cultic setting.

Genesis 17:9–14

Matthew Thiessen states, "Genesis 17 serves as the canonical introduction to the rite of circumcision, thereby influencing our understanding of all later passages."[3] In a series of speeches, God announces that he will establish an eternal covenant with Abraham and his offspring. Genesis 17:3b–21 is the second divine speech. It has three sections (vv. 3b–8; 9–14; 15–21). John Sailhamer notes that each section begins with the phrase, "And God said to him [Abram]," and introduces each of the parties involved in the covenant (i.e., Yahweh, Abram, and Sarai).[4] In the second section (vv. 9–14), there are three groups of people listed with respect to circumcision: (1) a male "born in the house of Abraham," (2) a male "bought with money" from a foreigner, and (3) "a foreigner."

---

1. The stipulation states that the Edomites and the Egyptians can be admitted in their third generation. Friedl, *Brüderliches Volk*, 50. Friedl sees the Edomites and the Egyptians as immigrants, distinct from foreigners.

2. Thiessen, "Genealogy, Circumcision, and Conversion," 131. Ross, *Creation and Blessing*, 333. Ross states, "The fact that circumcision existed in the ancient world before it was instituted as the covenant sign does not detract from its meaning," as he regards it as "a symbol of separation, purity, and loyalty to the covenant."

3. Thiessen, "Genealogy, Circumcision, and Conversion," 55.

4. Sailhamer, "Genesis," 180.

Three ways to identify these groups are described in this section. First, the covenant rite of circumcision applies to the first two groups. From an ethnic perspective, the first group (those born as Abraham's descendants) consists of the ethnic insiders, whereas the second group (those bought as Abraham's slaves) consists of the ethnic others. The household slaves now reside in the house of Abraham; this presumes their circumcision. Provided that their practice of circumcision presupposes their commitment to Yahweh, these ethnic others now affiliate in Yahweh's covenant relationship along with Abraham and his ethnic offspring.

Second, the phrase בֶּן־נֵכָר ("foreigner") indicates that the foreigner has no ethnic or geographic association with Abraham, as evidenced in its modifying phrase "who is not from your offspring" (v. 12). The phrase connotes the person's origin from a geographically foreign land. According to Bruce Waltke and Michael O'Connor, the preposition מִן can indicate "the place where a thing or person originated."[5] Thus, the phrase מִכֹּל בֶּן־נֵכָר ("from any foreigner") retains the sense of geographic distance from Abraham and his offspring.

Third, the group of ethnic others can be further categorized: (1) included others (i.e., circumcised foreign slaves in the household of Abraham) and (2) excluded others (i.e., uncircumcised foreigners), as indicated in the prohibition of uncircumcised ones from becoming Yahweh's people (v. 14).

Hence, Gen 17:9–14 indicates that there are three factors to be considered for categorizing people based on the stipulation of circumcision: (1) ethnic, (2) geographic, and (3) cultic. Based on these factors, the three groups of people listed in Gen 17:9–14 can be categorized into (1) ethnic, cultic, and geographic insiders (i.e., males born in the house of Abraham), (2) ethnic others but cultic and geographic insiders (i.e., males bought from a foreigner), and (3) ethnic, cultic, and geographic outsiders (i.e., foreigners).

Exodus 12:43–49

Two Settings in View

Exodus 12:43–49 expands the household of Abraham in Gen 17:9–14 to the Israelites and the nation of Israel. Yahweh's commissioning has two settings in view: (1) the exodus and (2) the land of Canaan. During the time of their departure from Egypt, two ethnic groups are mentioned: "the people of Israel" (בְּנֵי־יִשְׂרָאֵל, v. 37) and "a mixed multitude" (עֵרֶב רַב, v. 38). The Lord's commissioning also projects the time when the Israelites would be in

---

5. Waltke and O'Connor, *Introduction to Biblical Hebrew Syntax*, 212.

the land of Canaan. This is evident in the statute of the unleavened bread, which implies two groups of people as eligible for the feast: the "sojourner" (גֵּר) and the "native of the land" (אֶזְרַח הָאָרֶץ, v. 19). The phrase "native of the land" would be the descendants of Israel in the land of Canaan.[6]

Five Groups of Ethnic Others

The role of circumcision and its ethnic, cultic, and geographic implications, as mentioned in Gen 17:12b–13a, are more clearly revealed in Exod 12:43–49. This account is about institutionalizing the Passover feast and regulating who is eligible for participation in the feast. There are five groups of ethnic non-Israelites listed in this account: (1) the foreigner (בֶּן נֵכָר), (2) the purchased slave (עֶבֶד), (3) the temporary resident (תּוֹשָׁב), (4) the hired worker (שָׂכִיר), and (5) the resident alien (גֵּר). According to Thomas B. Dozeman, all the listed groups are non-Israelites who "reside for different reasons among the Israelite people in the land of Israel."[7] This detailed categorization of non-Israelites points to the eventual presence of these groups in the land of Canaan.

The first group of ethnic others is the foreigner (בֶּן נֵכָר, v. 43). It appears to be inclusive of all four other ethnic non-Israelite groups. That is, its referent could be one of the four groups depending on its given context. Based on this logic, בֶּן נֵכָר could refer to a circumcised resident alien in the land of Israel. Although this comprehensive notion cannot be excluded, it seems more appropriate to render the phrase as an individual group, distinct from the other non-Israelite groups. Just as noted in the section of Gen 17:9–14, it contains the nuance of its referent's ethnic, geographic, and cultic distance from the Israelites.

The adjective "foreign" (נֵכָר) occurs in the MT in relation to "person," "god," "idol," "land," and "object."[8] All these items that the adjective modifies are of foreign origin, indicating an absolute sense of foreignness to the Israelites. Eugene Carpenter argues that the Hebrew phrase בֶּן־נֵכָר describes:

> the excluded person who is essentially a non-Israelite and is basically a description of someone dangerous or hostile to God's

---

6. Davies, *Critical and Exegetical Commentary*, 59.

7. Dozeman, *Commentary on Exodus*, 286.

8. The term "foreign" (נֵכָר) in the MT: (1) "person" (Gen 17:12, 27; Exod 12:43; Lev 22:25; 2 Sam 22:45, 46; Neh 9:2; Pss 18:45, 46; 144:7, 11; Isa 56:3, 6, 60:10; 61:5; 62:8; Ezek 44:7, 9); (2) "god" (Gen 35:2, 4; Deut 31:16; 32:12; Josh 24:20, 23; Judg 10:16; 1 Sam 7:3; 2 Chr 33:15; Jer 5:19; Dan 11:39; Mal 2:11); (3) "idol" (Ps 81:10; Jer 8:19); (4) "land" (Ps 137:4); and (5) "object" (Neh 13:30; 2 Chr 14:2 ["altars"]).

people and certainly not qualified to take part in Israel's Passover celebrations. His time among the Israelites is temporary, and his relationship with the Israelites on a covenantal level is nonexistent.[9]

Carpenter's statement appears to be contradictory to how Isaiah uses the phrase. Isaiah portrays the roles of the foreigners in the context of the Lord's promise to bless the Israelites.[10] With this point in view, Isaiah's portrayal of "foreigner" in the context of Isa 56:1–8 is notably unique, still indicating its antagonistic nuance. This aspect raises the question of what lies behind Isaiah's use of "foreigner" in Isa 56:1–8. This issue can be dealt with from a polemical perspective, which will be discussed in the section on Isa 56:1–8.

The second grouping in the list is the purchased "slave" (עֶבֶד, v. 44). Their participation in the Feast of Passover is conditioned on their obedience to the rite of circumcision. The position of this group right after the foreigner (בֶּן־נֵכָר) recalls Gen 17:12b, which shows that the household slave was purchased from a foreigner.

The next two groups of ethnic others, the juxtaposed nouns תּוֹשָׁב and שָׂכִיר, can be explained together.[11] Both are ethnic non-Israelites, along with the purchased household slaves and the resident aliens in the land of Israel. Their residence with the Israelites is not as long compared to the household slaves and the resident aliens; that is, they are not permanent settlers among the Israelites.[12] They are not part of Yahweh's covenant people. Their lack of circumcision indicates their lack of faith in Yahweh and lack of commitment to his covenant. This leads to their ineligibility for the Feast of Passover. Hence, both groups, תּוֹשָׁב and שָׂכִיר, can be categorized as ethnic others, temporary dwellers, and cultically excluded.

The final grouping in the list of ethnic others is the "resident alien" (גֵּר). This term is used with the verbal phrase יָגוּר אִתְּךָ ("sojourns with you,"

---

9. Carpenter, *Exodus*, 477.

10. Isaiah sees foreigners as those who help and serve the Israelites (as builders of the walls and servants [60:10] and as shepherds of flocks and plowmen and vinedressers [61:5]). According to Andrew Abernethy, Isa 61:5–6 is "a reversal of status between the oppressed and the oppressive nations," and Isa 62:8 is "a new era of hope for a people wounded by a reality where empire prohibits God's people from the basic right of enjoying the fruits of their labors." Abernethy, *Eating in Isaiah*, 171.

11. תּוֹשָׁב denotes someone "who comes from the original Canaanite population of the territory occupied by Israel, or alternatively who has become resident in such a locality" (*HALOT*, 1712). The term שָׂכִיר denotes "hireling, day-labourer" or "mercenary, hired soldier" (*HALOT*, 1327). Victor Hamilton sees both nouns as a hendiadys. Hamilton, *Exodus*, 197.

12. Carpenter, *Exodus 1–18*, 478.

v. 48). Its occurrence is followed by the practice of circumcision on the "sojourning" male. Two characteristics identify this sojourner. First, he is living among the Israelites. Second, he needs to practice the rite of circumcision in order to participate in the Feast of Passover. Hence, the term גֵּר carries a geographic and religious association with the Israelites.

Conceptualized Term גֵּר

As noted above, each of the non-Israelite groups listed in Exod 12:43–49 retains its own characteristics regarding ethnic background, geographical cohabitation, and religious affiliation. When it comes to the term גֵּר, Exod 12:48 reads:

> If a stranger (גֵּר) shall sojourn (יָגוּר) with you and would keep the Passover to the Lord, let all his males (לוֹ כָל־זָכָר) be circumcised. Then he may come near and keep it, he shall be as a native of the land. But no uncircumcised person shall eat of it.[13]

The גֵּר is related to the Hebrew verb גּוּר, which means "to dwell as alien and dependant."[14] Considering this etymology, the noun refers to a resident alien, denoting the person's physical residence in a foreign land. Based on Exod 12:48–49, the noun גֵּר also shows a solid sense of affiliation with a religion in that land. In terms of a logical sequence, it would be more appropriate to see "foreigner" (בֶּן נֵכָר) in the place of "resident alien" (גֵּר). That is, a foreigner would come to the land, reside among the Israelites, and be circumcised. Instead, the use of גֵּר even for the uncircumcised ethnic foreigner suggests that the noun is such a conceptualized term as to denote or presuppose his physical residence and religious affiliation among the Israelites.

In Exod 12:19, the prohibition of eating leavened bread is applied to both "a resident alien" (גֵּר) and "a native of the land."[15] Given this stipulation, it is reasonable to suggest that the term גֵּר in Exod 12:48 presumes the concept of a circumcised yet non-Israelite condition. In this respect, the noun גֵּר is a technical term. According to William H. C. Propp, the resident alien (גֵּר) is "almost always a non-Israelite man living among Israelites and

13. LXX uses προσήλυτος ("proselyte") for גֵּר.
14. *HALOT*, 185.
15. In Exod 12:19 LXX, the Greek term "γειώρας" is used for the term גֵּר. Its basic meaning is "resident alien." It is clear that the LXX translation is focused on the alien's cohabitation with the Israelites ("the natives of the land"). However, the context of the Hebrew word's occurrence is the prohibition of eating what is leavened. With this focus in view, the Hebrew noun גֵּר implicates a religious affiliation.

participating in their religion."[16] R. J. D. Knauth states, "[I]n many legal contexts *gēr* is used as a technical term for a particular social status, carefully distinguished from and standing between the 'native' (*'ezraḥ*) and 'brother' (*'āḥ*) on the one hand, and the 'foreigner' (*nokrî*) on the other hand."[17] Hence, the term גֵּר presupposes the resident alien's habitation among the Israelites. In addition, it connotes his religious affiliation with Yahweh's covenant by following the rite of circumcision.

If so, does the term גֵּר always presume a religious affiliation in the foreign land? The LXX translation of the Hebrew term sheds light on this question. The term גֵּר occurs in the MT 92 times. The LXX translates it into five different Greek words: (1) πάροικος, (2) προσήλυτος, (3) γειώρας, (4) γιώρας, and (5) ξένος.[18] For πάροικος, when its instances are contextually evaluated, it does not have a religious connotation, that is, the person is not a proselyte (a religious convert). Its emphasis is on the resident alien's physical dwelling in the land of Israel. Based on this usage of the Greek translation, W. C. Allen states that the Hebrew term could refer to "members of a tribe or nation sojourning in a strange land."[19]

For προσήλυτος, this translation has a connotation of religious conversion. However, a few cases must be considered in detail (Exod 22:21 [22:20 in the MT and LXX]; 23:9; Lev 19:34; Deut 10:19). The use of the Hebrew term גֵּר in these cases is to remind the Israelites of their status when they were in the land of Egypt and is related to the Lord's demand for them not to oppress ethnic others dwelling in their land. In Exod 22:21, the Lord commands the Israelites not to oppress גֵּר because the Israelites themselves were גֵּר in the land of Egypt. The LXX translates both the non-Israelite and the Israelites as προσήλυτος ("proselyte"). Based on this, Matthew Thiessen states, "The use of προσήλυτος to refer to the identity of the Israelites in Egypt suggests that the first occurrence of προσήλυτος in these verses cannot refer to a

---

16. Propp, *Exodus 1–18*, 419.

17. R. J. D. Knauth, "Alien, Foreign Resident," in *DOTP*, 27.

18. πάροικος (Gen 15:13; 23:4; Exod 2:22; 18:3; Deut 14:21; 23:7; 2 Sam 1:13; 1 Chr 29:15; Pss 39:13; 119:19; Jer 14:8). Deut 23:7 (23:8 in the MT and LXX) is unique in that the LXX uses πάροικος to describe the status of the Israelites in the land of Egypt, not προσήλυτος (cf. Exod 22:21 [LXX 22:20]; 23:9; Lev 19:34; Deut 10:19). γειώρας (Exod 12:19) is identical to γιώρας (Isa 14:1), which refers to "resident alien" (*GELS*, 132). ξένος refers to "not belonging to and being outside of a company of people"; in Job 31:32, it refers to the "newly arrived immigrant" (*GELS*, 480).

19. Allen, "On the Meaning of ΠΡΟΣΗΛΥΤΟΣ," 266. Allen notes that Deut 14:21 could be an exception. Yet, as he notes, it seems odd to refer to such a resident alien who partakes in a carcass of animals as προσήλυτος. Hence, this is the case for proof that the term προσήλυτος implies a solid sense of religious affiliation when it is translated from the Hebrew term גֵּר.

convert."²⁰ Thiessen's point of view is that the Greek word προσήλυτος is not a religious convert; rather, it is a physical resident.²¹

However, if προσήλυτος is a physical resident or religious convert can be approached from a contextual standpoint. The main purpose of the Lord's command in Exod 22:21 is not to oppress ethnic others in the land. This is a legal code. This command is addressed to the Israelites for the sake of resident aliens in the land. With this context in view, the Hebrew writer refers to both (the Israelites in Egypt and the resident aliens in the land) as גֵּר and the LXX translates it into προσήλυτος. As W. C. Allen notes, the Israelites "were in the land of Egypt in the same position of homeless strangers as are proselytes among yourselves [themselves]."²² In this sense, the Greek word προσήλυτος still has a sense of religious connotation in view.

Hence, the noun גֵּר basically refers to a resident alien who lives among the Israelites. It can also imply the person's religious affiliation to the Israelites through his practice of the covenant ritual circumcision. These two aspects, in general, are reflected in the LXX translations of that Hebrew term (πάροικος and προσήλυτος); the former emphasizes the alien's physical cohabitation and the latter his religious affiliation. If the Hebrew word גֵּר and its Greek translation προσήλυτος are used in the text, this is a strong implication to the alien's religious affiliation, particularly if the setting is cultic and/or legal.

In conclusion, there are two main designations for ethnically non-Israelites: גֵּר and בֶּן־נֵכָר. The former conceptually denotes the non-Israelite's geographic cohabitation, practice of circumcision, and covenantal affiliation with the Israelites. In contrast, the latter connotes the non-Israelite's distant status from the Israelites in terms of geography and religion.

Deuteronomy 23:1–8

Deuteronomy 23:1–8 [MT 23:2–9] begins a new section of the law focused on קְהַל יְהוָה ("the assembly of the Lord," vv. 1, 2 [2x], 3 [2x], 8).²³ The issue of who is not eligible for admission into the assembly dominates this section. According to Gerhard von Rad, "It [Deut 23:1–8] consists of a series in five

---

20. Thiessen, "Revisiting the προσήλυτος in 'the LXX,'" 342. Thiessen's article is a critical review of W. C. Allen's article.

21. Thiessen, "Revisiting the προσήλυτος in 'the LXX,'" 342.

22. Allen, "On the Meaning of ΠΡΟΣΗΛΥΤΟΣ," 269.

23. Christensen, *Deuteronomy 21:10–34:12*, 532. According to Christensen, Deut 22:30 [MT 23:1] functions "as the conclusion to the previous section of laws on marital and sexual misconduct."

parts in apodictic style; it is thus a text which must be considered first as a definite unit."[24]

Recontextualization of the Assembly in Canaan

According to *HALOT*, the noun קָהָל refers to "Israel, in particular the עַם equivalent to קְהַל יהוה Yahweh's contingent."[25] One notable distinction in its occurrence in Deut 23:1–8 is the attachment of the phrase "of the Lord." This is unique apart from Num 20:4, which is the first occurrence of the entire phrase (קְהַל יְהוָה) in the MT. Numbers 20:4 illustrates the Israelites' complaint to Moses at Meribah. Given its usage in this context, it appears that the addition "of the Lord" makes no significant difference to the notion that the noun קָהָל itself refers to the general gathering of the Israelites.

However, the assembly in Deut 23:1–8 cannot be identified as the people of Israel. In the book of Deuteronomy, the noun קָהָל occurs four times before Deut 23:1–8 (5:22; 9:10; 10:4; 18:16). In all these occurrences, the noun "assembly" is used to refer to the previous gathering of the Israelites before the Lord at Horeb. Now the Israelites are on the plains of Moab. Moses gives three sermons at the end of his life, and while doing so, he reminds his current audience of the Horeb gathering, recalling what God had done and instructed in the past. In this context, the phrase "the assembly of the Lord" occurs six times in Deut 23:1–8.

In comparison to the other occurrences of "the assembly" in Deuteronomy, Deut 23:1–8 defines a new assembly and constitutes its eligible members. It does so by prohibiting certain groups of people from admission. In this regard, Edward J. Woods states, "Thus, here the worshipping community is defined in a more limited fashion with the exclusion of the following three groups of people [the emasculated man, the child of a forbidden marriage, and Ammonite and Moabite]."[26] This new stipulation does not describe the current assembly at the plains of Moab. Rather, it projects a new congregation to be instituted in the land of Canaan. J. G. McConville states, "[T]he question of admission to the assembly is raised at this point, since Israelites would rub shoulders with non-Israelites during the nation's life in Canaan."[27] Michael D. Fiorello also states, "While the theme of Deuteronomy 23 is the assembly (קָהָל) of the Lord, the usage of this term

24. von Rad, *Deuteronomy*, 145.
25. The noun קָהָל occurs in the setting of "battle," "summons to court," and "Israel" (*HALOT*, 1079–80).
26. Woods, *Deuteronomy*, 243.
27. McConville, *Deuteronomy*, 348.

in verse 2 [MT] indicates that the expression is somewhat narrower in its intent than the whole nation of Israel."[28] Hence, Deut 23:1–8 is about constituting a new assembly in the land of Canaan, distinct from the assembly at Horeb, as well as at Moab.[29]

This idea can be supported by Deut 23:9–14 (MT 23:10–15), which deals with the Lord's demand for holiness in the military camp. Given its proximity to the stipulation regarding "the assembly of the Lord" (Deut 23:1–8), the camp rules can be used to illumine the nature of "the assembly of the Lord." The Lord demands that the camp be holy (קָדוֹשׁ) because "he [the Lord your God] walks in the midst of the [your] camp" (23:14). Based on the assumption of the Lord's holy presence in the camp, Israel's military camp is to reflect his holiness and completeness. According to Mary Douglas, "The idea of holiness was given an external physical expression in the wholeness of the body seen as a perfect container."[30] Likewise, the prohibition of the castrated male and the forbidden-union child from admission to the assembly of the Lord (Deut 23:1) can be interpreted in terms of God's holiness and completeness in that assembly.

The rules regarding camp holiness are analogous to the stipulation regarding the assembly of the Lord. The members of the camp are a narrow group gathered for a military campaign, like an inner circle within a broad circle. Similarly, the stipulation placed on the assembly of the Lord restricts the assembly to an inner circle within the broad circle of God's covenant people.

Nature of the Assembly of the Lord in Deuteronomy 23:1–8

Concerning the issue of entry into the assembly of the Lord, Deut 23:1–8 is divided into three units, each of which introduces two specific groups of people. The first unit prohibits the emasculated male and the child of a forbidden union from entering the assembly of the Lord (vv. 1–2). The second unit introduces Ammonites and Moabites and stipulates their exclusion "forever" (vv. 3–6). For each of these four groups, the stipulation uses

---

28. Fiorello, *Physically Disabled in Ancient Israel*, 95. However, there are scholars who see "the assembly of the Lord" (Deut 23:1–8) broadly as the nation of Israel. Jeffrey Tigay states, "Eligibility for membership in the Assembly seems to have been tantamount to eligibility for full citizenship." Tigay, *Deuteronomy*, 210.

29. Awabdy, *Immigrants and Innovative Law*, 74. Awabdy acknowledges that the assembly of the Lord in Deut 23 is "not coterminous" with the cultic festivals "at Sukkoth (Deut 16:13–14) and Shavuot (16:10–12)." In this sense, he supports the view that the assembly of the Lord in Deut 23 is distinct from the assembly at Horeb and Moab.

30. Douglas, *Purity and Danger*, 53.

the negative particle לֹא and the Qal use of בוא. The third unit introduces Edomites and Egyptians, and for each, the stipulation begins with the negative particle לֹא and the Piel use of תעב. The stipulation permits their third-generation children to enter the assembly of the Lord. The main concern of the stipulation with the first four groups in the list is its prohibition. The stipulation stresses the admission of the last two groups, the Edomites and the Egyptians, even though it is effective in their third generation.

The section of Deut 23:1–8 also seems to categorize the groups of people based on ethnicity. Although this is the beginning of a new section and deals with a new subject matter, its first two verses appear to be in parallel with the last verse of the preceding section (Deut 22:13–30). Both begin with the negative particle לֹא and its following Qal imperfect verb and have no disjunctive textual element between them. Thus, Deut 23:1–2 has continuous and discontinuous aspects with respect to their textual relatedness to the preceding section. Also, the rest of the section introduces four non-Israelite ethnic groups (Ammonite, Moabite, Edomite, and Egyptian). This textual piece can suggest that the emasculated male and the forbidden-union child are the groups ethnically regarded as of Israel.

There is no clear ethnic or cultic designation mentioned for the emasculated male and the child of a forbidden union. Some scholars maintain that the stipulation of Deut 23:1–2 is a response to Canaanite cult practice involving castrating males and prostituting females.[31] Two proof texts, Deut 14:1 ("You shall not cut yourselves nor shave your forehead for the sake of the dead") and Deut 23:17 ("None of the daughters of Israel shall be a cult prostitute, and none of the sons of Israel shall be a cult prostitute"), are believed to allude to this kind of cultic practice. The prohibition of the two groups can be interpreted as protecting the Israelites from becoming connected to or involved in these cultic practices. Based on this view, the two groups introduced here can be regarded as ethnic non-Israelites.

However, although its polemical aspect cannot be completely rejected, this stipulation should be reexamined. The phrase "assembly of the Lord" occurs as a prepositional phrase with the preposition בְּ along with the Qal imperfect form of the verb בוא. Concerning the meaning of the verb בוא, Eugene H. Merrill states:

> The "assembly" (*qāhāl*) refers here to the formal gathering of the Lord's people as a community at festival occasions and other times of public worship and not to the nation of Israel as such. This is clear from the occurrence of the verb "enter"

---

31. Cairns, *Word and Presence*, 201. Thompson, *Deuteronomy*, 239. McConville, *Deuteronomy*, 348. Maxwell, *Deuteronomy*, 264–65.

(bō') throughout the passage (vv. 1–3, 8), a verb that suggests participation with the assembly and not initial introduction or conversion to it.³²

The act of entrance into the "assembly of the Lord" could be what the usual congregation of the Israelites would normally expect. In contrast, the prohibition of the emasculated male and the forbidden-union child from the assembly is interpreted as something new, a new restriction pronounced to all of God's covenant people. Hence, the two groups are part of the broad concept of assembly but not part of the narrow concept of assembly.

Deuteronomy 23:1–8 is about reconstituting the formal cultic gathering of Israel in the land of Canaan. Circumcision was the distinguishing characteristic of the Israelites and was even practiced by ethnic non-Israelites. Particularly in the cultic worship setting, the term גֵּר was a technical designation for those who were ethnic others yet cohabitants and cultic insiders.³³ The rite of circumcision is what defined God's covenant people in a broad sense. On the other hand, the restricting measures in Deut 23:1–8 for the assembly of the Lord defined a specific assembly to manifest God's holiness. Hence, Deut 23:1–8 did not define a general assembly of God's covenant people but defined a specific assembly in the cultic setting.

Leviticus 21:16–24 and 22:17–25

In this study of Deut 23:1–8 and its nature of application, it is evident that the ritually unclean or incomplete and the ethnically foreign, although being part of God's covenant people, have a certain degree of restriction in the cultic setting. This feature is identified in the case of priests who have physical blemishes, people who belong to the priesthood family but are restricted from participating in the cultic worship.

Leviticus 21:16–24 provides rules concerning the descendants of Aaron and their priestly roles. A priest would offer bread and go through the veil or approach the altar in the Tent of Meeting. In addition to defining the priest's role, the rules stipulate that a priest should not do the job if he has a blemish (21:18–20); the list of "blemishes" (מאוּם 21:17, 18, 21, 23]) includes the following physical defects: blind, lame, mutilated face, long

---

32. Merrill, *Deuteronomy*, 307.

33. Awabdy, *Immigrants and Innovative Law*, 77. Awabdy states, "Deut 23:4–9 does not reproduce the culture's socio-religious dynamics, but attempts to reconfigure—and in reconfiguring conceals—those dynamics by means of new laws." He regards Ammonite and Moabite as נכרי "a non-resident outsider." On the other hand, he regards Edomite and Egyptian as גֵּר.

limb, injured foot, injured hand, hunchback, dwarf, defect in his sight, itching disease, scabs, and crushed testicles. Michael D. Fiorello states, "It is possible that biblical writers saw these physical disabilities as a distinctive but normal aspect of a person's living experience."[34] Thus, this defect could be "due to a birth defect, deliberately inflicted for pagan religious ritual, or [have] accidentally incurred."[35] Hence, the blemish of "crushed testicles" cannot be limited to the practice of castration.

Leviticus 22:17–25 is a rule concerning the animal offering, prohibiting the unacceptable animal with a "blemish" (מאום [22:20, 21, 25]), which is the same term used to describe the twelve blemishes in Lev 21:16–24. The four Qal passive participles of מָעוּךְ, כָּתוּת, נָתוּק, and כָּרוּת ("bruised," "crushed," "torn," and "cut") describe the animal's impaired condition in relation to its testicles. All these words are in the passive form, a fact that the blemish is the result of outside effect; the practice of the "foreigner" (v. 25) would have caused this blemish—male animal mutilation. Given that the four different descriptive passive verbs appear for this blemish, however, it seems unreasonable to confine all these injuries to the practice of castration.

Parallel Relationship between the Priest and the Sacrificial Animal

Leviticus 21–22 deals with the Lord's demand for holiness in the priesthood and in the offerings. This section consists chiefly of four parts: (1) the priest's genealogical purity and physically unprofane state (21:1–15), (2) the prohibition of the blemished priest from the priestly role (21:16–24), (3) the priest's ritual cleanness (22:1–6), and (4) the prohibition on using a blemished animal for sacrifice (22:7–33). The structure and proximate locations of these passages require taking into consideration both the priest and the sacrificial animal with respect to their wholeness and completeness: The priest should be קֹדֶשׁ ("holy," 21:6) and the sacrificial animal תָּמִים ("perfect," 22:21).

According to Leigh M. Trevaskis, the unqualified priest (21:16–24) and the unacceptable sacrificial animal (22:17–25) have a parallel relation.[36] First, the Hebrew term מאום ("blemish") appears in both accounts. Second, each of the "blemish" lists has twelve specific blemishes (21:18–20; 22:22–24). Third, each list begins with "blind" and ends with "testicles." Fourth, it appears that the blemishes that affect the blemished priest also occur in

---

34. Fiorello, *Physically Disabled in Ancient Israel*, 82.
35. Fiorello, *Physically Disabled in Ancient Israel*, 84.
36. Trevaskis, *Holiness, Ethics and Ritual in Leviticus*, 210–13. Trevaskis presents five possible parallels between Lev 21:16–24 and 22:17–25.

the list of the blemished sacrificial animal. Fifth, both lists are related to the invalidation of the priest and the sacrificial animal. Sixth, the setting for both lists and their resulting prohibitions is the most holy place in the sanctuary (מִקְדָּשׁ). A legitimate priest could "go through the veil" (21:23) and "approach the altar" (21:23) to offer the sacrificed animal in that sacred precinct; the legitimate priest and the legitimate sacrificial animal are exposed to the Lord's holy presence.[37]

The seventh commonality is that their invalidation does not mean their excommunication. In the case of the priest, "he [the blemished priest] may eat the bread of God, both of the most holy and of the holy things" (21:22). Despite his state and his inability to perform his duty, the blemished priest still belongs to the priesthood. His status lies in the middle area between the inner circle of priesthood and the broad circle of priesthood. Concerning the cultically unacceptable animal, "a bull or a lamb that has a part too long or too short" can be offered "for a freewill offering" but not for "a vow offering" (22:23).[38] Even though the animal with "a part too long or too short" is not in perfect condition and fully eligible for sacrifice, it is regarded as acceptable in the freewill offering. Concerning the nature of this defect, Richard S. Hess states, "Such a defect does not achieve the ideal sense of balance required for sacrifices involving the perfect fulfillment of a vow, but neither does it call into question the wholeness of the animal as the other 'defects' do."[39] Hence, although the priest and sacrificial animal are not acceptable in the most complete sense of qualification, they have a limited degree of accepted state.

Comparison between Lev 21:20 and Deut 23:1

One of the listed blemishes that could impair a priest is "crushed testicles" (מְרוֹחַ אָשֶׁךְ, Lev 21:20). This Hebrew phrase only occurs at this place in the MT, so it has no textual connection with that of Deut 23:1. One of the words describing the impaired testicles of an animal (Lev 22:24) is the Qal passive participle form of כרת ("to cut"), which also occurs in the description of the emasculated male in Deut 23:1. Can the cultic setting of Lev 21 and 22 be identified with the setting of Deut 23:1–8? Both accounts have a cultic setting. However, the priest and the sacrificial animal enter the most sacred area in the sanctuary. On the other hand, the setting of Deut 23:1–8

---

37. מִקְדָּשׁ here refers to "the entire sacred precinct" (*HALOT*, 626).

38. Lev 7:11–36 is about the law of the sacrifice of peace offerings. This peace offering is either a thanksgiving offering, a vow offering, or a freewill offering.

39. Hess, "Leviticus," 778.

represented in "the assembly of the Lord" is different from the priest and the sacrificial animal's setting; it is a reduced form of the entire congregation of God's covenant people.

One common characteristic is identifiable in Lev 21–22 and Deut 23:1–8. The ineligible priest, the unacceptable sacrificial animal, the excluded groups of people from the assembly of the Lord—all are prohibited from participating in their cultic activities or duties, but none are excluded from their given statuses. Eugene H. Merrill states:

> Israelites with such handicaps are elsewhere assumed to have been full members of the community with the only restriction being their ineligibility for the priesthood (Lev 21:20). Our text [Deut 23:1], then, more fully clarifies the extent to which deformed Israelites could participate in the cultus and does not speak to the issue of whether or not they belonged to the covenant community. It is everywhere assumed that they did.[40]

Summary

Scholars commonly maintain that Deut 23:1–8 is a polemic against the pagan cultic practice of the Canaanites intended to protect the cultic setting of the Israelites from pagan intrusion. This point of view, however, presupposes that those excluded groups of people are ethnic non-Israelites who have no concern with the covenant people of Yahweh, that is, they are uncircumcised ethnic others. However, their entrance into the assembly of the Lord is not an initial stage of conversion. Instead, Deut 23:1–8 indicates their status as belonging to Yahweh's covenant people; this presumes their circumcision. That is, these excluded groups lie in the area between the inner circle and the broad circle. The first two groups belong to this area because of their physiological factors, whereas the last four groups belong to this area because of their ethnic foreign origins. Given that Deut 23:3–8 introduces Ammonite, Moabite, Edomite, and Egyptian (i.e., ethnic others), it is likely that the emasculated male and the forbidden-union children could be ethnic Israelites.

Textual Tradition of Deut 23:1–8 in the Old Testament

According to Gary E. Schnittjer, Deut 23:1–8 appears, in an implicit allusion or a direct citation, in Ruth 2:8, 10; 1 Kgs 11:1–2; Ezra 9:1–2; Neh 10:30;

---

40. Merrill, *Deuteronomy*, 307.

13:23–27; Isa 52:1; 56:1–7; Lam 1:10.[41] From those texts, I will explore the Ezra-Nehemiah text and Isa 56:1–8. As shown, Deut 23:1–8 is a text to reconstitute the setting of cultic worship by excluding the ritually unclean or incomplete and the ethnically foreign. Although the other texts reflect the conceptual world of exclusion, as implied in Deut 23:1–8, they do not show this aspect of reconstitution.

Ezra and Nehemiah

People of the Land

In the MT, the phrase "people of the land" has five different forms. First, the nouns "land" (אֶרֶץ) and "people" (עַם) are both singular (Ezra 4:4; Neh 9:10). Second, the noun "land" (אֶרֶץ) is singular, but the noun "people" (עַם) is plural (Ezra 10:2, 11; Neh 9:24; 10:31–32 [MT]). Third, both nouns are plural (Ezra 3:3; 9:1, 2, 11; Neh 9:30; 10:29 [MT]). Fourth, Ezra 6:21 uses the plural of "people" (גוֹי) with the singular of "land" (אֶרֶץ). Fifth, Neh 9:24 uses the plural of "man" (יֹשֵׁב) with the singular of "land" (אֶרֶץ).

The following four referents for "people of the land" are identifiable or inferable based on the context: (1) the current inhabitants of the land (Ezra 3:3; 4:4; 6:21; 9:1–2; 10:2, 11, 31–32 [MT]; Neh 10:29 [MT]), (2) the historical inhabitants of the land during the Canaan conquest (Ezra 9:11; Neh 9:24 [2x]), (3) the Egyptians (Neh 9:10), and (4) the Babylonians (Neh 9:30). Nehemiah sees the people of the land as ethnically foreign to the Israelites, for he refers to "the peoples of the lands" (עַמֵּי הָאֲרָצוֹת) as "foreigners" (בְּנֵי נֵכָר). Nehemiah uses the verb בדל ("to separate") in 9:2 and 10:28; in the former, he uses the phrase "the peoples of the lands," and in the latter, "foreigners."

---

41. Schnittjer, *Old Testament Use of Old Testament*, 876. Ruth is addressed as a Moabite (1:4, 22; 2:2, 6, 21; 4:5, 10). Ruth calls herself "foreigner" (נָכְרִי). These elements in Ruth recalls Deut 23:3. First Kings 11:1–2 is what recalls Solomon's intermarriage with foreign (נָכְרִי) women ("the daughters of Pharaoh, Moabite, Ammonite, Edomite, Sidonian, and Hittite"). All of the four ethnic others listed in Deut 23:3–8 (Ammonite, Moabite, Edomite, and Egyptian) are found here. In Isa 52:1, three adjectives are meaningful. קֹדֶשׁ ("holy") describes Jerusalem. The other two, עָרֵל ("uncircumcised") and טָמֵא ("unclean"), describe the foreign invading nations. The "uncircumcised" recalls the Abrahamic covenant, so it refers to a total distancing from Yahweh's covenant people. The "unclean" appears to be related to the Mosaic covenant in a ritual sense. In Lam 1:10, the sentence לֹא־יָבֹאוּ בַקָּהָל לָךְ ("not enter your assembly") recalls the stipulation of the assembly of the Lord in Deut 23:1–8. Schnittjer states, "Isa 52:1 interpretively alludes to the law of the assembly in Deut 23:1–8 [2–9] in accord with Lam 1:10 to affirm permanently excluded others" (250).

Ezra 6:21 and Neh 10:28

Both texts indicate that there are non-Israelite converts, classified as גֵּר. In general, Ezra and Nehemiah focus on the returned Israelites and the non-Israelite residents in the land. Although Ezra and Nehemiah neither use גֵּר nor focus on the non-Israelite converts, there are two passages in which Ezra and Nehemiah include ethnic others who affiliate in the worship of Yahweh.[42] Ezra 6:21 reads,

וַיֹּאכְלוּ בְנֵי־יִשְׂרָאֵל הַשָּׁבִים מֵהַגּוֹלָה
וְכֹל הַנִּבְדָּל מִטֻּמְאַת גּוֹיֵ־הָאָרֶץ אֲלֵהֶם
לִדְרֹשׁ לַיהוָה אֱלֹהֵי יִשְׂרָאֵל

> The sons of Israel who returned from the exile ate it
> and everyone who separated himself from the uncleanness of
> the peoples of the land to them
> to seek the Lord God of Israel.

Ezra 6:21 seems to have in mind three groups of people: (1) the returned Israelites, (2) all who separated from the uncleanness of the peoples of the land and attached themselves to the Israelites to worship the Lord God of Israel, and (3) the peoples of the land.[43] Given that Ezra and Nehemiah focus on the general distinctions between the Israelites and the peoples of the land, Ezra's mention of the second group is intriguing.

Likewise, Neh 10:28 [MT 29] reads, וְכָל־הַנִּבְדָּל מֵעַמֵּי הָאֲרָצוֹת אֶל־תּוֹרַת הָאֱלֹהִים ("And everyone who separated from the peoples of the lands to the law of God"). Nehemiah makes a lengthy list of people who put their names to the sealed covenant (Neh 10:1–27). Nehemiah 10:28 [MT 29] is an additional note that Nehemiah puts to that list. Ezra 6:21 and Neh 10:28 both use בדל ("to separate") to describe an act of separation from the uncleanness of the peoples of the land and a decision to seek Yahweh.

Ezra and Nehemiah see this newly affiliated group of people as newly converted to the worship of Yahweh.[44] The setting of Ezra 6:19–22 is the returned Israelites' celebration of the Passover and the Feast of Unleavened Bread. If so, based on Exod 12:43–49, these new converts should undergo

---

42. Schnittjer, "Bad Ending of Ezra-Nehemiah," 44. Schnittjer states, "Twice, Ezra-Nehemiah refers to foreigners who rightly became part of the Yahwistic community."

43. There is no verb for "to join" in the text. The prepositional phrase אֲלֵהֶם ("to them" [the returned Israelites]) indicates their act of joining the Israelites.

44. Harrington, *Books of Ezra and Nehemiah*, 404. By her comparison of the list of Neh 10:1–27 with those of Ezra 2 and Neh 7, Harrington points out the growth of the community—a possible indication that new members have been added from local residents.

the rite of circumcision as their expression of faith in Yahweh. There is no mention of גֵּר in Ezra and Nehemiah, yet its concept is in Ezra-Nehemiah's descriptions of those newly affiliated foreigners in the land. Hence, it is reasonable to assume that some local residents in the land joined the returning Israelites to worship Yahweh.[45]

Ezra 9:1–2 and 10:2

On his return to Jerusalem, Ezra received a report about the people of Israel in Jerusalem: "The people of Israel, the priests, and the Levites did not separate (בדל) from the peoples of the lands in their abominations (כְּתוֹעֲבֹתֵיהֶם)" (Ezra 9:1). When the noun תּוֹעֵבָה ("abomination") appears in relation to the Canaanites, it refers to their "abhorrent customs" (Lev 18:30), including sexual sins (Lev 18:22; 22:13).[46] Based on this report, Ezra's concern is not just about the returned Israelites' intermarriage with the local residents. It also includes their adoption of pagan customs in the land. To consider the nature of Ezra's reform as restricted to the issue of ethnicity does not fully appreciate what lies behind this reform: the customs of the local residents introduced through intermarriage.

Ezra 9:1–2 identifies "the peoples of the lands" as "the Canaanites, the Hittites, the Perizzites, the Jebusites, the Ammonites, the Moabites, the Egyptians, and the Amorites." The Jebusites and the Amorites were inhabitants of the land of Canaan during the time of conquest (Deut 7:1–6). Three of the groups in the list (the Ammonites, the Moabites, and the Egyptians) were the ethnic non-Israelites to be excluded from the assembly of the Lord (Deut 23:3–8).[47] According to Ezra 9:1–2, the intermarriage of returning Israelites with non-Jewish people diluted the Jews' ethnic identity. As a result, "the holy seed" (זֶרַע הַקֹּדֶשׁ) was mixed with "the peoples of the lands" (v. 2).

The book of Ezra ends with Ezra's separation of "all the men of Judah and Benjamin" from their "foreign (נָכְרִי) wives" (10:2). Shecaniah (10:2) acts in obedience to Ezra, indicating that his obedience is based on "commandment" (מִצְוָה) and "law" (תּוֹרָה, v. 3). What is the commandment or law in view here? Textually, there is no evidence that Ezra's separating act and

---

45. Yamauchi, "Ezra and Nehemiah," 431. On the other hand, Breneman argues that those people are "Jews living in Judah other than the ones who returned from the exile." Breneman, *Ezra, Nehemiah, Esther*, 121.

46. *HALOT*, 1703. Its general usage relates to the cultic practices of pagan nations and the Israelites' practice of those things. Most of its occurrences are in Ezekiel. Ezek 44:7 states that the act of admitting "foreigners" (בְּנֵי־נֵכָר) who are "uncircumcised in heart and flesh" is the Israelites' abomination.

47. Harrington, *Ezra and Nehemiah*, 231.

Nehemiah 13:1–3

Nehemiah 13:1b–2a is the citation of Deut 23:3–5 (MT 23:4–6).[48] It is introduced with the phrase "from the Book of Moses" (v. 1a). The content includes the Ammonite and Moabite, two of the six groups of people prohibited from admission to the assembly of the Lord (Deut 23:1–8). It is not clear if Nehemiah has all six groups in mind; his focus is on the Ammonite and Moabite. Verse 3 states that the Israelites "separated (בדל) all those of foreign descent (עֵרֶב) from Israel." The noun עֵרֶב occurs five times in the MT (Exod 12:38 [non-Israelites who joined the Hebrews at the time of the Exodus]; Neh 13:3 [people of foreign origin in post-exilic Judah]; Jer 25:20 and Ezek 30:5 [groups of foreign mercenaries]; and Jer 50:37 [the mixture of races in the population of Babylon]).[49] Its related verb ערב occurs in a Hitpael perfect form in Ezra 9:2 ("the holy race *has mixed itself* with the peoples of the lands," emphasis added). To put these together, the phrase כָּל־עֵרֶב indicates the ethnically mixed people resulting from intermarriage.[50]

Nehemiah rebukes his people for marrying with "women of Ashdod, Ammon, and Moab" (Neh 13:23). Schnittjer suggests that Ashdod was "a place known for its *mamzer* (מַמְזֵר) inhabitants in this period," meaning "persons of illegitimate birth."[51] If Ashdod represents the children of a forbidden union, as listed in Deut 23:2, Nehemiah's citation of the Deuteronomy text is a little broader. In his rebuke, Nehemiah recalls Solomon and his marriage with foreign women (Neh 13:26). According to 1 Kgs 11:1, those foreign women were "the daughter of Pharaoh [Egyptian], Moabite, Ammonite, Edomite, Sidonian, and Hittite."[52]

What is the rationale for Nehemiah's citation of Deut 23:3–5? Given his situated context, Nehemiah could refer to the Ammonite and Moabite because he has in view Tobiah and Sanballat, his two main opponents. He introduces Tobiah as an Ammonite (Neh 2:10, 19; 4:3), and Sanballat as a

---

48. There are a few textual differences between Neh 13:1b–2a and Deut 23:3–4. One of them is the phrase "assembly of the Lord," which changes to the phrase "assembly of God."

49. *HALOT*, 878.

50. Harrington, *Ezra and Nehemiah*, 457. According to Harrington, the Hebrew term in the context of Neh 13:3 refers to "the intermarriages that had produced an ethnic and religious mixture."

51. Schnittjer, "Bad Ending of Ezra-Nehemiah," 43.

52. Schnittjer, "Bad Ending of Ezra-Nehemiah," 44.

Horonite (חֹרֹנִי, 2:10, 19; 13:29). According to Hannah K. Harrington, the term Horonite could relate to a place in Moab called Horonaim.[53] Harrington's view is that Nehemiah's citation of the Ammonite and Moabite from Deut 23:3–5 has a direct contextual application targeting Tobiah and Sanballat.

However, Benedikt Hensel sees Ezra-Nehemiah's reform—separating the returned Israelites and their descendants from the people of the land—as a polemic "cipher" toward the Samaritans and their cultic worship at Gerizim.[54] One basis for this view is an Elephantine letter to Bagoas which states that Sanballat was the governor of Samaria and had two sons, Delaiah and Shelemiah. According to Harrington, "Sanballat's name includes the moon god, Sin, but his sons' names end within 'iah,' which is a shortened form of Yahweh."[55] Nehemiah gives no detailed descriptions on the involvement of Sanballat and the Samaritans in the cultic worship of Yahweh.

Whether Nehemiah refers to Sanballat as Moabite or Samaritan, it is clear that Nehemiah sees him as ethnically foreign, so he separates Sanballat's daughter from her Israelite husband, "one of the sons of Jehoiada, the son of Eliashib the high priest" (13:28). Nehemiah sees this intermarriage as a desecration of the "priesthood" and a violation to "the covenant of the priesthood and the Levites" (v. 29).

Summary

There are five points of significance to glean from Ezra and Nehemiah. First, their purpose is to inaugurate the cultic worship of Yahweh by the returned Israelites in the rebuilt temple. This is similar to Deut 23:1–8 in that during their wilderness time, the Israelites inaugurated the assembly of the Lord, an inner circle within the entire congregation of God's covenant people. The stipulation prohibited six groups of people from entering the assembly of the Lord. By nature, this inner circle represented God's wholeness and completeness. This would be a rationale for Ezra and Nehemiah to use Deut 23:2–5, as attested in Neh 13:1–2. Second, Ezra and Nehemiah see the people of the land as ethnically and religiously foreign to the Israelites. Nehemiah specifically identifies them as "foreigners" (בְּנֵי נֵכָר). Third, Ezra and Nehemiah both acknowledge the presence of people like גֵר, who are

---

53. Harrington, *Ezra and Nehemiah*, 456. Harrington suggests another option regarding the origin of the term "Horonite"; it could be "Hauran, an area east of the Sea of Galilee (Ezek 47:16, 18)" (288).

54. Hensel, "Ethnic Fiction and Identity-Formation," 144.

55. Harrington, *Ezra and Nehemiah*, 154–55.

ethnically heterogeneous but religiously and geographically homogeneous to the Israelites. Fourth, on the surface, Ezra and Nehemiah's reform is an ethnic separation of the Israelites from the residents of the land. It is clear, however, that this reform is based on the understanding that intermarriage introduces pagan customs. Fifth, Ezra and Nehemiah's reform is chiefly targeted at religious leaders such as priests and Levites. This point of view might be helpful in understanding that their reform is chiefly focused on the reconstitution of the cultic worship in the rebuilt temple.

Isaiah 56:1–8

Isaiah 56:1–8 begins with the adverb כֹּה. This indicates the oracle's relatedness to what precedes it. Isaiah 55 portrays the Lord's salvation as his sovereign act, as indicated in verse 3 ("I will make with you an everlasting covenant, my steadfast, sure love for David"). However, as Jacob Stromberg argues, from Isa 56:1–8 on, Isaiah portrays the Lord's salvation as delayed and yet to come while at the same time emphasizing justice and righteousness to be practiced among the Lord's covenant people.[56] The fact that Isa 56:1–8 introduces the Lord's salvation and righteousness along with his demand for justice and righteousness among his covenant people (v. 1) identifies Isa 56:1–8 as a bridge between the Lord's sovereign act and his people's responsibility in anticipation of it.[57]

Isaiah 56:1–8 has a symmetrical structure with four layers: (1) the Lord's demand for justice and righteousness (v.1) and the Lord's gathering of his people (vv. 7–8); (2) the principle of the Lord's blessing as the Sabbath observance (v. 2) and the Sabbath observance as principal (v. 6b); (3) the foreigner's lament (v. 3a) and his acceptance (v. 6a); and (4) the eunuch's lament (v. 3b) and his acceptance (vv. 4–5). The phrases "Thus says the Lord" (v. 1) and "the utterance of the Lord" (v. 8) function as a parenthesis to make Isa 56:1–8 an individual unit.[58] In this structure, the eunuch's lament and his acceptance are positioned in its center, so it appears that the eunuch is part of the foreigner group. However, the oracle regards them as distinct groups with the common characteristic of being vulnerable to exclusion.

---

56. Stromberg, *Isaiah after Exile*, 75. Stromberg argues that the author of the Trito-Isaiah looks at the Lord's promise of salvation in the Deutero-Isaiah "through the lens of a post-exilic delay."

57. Childs, *Isaiah*, 456. Childs states, "From the narrative perspective of the Third Isaiah corpus, the prophetic writer is offering a theological reformulation, but he has not altered his point of standing from that of the Second Isaiah."

58. Childs, *Isaiah*, 455.

Yahweh's Demand of Justice and Righteousness

Isaiah 56:1–8 begins with the Lord's command, "Keep justice and do righteousness" (v. 1). The verbs שמר and עשה in the command are in the second-person plural. According to Curtis W. Fitzgerald, the two imperative verbs are "directed toward those who are presently keeping the covenant of Yahweh," including Jews, foreigners, and eunuchs.[59] The Lord is the speaker of this oracle, and his audience is a multitude of listening people. The Lord demands that they put into practice מִשְׁפָּט ("justice") and צְדָקָה ("righteousness"). The noun צְדָקָה occurs twice in verse 1. Its first occurrence refers to the audience's need to do "righteousness." The second refers to the Lord's "righteousness" to be revealed along with his salvation. The LXX text distinguishes the two occurrences by using different Greek words, δικαιοσύνη and ἔλεος. Based on this, the word צְדָקָה can be differentiated based on context. Thus, the Lord's demand for justice and righteousness should be interpreted in light of God's imminent revelation of his own "salvation" and "righteousness."[60]

In Isaiah, the Hebrew nouns מִשְׁפָּט and צְדָקָה often occur together (1:27; 5:7, 16; 9:6; 28:17; 32:16; 33:5; 54:17; 56:1; 58:2; 59:9, 14). According to Joseph Blenkinsopp, the former refers to "a social concept and has particular reference to the protection of the classes in society that are least able to look after themselves—widows, fatherless, destitute (Isa 1:17; 10:2). Of particular importance is safeguarding the access of the powerless in society to judicial process (Amos 5:10–13; Mic 3:9–12; Isa 5:23; 33:15)."[61] The latter term refers to "doing what is right in the sphere of social relations."[62] According to Blenkinsopp, when both nouns are in combination, as in Isa 56:1, the basic meaning of מִשְׁפָּט is still valid. John Goldingay sees the combination of the nouns as the hendiadys, meaning "something like faithful

---

59. Fitzgerald, "Rhetorical Analysis of Isaiah 56–66," 41.

60. There is a debate about how to understand the Lord's salvation and his people's practice of justice and righteousness. Stromberg sees the conjunction כִּי (v. 1) as conditional, stating, "One would enjoy the salvation of v.1b only through obedience to the imperative of v. 1a, the basis for obedience therefore being enjoyment of salvation." According to him, Isaiah introduces the foreigner and the eunuch as "rhetorically powerful examples of it [obedience]." Stromberg, *Isaiah after Exile*, 76. In contrast, John Oswalt does not see it as conditional but as causative; the Lord's salvation is at hand, and that is the reason that justice and righteousness are to be done. Oswalt, *Book of Isaiah*, 455. Schramm, *Opponents of Third Isaiah*, 119. Schramm also sees the conjunction as causitive.

61. Blenkinsopp, *Isaiah 56–66*, 134.

62. Blenkinsopp, *Isaiah 56–66*, 134.

exercise of authority."⁶³ Goldingay emphasizes the role of leaders with authority and their need for justice and righteousness. With this meaning in view, Yahweh's demand for "justice" and "righteousness" to his audience lies in the social and relational realm of the Lord's covenant community, although their relationship to God's character cannot be neglected.

Principle of Yahweh's Blessing

Verse 2 states that to receive the Lord's blessing, the Sabbath must be kept and not profaned.⁶⁴ אֲשֶׁר ("blessed") is syntactically connected to the two nouns אֱנוֹשׁ ("man") and בֶּן־אָדָם ("son of man"). Both nouns have a universal connotation, with no differentiation for ethnic or religious identities. Both nouns function as subjects to the verbal phrases יַעֲשֶׂה־זֹּאת ("[who] does this") and יַחֲזִיק בָּהּ ("[who] holds it fast"); to these phrases, a pronoun זֹאת ("this") and a pronominal feminine singular suffix ה ("it") are respectively attached.

Which text does the phrase "doing this and holding it fast" (v. 2a) refer to? It could refer to either the Lord's demand for justice and righteousness among his covenant people (v. 1a) or the Sabbath observance (including the Lord's covenant). There are three factors in this issue. First, the feminine pronoun "this" and the feminine pronominal suffix "it" can refer to "justice" (masculine) and "righteousness" (feminine), although their genders do not exactly match. Their function is anaphoric. However, the pronoun and the pronominal suffix can point to what follows: "keeping the Sabbath from profaning it and keeping his hand from doing any evil" (v. 2b). Their function is proleptic, although their exact referencing nouns are not identifiable; in this case, their proleptic function is rather conceptual.⁶⁵

Second, the Hebrew words שמר and עשה occur in both verses; the former points to "justice" (v. 1a) and "the Sabbath" (v. 2b) and the latter to "righteousness" (v. 1a) and "any evil" (v. 2b). Based on this, R. Reed Lessing

---

63. Goldingay, *Critical and Exegetical Commentary*, 66.

64. Exod 31:12–17 is the law of the Sabbath. Keeping the Sabbath as holy is described as not profaning it, with the command, "Whoever does any work on it, that soul shall be cut off from among his people" (v. 14). According to this text, profaning the Sabbath means doing work on that day. Isa 56:2b puts the two main participle phrases in juxtaposition: (1) "keeping the Sabbath from profaning it" and (2) "keeping his hand from doing any evil." Based on Exod 31:12, it can be interpreted that the two participle clauses function as a two-fold illustration to the Sabbath observance. Oswalt defines their relationship as complementary, stating that "avoidance of evil is to be an expression of worship." Oswalt, *Isaiah 40–66*, 455–56.

65. Delitzsch, *Biblical Commentary on the Prophecies of Isaiah*, 2:332.

sees Isa 56:1–2 as "tied together by the repetition of the verbs."⁶⁶ However, the act of "holding fast" (חזק, v. 2a) occurs in relation to the Lord's covenant in verses 4 and 6. With this point in view, the act of "holding fast" can be viewed as proleptically stated in verse 2a and then clarified in the following context.

The third factor is the Sabbath observance (v. 2b). Is it related to the Lord's demand for justice and righteousness (v. 1a) or to the Lord's promise of blessing (v. 2a)? According to Lessing, by "keeping the Sabbath undefiled and guarding one's hand from doing any evil," the Lord's covenant people fulfill his demand for justice and righteousness.⁶⁷ In fact, the Sabbath observance is rooted in the faith of the Lord's covenant people, so viewed as their act of justice and righteousness. As noted above, however, the primary usage of the Hebrew terms מִשְׁפָּט and צְדָקָה relates to the human realm; as John Calvin suggests, doing justice and righteousness belongs to the second table of the Ten Commandments, whereas the Sabbath observance belongs to the first.⁶⁸

Hence, the acts of "doing this" and "holding fast" (v. 2a) point more toward what follows them (the Sabbath observance) than toward what precedes them (the Lord's demand for justice and righteousness). That is, what appears unclear is gradually clarified. If so, the Sabbath observance is the basic condition of the Lord's blessing and the sign of the Lord's blessed covenant people; thus, it works as the fundamental guide by which to evaluate God's covenant people, including "foreigners" and "eunuchs." Brooks Schramm states, "The particular role played by Sabbath observance in this oracle is unique in the Hebrew Bible, for in this passage Sabbath observance appears to be the primary criterion by which membership in the community is defined, and in that sense, it functions in a manner similar to that of circumcision in Genesis 17."⁶⁹ As will be discussed, the Lord's demand for justice and righteousness—an imperative to his audience—can be illumined from this point of view.

---

66. Lessing, *Isaiah 56–66*, ConcC, 42.

67. Lessing, *Isaiah 56–66*, 46. See also Gary Smith, *Isaiah 40–66*, NAC 15B (Nashville: Broadman & Holman, 2009), 530. JiSeong James Kwon, "Re-Examining the Torah in the Book of Isaiah," 557.

68. Calvin, *Commentary on the Book of the Prophet Isaiah*, 4:177.

69. Schramm, *Opponents of Third Isaiah*, 117–18.

Foreigners and Eunuchs

The symmetrical structure of Isa 56:1–8 narrows to the lament of the eunuch and the Lord's promise to bless eunuchs. The eunuch text appears bracketed by the foreigner text. This suggests that Isaiah views the eunuch as part of the ethnic others (i.e., foreigners).[70] However, a careful investigation of the text provides evidence that the eunuch and the foreigner are distinct groups. Their common status, particularly as the most marginalized or vulnerable to exclusion in the cultic setting, necessitates considering them in parallel relation.

There are three distinctions between these groups. First, their laments are different. The eunuch describes himself as a "dry tree" (v. 3b). This figure of speech is related to the eunuch's inability to produce fruit, that is, descendants. He laments his physical incompleteness. The foreigner's lament is more apparent, as he fears his rejection by God's people (v. 3a). He laments his ethnically foreign status. What lies beneath the two laments is their potential exclusion from God's covenant people, in the setting of cultic worship in the temple.[71]

From their laments, it is inferable that the eunuch and the foreigner are already associated with God's covenant people. This state presumes their practice of the covenant rite of circumcision according to the Abrahamic covenant (Gen 17). Based on his lament, the foreigner should be classified as a circumcised resident alien (גֵּר, the proselyte), not as a foreigner (בֶּן־הַנֵּכָר).[72] Also, in Isa 52:1, it is stated in a declarative mode that "the uncircumcised and the unclean" will no longer enter Jerusalem ("the holy city"). This degree of antagonism toward foreigners ("the uncircumcised and the unclean") is not in Isa 56:1–8. This fact supports the view that the phrase בֶּן־הַנֵּכָר does not denote "the uncircumcised and the unclean." According to Joseph Blenkinsopp, it would be meaningless if Isa 56:1–8 deals with the subject matter of "the exclusion of the uncircumcised and ritually

---

70. Andreas Schüle, "Tora für Fremde und Eunuchen," 445. Schüle argues that eunuchs in Isa 56:1–8 formed a separate subgroup of foreigners.

71. De Hoop, "Interpretation of Isaiah 56:1–9: Comfort or Criticism?," 681–82. Hoop argues that the laments of the eunuch and the foreigner contain "an implicit criticism of leaders who apparently follow certain laws of the Torah but neglect more important ones. This becomes clear when we examine Isa 56:1–9 in its Trito-Isaianic context."

72. Kwon, "Re-Examining the Torah in the Book of Isaiah," 558. Kwon regards the status of foreigners and eunuchs in Isa 56:1–8 as "proselytes."

unclean from the Jerusalem of the future."[73] In fact, Blenkinsopp interprets the Hebrew phrase as a "foreign proselyte."[74]

The second distinction between the eunuch and the foreigner is how each of them responds to the Lord. The eunuch's faithfulness to the Lord is evident because of his Sabbath observance, his choice of things pleasing to the Lord, and his holding fast to the Lord's covenant ("eunuchs" v. 4). The three verbs used in this description—בחר, שמר, and חזק—indicate the eunuch's persistent faithfulness. By comparison, the foreigner responds to the Lord through his volitional decision to join himself to the Lord. The Niphal form of לוה (vv. 3, 6) marks this feature as notable.[75] For the eunuch, the Sabbath is mentioned, but there is no mention of the Sabbath for the foreigner.[76] A foreigner would be ethnically, religiously, and even geographically distant from the Israelites. Considering the foreigner's status, joining oneself to Yahweh is a radical decision. This oracle emphasizes this aspect. In the literary setting of the oracle, however, as implied in the foreigner's lament (v. 3a), the foreigner is not a pre-conversion foreigner.

The third distinction is the Lord's promise to the faithful eunuch and to the converted foreigner. The Lord promises to bestow on the eunuch a notable status even in the temple setting (v. 5, "a name better than sons and daughters" and "an everlasting name"). Given that the faithful eunuch's honorable name is connected with "sons and daughters," those who would typically memorialize their deceased father, it is assumed that metaphorically Yahweh will fulfill that role for the eunuch.[77]

For the converted foreigner, according to Dalit Rom-Shiloni, the five types of the foreigner's service for the Lord (v. 6) are identical to the things "required by any lay member of Israel": (1) to minister to him, (2) to love his name, (3) to be his servant, (4) to keep the Sabbath holy, and (5) to hold

---

73. Blenkinsopp, *Isaiah 56–66*, 135.

74. Blenkinsopp, "Second Isaiah, Prophet of Universalism?," 61. This disagreement—between Isaiah's use of the Hebrew phrase בֶּן־הַנֵּכָר and this foreigner's reality of religious affiliation to Yahweh—will be discussed from a rhetorical perspective.

75. The MT reading is a Niphal perfect with an article (i.e., הַנִּלְוָה). However, BDB suggests a Niphal participle of לוה (BDB, 530). The LXX translates it into a participle (προσκείμενος). Also, in 56:6, the Niphal participle is used. Textually, the Niphal participle is preferred.

76. Isa 56:6b states, "all who keep the Sabbath from profaning it and hold fast my covenant." The word "all" can be inclusive of foreigners and eunuchs. With this in view, the Sabbath observance, as a principle, is also applied to faithful foreigners. Isaiah's mention of the Sabbath, in a textual sense, is directly related to the eunuch, as seen in verse 4a.

77. Goldingay, *Isaiah 56–66*, 79.

fast to his covenant.⁷⁸ The last two types seem to be applied not just to the foreigner but also to the eunuch, as shown in the use of "all" (כָּל)—along with its related two participles (שֹׁמֵר and מַחֲזִיקִים) with regard to the Sabbath and the Lord's covenant (v. 6b).

As indicated in their laments, the eunuch and the foreigner are associated with God's covenant people but are also vulnerable to exclusion. The eunuch is physically incomplete, and the foreigner is an ethnic other; either state may cause their exclusion. Their demonstration of faithfulness, as noted in verse 6b, is concerned with the Sabbath observance. That is, God promises that all who keep the Sabbath and who hold fast to his covenant will be blessed. The Sabbath principle is an obligation for "all," which draws attention to the principle of the Lord's blessing for the "man" and "son of man" (v. 2a).

Rhetorical Features of Isa 56:1–8

As mentioned, Isaiah has a rhetorical intent for using the term "foreigner." First, the Hebrew term does not reflect the foreigner's affiliated status of being a member of God's covenant. Technically, גֵּר is more appropriate than בֶּן־הַנֵּכָר. Also, Isaiah's critique of the exclusive mood against the cultically less privileged, such as ethnic foreigners and physical eunuchs, is evident. In this regard, Katherine E. Southwood argues, "The text here is clearly a critique of the way that those constructed as 'foreigners' and other groups are treated. It has a hortatory quality beseeching listeners to change their attitudes through greater recognition of the way that groups such as the 'foreigner' and eunuch align themselves to the dominant group."⁷⁹

Another proof of Isaiah's rhetoric is that the oracle directly addresses the audience using the second-personal plural form (v. 1a), whereas the oracle indirectly addresses the "foreigner" and "eunuch" in third-person plural form (v. 3). While Isaiah uses an imperative to communicate the Lord's command for justice and righteousness (v. 1a), he uses the jussive form for the foreigner and the eunuch (וְאַל־יֹאמַר, "Let not say [the foreigner] or [the eunuch]," v. 3). The negation particle אַל with the third-person singular imperfect of אמר occurs in relation to "foreigner" and then "eunuch."⁸⁰ This

78. Rom-Shiloni, *Exclusive Inclusivity*, 123.

79. Southwood, "'Foreigner' and the Eunuch," 442.

80. The phrase "let the foreigner do not say" appears to be in parallel with the phrase "let the eunuch say." For the foreigner, there is a description ("who joins himself to the Lord"). However, for the eunuch, there is no such description. The parallel relation leads to the assumption that for the eunuch, the phrase "who joins himself to the Lord" is not included in the text because of the redundancy identifiable in this parallelism.

combination brings about a jussive idea; its function here is a prohibitive command indirectly given by Yahweh to the foreigner and the eunuch.[81] Isaiah's use of the third-person subject with the jussive idea for the foreigner and the eunuch (v. 3) makes this prohibitive command ("Let not say") less directed toward them.

Third, the Lord's promises to the eunuch and the foreigner (vv. 4–6) begin with אָמַר יְהוָה לַסָּרִיסִים ("the Lord says to eunuchs"). This appears to be a direct utterance made by the Lord to eunuchs and foreigners.[82] However, there is no use of the second-person pronoun to address eunuchs and foreigners. Also, in these verses, there is a long attributive description attached to each of them (i.e., "to the eunuchs who keep my Sabbaths" [v. 4] and "[to] the foreigners who join themselves to the Lord" [v. 6]). The form of the Lord's utterance appears like a direct speech to eunuchs and foreigners, but its actual nuance is more like an announcement made to an audience. Hence, although it cannot be denied that "Let the foreigner [the eunuch] say" (v. 3) and "Thus says the Lord" (v. 5) are uttered to the eunuch and the foreigner, the entire oracle is more directed toward the second-person plural audience of the oracle (v. 1).

Echoic-Allusion Study of Isaiah 56:1–8

As shown, there is considerable evidence supporting the view that Isa 56:1–8 is a polemic against exclusion and a rhetorical message to the audience delivering Yahweh's demand for justice and righteousness. To paint a more vivid picture of the context in which Isa 56:1–8 is situated, this section will examine the Isaiah text in relation to Deut 23:1–8. This examination uses an echoic allusion method, as introduced in the chapter "Methods of the Study."

Echoic allusion is a literary device in which the author alludes to one text in another text via a textual signal, which works formally to indicate the alluded text and functionally to recall, or echo, its original context. The author uses echoic allusion to enrich the intended meaning of the alluding

---

However, as noted, the act of joining oneself to the Lord, as the oracle emphasizes, is related to the foreigner alone, not to the eunuch. Hence, applying the redundancy here is not appropriate.

81. The presence of the particle אַל is an indicator of jussives. Chisholm, *From Exegesis to Exposition*," 104.

82. In the Hebrew text, "the eunuchs" has the preposition לְ, but "the foreigner" does not. However, in the Greek text, "the foreigners" are in dative, just as "the eunuchs." Based on this Greek text, it seems that the Lord's utterance is made to "the eunuchs" and then to "the foreigners."

text. The meanings of the alluding text and the original context can be antithetical (i.e., ironic). In this ironic relationship, which exists in the textual relationship of Deut 23:1–8 and Isa 56:1–8, it is possible that the alluding text (Isa 56:1–8) is a polemic to the original context of the alluded text (Deut 23:1–8). Echoic allusion is an implicit means of delivering a polemic when an author intends to propose his own ideal to his audience, an idea that is superior to that of the original context.

As noted, the basic requirement for Yahweh's blessing is the Sabbath observance (Isa 56:2, 6b). It is applicable to all God's covenant people ("man" and "son of man" in v. 2; "all" in v. 6b). As expressed in their laments, the foreigner and eunuch are vulnerable to exclusion. It is likely that Deut 23:1–8, among other passages, functions as the theoretical basis of this exclusion, particularly in the cultic setting of the temple. The Isaiah text is a polemic against this exclusion and delivers to its audience Yahweh's demand for justice and righteousness. The text promotes an attitude of inclusiveness in the cultic setting, particularly toward the most vulnerable groups of people. God's covenant people need this attitude in anticipation of the Lord's salvation and righteousness.

Foreigner and Eunuch: Echoic-Allusion Signal to Deut 23:1–8

The Hebrew phrase בֶּן־הַנֵּכָר and noun סָרִיס function as a two-fold textual signal alluding to the text of the assembly of the Lord (Deut 23:1–8). This point of view can be persuasive in several ways. First, both occur in the section of Isa 56:1–8, structurally in the center of the section. This pattern is unique in the Old Testament. Nehemiah 13:1 could have in view the entire stipulation of the assembly of the Lord (Deut 23:1–8), but its citation (and actual application) is about the ethnic non-Israelite (i.e., Ammonite and Moabite).

Second, Deut 23:1–8, in a categorical sense, has two groups: (1) the emasculated male (including the forbidden-union children) and (2) ethnic non-Israelite foreigners (Ammonite, Moabite, Edomite, and Egyptian). Isaiah's use of the terms "foreigner" and "eunuch" is a result of his simplified categorization of the six groups in the Deuteronomy text. Third, the laments of the foreigner and the eunuch (Isa 56:3) reflect the principle of exclusion, for which Deut 23:1–8 functions as a theological basis. For the eunuch, his physically incomplete and unfruitful state appears as an obstacle to his participation in the cultic setting of worship. For the foreigner, his ethnic otherness is a hindrance to his participation. This notion of exclusiveness, as evidenced in Neh 13:1, is evident in the Deuteronomy text.

Fourth, Isaiah's use of the Hebrew phrase בֶּן־הַנֵּכָר and noun סָרִיס reflects his rhetorical use of the terms. In a broad sense, an ethnic non-Israelite foreigner could be either בֶּן־נֵכָר or גֵּר. As evidenced in Exod 12:43–39, the phrase בֶּן־הַנֵּכָר indicates the person's foreignness to the Israelites regarding ethnicity, religion, and geography. In contrast, the latter is an ethnic non-Israelite who resides among the Israelites and joins the cultic worship of Yahweh as a member of God's covenant people; this religious status presumes his practice of the rite of circumcision.

To refer to a foreigner, Isaiah uses בֶּן־הַנֵּכָר rather than גֵּר. He also describes this foreigner with the participle phrase "who joins himself to the Lord" (vv. 3, 6 [plural]). In fact, this act of joining can refer to the person's conversion to Yahweh.[83] However, his lament (v. 2) indicates that he is not in a pre-conversion state but in a post-conversion state. Isaiah's use of the phrase בֶּן־הַנֵּכָר for the foreigner's state as one of God's covenant people reflects his rhetorical purpose. In this respect, Blenkinsopp states, "The combination of eunuchs and foreign proselytes suggests strongly that the misgivings expressed in Isa 56:1–8 arose from the threatened application of this law [the assembly of the Lord in Deut 23:1–8]."[84]

Isaiah's use of the noun סָרִיס (vv. 3–4) also reflects his intention to rhetorically introduce the eunuch by focusing on the eunuch's castrated state. The Hebrew noun occurs three times in Isaiah (39:7; 56:3, 4). Isaiah prophesied to Hezekiah about his sons: "They shall be eunuchs (סָרִיסִים) in the palace of the king of Babylon" (Isa 39:7; cf. 2 Kgs 20:18). There is debate as to the meaning of the סָרִיס in this prophecy.[85] For its occurrence in Isa 56:3–4, however, Isaiah's use of the Hebrew term סָרִיס clearly has in view the castrated condition (v. 3, "I am a dry tree"). The metaphor "dry tree" refers to the incapability of bearing fruit. In this regard, the Lord's promise to bless eunuchs ("a name better than sons and daughters," Isa 56:5) can be understood.

The fact that Isaiah's use of the term "eunuch" points to the eunuch's physical castrated state is well-reflected in Deut 23:1, which does not use the Hebrew noun סָרִיס. Instead, it has the two passive participles פְּצוּעַ ("bruised") and וּכְרוּת ("and cut off") to describe the male's physical eunuch state. Although both participles cannot point to the ancient practice of castration, they can indicate the notion of the eunuch's castrated state. That is,

---

83. As argued, Exod 12:48 refers to גֵּר, in a conceptual or technical way, as an ethnic non-Israelite even before his conversion through the rite of circumcision.

84. Blenkinsopp, "Second Isaiah, Prophet of Universalism?," 61.

85. Johnston, "סָרִיס," NIDOTTE, 3:292.

the fact that Isaiah's use of the Hebrew noun סָרִיס here corresponds with the notion of castration most evidently reflects what Deut 23:1 has in view.

Hence, the identity labels "foreigner" and "eunuch" in Isa 56:1–8 function as a two-fold textual signal to recall the text of Deut 23:1–8 and to bring its context to the new context of Isa 56:1–8. Based on relevance theory, Isaiah's use of בֶּן־הַנֵּכָר and סָרִיס creates the optimal relevance to the audience in that these terms easily draw the attention of his audience in the most effective way in cognition but the least effort-demanding way in processing.[86] In terms of their form, בֶּן־הַנֵּכָר and סָרִיס are the conceptually simplified categories of the six groups of people in Deut 23:1–8. And in terms of their function, they are evocative enough to create a contextual interaction between the two texts.[87] Isaiah's use is clearly rhetorical, somehow reflecting the way the direct audience of the oracle (v. 2) uses them—as identity labels or slogans for exclusiveness.

Ironic Relation of Isa 56:1–8 to Deut 23:1–8

When one text alludes to another text, each of the texts has its own contextual meaning. As noted in the chapter "Methods of the Study," the meaning of the text in the original context can be antithetical to that of the alluding text in the new context. As identified in Neh 13:1–2, Deut 23:1–8 has its own textual tradition; the Nehemiah text utilizes the Deut 23:1–8 concept of exclusion. Isaiah 56:1–8 also uses the textual tradition of Deut 23:1–8 as the conceptual world, as indicated in Isaiah's use of the Hebrew terms "foreigner" and "eunuch." However, Isa 56:1–8 depicts a different picture; its inclusive depiction is antithetical to the exclusive concept of Deut 23:1–8.

The extent of admission by foreigners and eunuchs is unprecedented in the Hebrew Bible. To faithful eunuchs, the Lord promises to bestow "a monument and a name" and "everlasting name" within his "house and walls" (Isa 56:5); the words "house" and "walls" refer to the Lord's temple. He promises their full admission inside the cultic system of the temple. To faithful foreigners, the Lord promises that their status will be like what the Israelites have: (1) to minister to the Lord, (2) to love his name, and (3) to become his servants (Isa 56:6a). For all who are faithful to the Lord's Sabbath, that is, his covenant, the Lord promises to bring them to Zion and receive their sacrifices on his altar (v. 7), announcing that his house is "a house of prayer for all peoples." The phrase "all peoples" implicates the extent of the Lord's acceptance. In this regard, Gordon H. Johnston states, "God's offer of salvific

---

86. Wilson and Sperber, *Meaning and Relevance*, 200.
87. Smith, *Allusive and Elusive*, 38.

blessings are all-embracing and inclusive of those who were often viewed as excluded."[88] Hence, focusing on exclusion in the cultic setting of the temple, the entire picture of Isa 56:1–8 is clearly antithetical to that of Deut 23:1–8.

Polemic against the Idea of Exclusion

Dan Sperber and Dierdre Wilson suggest three conditions for an utterance to be considered an echoic allusion: (1) "a recognition of the utterance as echoic," (2) "an identification of the source of the opinion echoed," and (3) "a recognition that the speaker's attitude to the opinion echoed is one of rejection or dissociation."[89] As discussed, Isaiah's use of the Hebrew terms "foreigner" and "eunuch" in the context of his argument for the Lord's inclusive plan recalls, or echoes, the text of Deut 23:1–8. The exclusive idea of Deut 23:1–8 is in Neh 13:1–2, in which Nehemiah cites the Deuteronomy text and his audience responds in obedience. With the inclusive idea of Isa 56:1–8 in view, Isaiah rejects the echoed idea of exclusion. Though this rejection is not explicit in the text, it is clear that Isaiah is disassociating himself or his argument from the echoed idea of exclusion.

What is the foundation of Isaiah's polemic to the exclusive nature of Deut 23:1–8? Isaiah sees Sabbath observance as the fundamental sign for God's covenant people to demonstrate their faithfulness (Isa 56:2, 6b). He also exhorts his audience, particularly the ethnic Israelites and the cultically complete, to use that sign as a criterion to embrace the ethnically and cultically marginalized (i.e., foreigners and eunuchs).

Rhetoric to the Audience

The final implication of Isaiah's allusion to Deut 23:1–8 is in the rhetoric directed to his literary audience and focused on justice and righteousness. As mentioned, there are a few indicators that the oracle targets a second-person plural audience and that its main message is their practice of justice and righteousness (Isa 56:1). Yahweh's demand to his so-called included covenant people is parallel with his declaration—"My house shall be called a house of prayer for all peoples" (v. 7) and "I will gather yet others to him besides those already gathered" (v. 8). Thus, Yahweh's demand for justice and righteousness and his plan to gather all his faithful covenant people to his house comprises the framework of the entire oracle.

---

88. Johnston, "סָרִיס," *NIDOTTE*, 3:293.
89. Sperber and Wilson, *Relevance*, 237–40.

As Young-Sam Won suggests, the author's use of an allusion, and not a direct reference, reveals a rhetorical nature. That is, the allusion contains "a vital subtext that culminates in the main point" intended by the author.[90] Based on this point of view, Isaiah's use of allusion to Deut 23:1–8 presupposes his purpose to communicate his main point (i.e., his ideal) toward his audience. Through this oracle, Isaiah presents the ideal of "justice" and "righteousness" to God's covenant people, particularly in the setting of temple worship. In the context of the oracle, this virtue is related to the open-mindedness of God's covenant people toward those vulnerable to cultic exclusion, as represented by foreigners and eunuchs. With the echoic allusion idea in view, as Rom-Shiloni notes, Isaiah's implicit use of allusion regarding Deut 23:1–8 is "a polemical interpretive allusion."[91] Michael Fishbane calls the oracle of Isa 56:1–8 "new divine teachings."[92]

Summary

The oracle of Isa 56:1–8 portrays the eunuch and the foreigner as faithful to God's covenant, making it reasonable to see them as part of God's covenant people. Also, the audience of the oracle raises doubt about this status, particularly in the cultic setting of worship in the temple, being inclined toward an exclusion of these groups. Taking into consideration these pieces of information inferred from the oracle, there was a middle ground of people whose cultic status could not easily be defined. As noted, the assembly of the Lord in Deut 23:1–8 does not refer to the entire congregation of God's covenant people. It is a particular gathering of people for the cultic setting that manifests God's holiness. The context of Isa 56:1–8 suggests the same assembly of the Lord as its background.

The eunuch's lament indicates that his possible exclusion is due to his physical condition of incompleteness and unfruitfulness, which might present a hindrance to manifesting God's holiness. His exclusion is ritual, as identified in Deut 23:1–8. Both texts focus on his physical condition rather than his ethnic status. In contrast, the foreigner's possible exclusion is due to his ethnic non-Israelite background. Although his lament indicates that he is part of God's covenant people, the oracle's portrayal of his attachment to the Lord is more like his conversion. Hence, the social groups of eunuchs and foreigners are in the middle area between inclusion and exclusion, depending on their settings. It could be that in the setting of a local synagogue,

---

90. Won, *Remembering the Covenants in Song*, 87.
91. Rom-Shiloni, *Exclusive Inclusivity*, 124.
92. Fishbane, *Biblical Interpretation in Ancient Israel*, 128.

those groups were acceptable. In contrast, when in the setting of the temple, they could be unacceptable.

Textual Tradition of Deut 23:1–8 in Second Temple Literature

Dead Sea Scrolls

4QMMT

4QMMT is the text that the series *Discoveries of the Judean Desert* (DJD) produced through its collation of six fragment manuscripts (4Q394–399).[93] It is called *Maqsat Ma'aseh Ha-Torah* (MMT). According to Hanne von Weissenberg, MMT has three main literary divisions: (1) the calendar (Section A), (2) the halakhot (Section B), and (3) the epilogue (Section C).[94] Weissenberg proposes that the occurrence of Deut 23:2–4 (MT) in the halakhot section indicates Deuteronomy was one of the textual sources behind 4QMMT.[95] According to him, in the halakhot section, Deut 12 is vital because "the legal section (Deut 12–26) begins with a definition of the one and only correct cultic place. The command of cultic centralization is repeated several times in Deut 12."[96] That is, 4QMMT has in view Jerusalem and its temple as the cultic place of worship. It is within this broad framework that Deut 23:2–4 (MT) is located.

Deuteronomy 23:2–4 (MT) appears in three manuscripts (4Q394 8 III–IV, 4Q396 1–2, and 4Q397 5). In their combined text, there are five Hebrew words that bring attention to Deut 23:2–4 (MT): (1) "Ammonite" (עמוני), (2) "Moabite" (מואבי), (3) "bastard" (ממזר), (4) "penis" (שפכת), and (5) "congregation" (קהל).[97] It is clear that this text uses Deut 23:2–4 (MT) as its source. This text lists the four groups to be excluded from the congregation, just as prescribed in Deut 23:2–4 (MT). Furthermore, the text states that to keep oneself from any defiling union is "to show reverence for the sanctuary (מקדש)."

What is the rationale for using the Deuteronomy text in 4QMMT? It contains two subjects: (1) entering the sanctuary and (2) intermarriage. Intermarriage is regarded as defiling and unclean. Those prohibited people

---

93. Wearne, "Linguistic Remarks on the Unity of 4QMMT," 68.
94. von Weissenberg, "Deuteronomy at Qumran and in MMT," 527.
95. von Weissenberg, "Deuteronomy at Qumran and in MMT," 527.
96. von Weissenberg, "Deuteronomy at Qumran and in MMT," 529.
97. Wise, Abegg, and Cook, *Dead Sea Scrolls*, 458.

might use their marriage to enter the assembly of the Lord, the temple of Jerusalem.⁹⁸ The interrelation of both subjects is found in Ezra-Nehemiah. In addition, the concept of "holy seed" (זרע קדש) is embedded as a fundamental notion in 4QMMT, as evidenced in the phrase "holy [seed]" of 4Q396 1–2 IV, 75 (with 4Q397 6–13).⁹⁹ Christine E. Hayes argues, "The holy seed rationale of Ezra and Jubilees motivates the prohibition of intermarriage in 4QMMT."¹⁰⁰ Thus, based on 4QMMT's textual reliance on Deut 12, which regards Jerusalem as the cultic center for the Israelites, a prohibition on those groups and on their intermarriage with the Israelites fits well.

4Q174 III, 1–6

The author of 4Q174 III, 1–13 cites 2 Sam 7:10–14, Exod 15:17–18, and Amos 9:11, but the author's main concern is "a pesher interpretation of 2 Sam 7:10–14."¹⁰¹ That is, the author uses "the temple" in Nathan's oracle to David to illustrate an eschatological temple. 4Q174 III, 2 states, "This 'place' is the house that [they shall establish for Him] in the Last Days." The noun "place" (מָקוֹם) in 2 Sam 7:10 appears here. Given this textual relatedness, the author has in view the temple that God promised to David.

However, the author interprets the temple from an eschatological point of view. First, in his text, the author identifies that "strangers (זרים) have desolated formerly the sanctuar[y] of Israel because of their sin" (5–6). Second, Nathan's oracle (2 Sam 7:10–14) itself has a messianic nature. Third, the author uses a messianic phrase. He cites 2 Sam 7:14a, which ends with "to me [God] a son" and refers to this "son" as "the shoot of David" (11). He also cites Amos 9:11, "I will raise up the booth of David which has fallen." While realizing the fallen state of the original temple, the author anticipates a future messianic temple; this anticipation is attributed to his recognition of the eschatological nature of 2 Sam 7:10–14.¹⁰²

---

98. Loader, *Dead Sea Scrolls on Sexuality*, 61.

99. Wise, Abegg, and Cook, *Dead Sea Scrolls*, 460.

100. Hayes, *Gentile Impurities and Jewish Identities*, 82. Hayes suggests that 4QMMT prohibits the intermarriage of the Israelites with proselytes.

101. Dimant, *History, Ideology, and Bible Interpretation*, 272.

102. There is a debate about the usage of the noun בית in the Qumran sectarian texts. According to Devorah Dimant, it has two uses: (1) "an epithet of the Qumran community" and (2) "the Temple." Dimant suggests that the author of 4Q174 III, 1–13 has the latter in his citation of 2 Sam 7:10–14a. Dimant, "Vocabulary of the Qumran Sectarian Texts," in *Qumran und die Archäologie*, 362–63. On the other hand, Joseph M. Baumgarten states, "What the author of 4Q Florilegium envisions with his human sanctuary is not the rebuilt Temple, but the constitution of a circle of initiates whose

The author lists five groups of people prohibited from entering this temple: "Ammonite" (עמוני), (2) "Moabite" (מואבי), (3) "bastard" (ממזר), (4) "foreigner" (בן נכר), and (5) "alien" (גר). The first three are identical to the list in Deut 23:1–4. Also, the subject matter here is their prohibition because of God's glory. The author does not use the phrase "the assembly of the Lord" (Deut 23:1–8) but "the sanctuary of the Lord" (מקדש אדני).

In comparison with Deut 23:1–3, this text adds "foreigner" (בן נכר) and "alien" (גר). It seems that "Ammonite" and "Moabite" could be a metonymy for all the non-Israelites, but the author adds "foreigner." The phrase בן נכר indicates an absolute sense of foreignness in terms of ethnicity, religion, and even geography. The noun גר is a resident alien in a foreign land, yet it suggests an intense sense of religious affiliation among the natives in the land. With this connotation in view, it seems odd to see "resident alien" excluded from "the sanctuary of the Lord." Furthermore, CD XIV, 3–5 indicates that גר is the fourth status in the assembly of all the camps (מחנה), along with "priests," "Levites," and "the children of Israel." This means that גר is a member for the Qumran sect of Yahad.

How should one understand these opposing attitudes toward גר? First, their settings are different. CD XIV, 3–5 indicates that Yahad, the Qumran sect, has "camps" (מחנה), meaning that the sect has multiple regional settlements, just as Josephus indicates (J.W. 2.124). The גר lies in the area between the outer circle and the inner circle. On the level of a regional settlement, גר was a member of Yahad. However, in the eschatological temple, their full admission is not permissible.[103]

1QM VII, 3–7

The War Scroll is the reconstructed text of 1QM and six additional manuscripts found in Cave 4 (4Q491–496). 1QM VII, 4b–5a reads, "All lame or blind or girded or a man who has permanent blemish on his flesh or a man touched by uncleanness on his flesh—all of these should not go with them to battle." The text introduces five types of impairment. This recalls Deut 23:9–14, which prescribes purity and cleanness in the military camp. There

---

works of the Law and whose searching for deeper revelations of Torah would have the cultic significance associated with sacrifice." Baumgarten, *Studies in Qumran Law*, 83–84.

103. Gillihan, "גר Who Wasn't There," 262. Gillihan proposes that "while the גר of D does seem to be a Gentile convert, the category is a legal fiction crafted on the basis of Scripture–Gentiles did not actually join the sect" (264). He sees this approach as what accommodates "both the Covenanters' thoroughgoing anti-Gentile ideology, and the positive portrait of the גר in D, 4QLots, and 4QpNahum" (264).

is no mention of a male castrated or injured in his testicles or penis here in this scroll. Yet the list of blemishes certainly presupposes such a male. Part of the reason is that Deut 23:1–8, which defines the assembly of the Lord by restricting its eligible members, has a parallel with Deut 23:9–14, which defines the military camp by excluding the physically impaired or unclean. Just as in Deut 23:1–8 and 23:9–14, it seems that the War Scroll does not intend to exclude those listed people from Yahad.

1QSa II, 3–10

The unit of 1QSa I, 27–II, 10 has two distinct sections. The first section (I, 27–II, 2) addresses who is eligible for membership in the Qumran sect of Yahad. The second section (II, 3–10) addresses who should be excluded. The excluded list consists of those "crippled in both legs or hands, lame, blind, deaf, dumb, or possessed of a visible blemish in his flesh or a doddering old man." The setting of their exclusion is קהל ("assembly"), a Hebrew term used in Deut 23:2–9 (MT). The Hebrew term used here is identical to עדה ("congregation").

Also, the noun עדה is identified as the congregation (עדה) of "the m[en] of reputation" (שם, v. 8) and "holy" (קודש, v.9) congregation. Given the use of those descriptive phrases attached to the noun עדה, this congregation is an inner circle in the broad Yahad. Also, it is stated, "If [one] of these people has some[thing] to say to the holy congregation, let an oral [de]position be taken" (II, 9–10). This statement indicates that disabled people belong to the broad congregation of Yahad. It is notable that the author of 1QSa I, 27–II, 10 refers to "the assembly of the Lord" in Deut 23:1–8, as indicated in his use of the Hebrew קהל, and then applies the principle of cleanness to his own context by the means of exclusion.

Summary

The Dead Sea Scrolls alludes to Deut 23:1–3 by using words or phrases found in the Deuteronomy text. Also, the DSS uses a pesher interpretive method. That is, it applies Deut 23:1–3 in accordance with its situated context, that is, the Qumran sect of Yahad. The Qumran texts appear exclusive by nature in ethnic and ritual terms. However, this does not mean that the Yahad community, including its regional settlements, exclude all ethnic others and ritually unclean or impaired people. When the DSS text deals with the temple, the eschatological military camp, and the inner circle within the sect, its tone is exclusive. However, its actual constituents clearly include proselytes and ritually unclean or impaired people.

Flavius Josephus

The fourth book of *Jewish Antiquities* is part of Josephus's illustration of "the history of the Hebrews as described in the Pentateuch."[104] The section of *Ant.* 4.196-302 is about Josephus's review concerning the "constitution" delivered by Moses to the Israelites in the wilderness, as indicated in his use of the word πολιτείαν ("government") at its beginning and at its end.[105] According to David Nakman, "This [the section] mainly concerns the courts and laws of damages as they appear in Deuteronomy and is combined with integrated legal rulings from other locations in the Torah."[106] Given its location within this section, which depends chiefly on Deuteronomy, *Ant.* 4.290, although not a direct reference, is likely what Josephus wrote with Deut 23:1 in mind.

The text of *Ant.* 4.290-91 reflects Josephus's sense of detestation toward self-castrated males. He uses γάλλος to refer to a eunuch.[107] His basic exhortation is to avoid eunuchs and flee from being even "a travel companion" with them. Josephus describes them as cutting off not just their "manhood" but also their "fruit of the child-procreation." He even disregards them as "a slaughter of children" who removed their "source."

One fundamental principle behind this point of view is that "God granted [the fruit] to humans for the increase of our race." This is an implicit reference to the account of God's human creation (Gen 1:28). In addition to this biblical principle, Josephus also provides a philosophical rationale for his argument. The act of castration on the body (σῶμα) is the change of their soul (ψυχή) to the effeminate state (291).[108] Finally, Josephus states, "It is not lawful to make men or other animals 'castrated' (ἐκτομίας)" (291). This statement recalls Lev 22:24, which forbids an animal for an offering if it has a blemish ("bruised," "crushed," "torn," and "cut") regarding its testicles.

Josephus does not refer to Deut 23:1-8 in an explicit sense. However, as implied in *Ant.* 4.290-291, he uses Deut 23:1 as the conceptual basis for his point of view concerning the self-castrated males and the practice of

---

104. Nakman, "Josephus and Halacha," 283.
105. Josephus, *Jewish Antiquities*, 94-95; 146-147.
106. Nakman, "Josephus and Halacha," 283.
107. Josephus, *Jewish Antiquities*, 2:140-41. Josephus uses the following terms for a castrated eunuch: (1) γάλλος, (2) ἐκτομίας, (3) εὐνουχίζω, and (4) εὐνοῦχος.
108. Josephus, *Jewish Antiquities*, 2:142-43.

castration. That is, he uses Lev 22:24 as a vehicle to argue against the practice of castration. In other words, Josephus uses the Leviticus text as not just a prohibition on offering such an animal but also on inflicting such a blemish on animals. Josephus applies this principle to human males, asserting that it is against the creation principle of God.

Philo of Alexandria

According to Hywel Clifford, Deut 23:1–8 is "quoted in at least ten of the many works attributed to Philo."[109] Philo introduces each of the six groups of people listed in Deut 23:1–8: (1) the eunuch, (2) the harlot's children, (3) the Ammonites, (4) the Moabites, (5) the Edomites, and (6) the Egyptians. His textual dependence on Deuteronomy is evident, in light of his use of key words or phrases, exact quotations, or paraphrasing.[110] He interprets characteristics unique to each of the groups and provides the rationales for their exclusion or inclusion. From a philosophical or theological point of view, Philo uses an allegorical method for interpretation. By doing so, Philo demonstrates two main concerns: (1) the God of Israel is the absolute God, and (2) his assembled people are to manifest him in godliness and virtue. This study will scrutinize the three main passages in Philo's works that deal with each of the groups listed. It will suggest Philo's allegorical conceptualization of the first four groups for exclusion and the last two groups, particularly the Egyptians, for inclusion.

On the Special Laws 1.324–45

In this passage, Philo thoroughly interprets the first four groups listed in Deut 23:1–6. The Ammonites and the Moabites do not appear by name. Yet, based on Philo's description of them in other places, Philo indeed has them in mind in this passage. According to Hywel Clifford, Deut 23:1–6 is "nowhere treated as a whole" as in this passage.[111] In *Spec.* 1.325, Philo writes:

> Therefore, as it was aware that no inconsiderable number of wicked men are often mingled in these *assemblies* [ἐκκλησίαις], and escape notice by reasons of the crowds collected there, in

---

109. Clifford, "From Exclusion to Inclusion?," 176. Clifford thoroughly deals with the textual tradition of Deut 23:1–8 in Second Temple Judaism literature. This study will use his suggested references.

110. Clifford, "From Exclusion to Inclusion?," 176.

111. Clifford, "From Exclusion to Inclusion?," 176.

order to prevent that from being the case in this instance, he [Moses] previously excludes all who are unworthy from the sacred assembly, beginning in the first instance with those who are afflicted with the disease of effeminacy, men-women, who, having adulterated the coinage of nature, are willingly driven into the appearance and treatment of the licentious women. He also banishes *all those who have suffered any injury or mutilation in their most important members* (my literal translation, *eunuchs* [θλαδίας] *who have cut off* [ἀποκεκοκομμένους] *the productive members*), and those who, seeking to preserve the flower of their beauty so that it may not speedily wither away, have altered the impression of their natural manly appearance into the resemblance of a woman.[112]

At the beginning of the text, it is notable that Philo has his own context in which to apply the principle of exclusion based on Deut 23:1–6. He states that "no inconsiderable number of wicked men are often mingled in these assemblies." From this statement, it is assumed that Philo distinguishes his own assembly from other assemblies.[113] Although not fully revealed in the text, Philo has indeed the background of his own assembly behind his interpretation of Deut 23:1–6.[114] In *Spec.* 1.324–45, Philo refers to his own assembly as "the followers and disciples of the prophet Moses" (345).[115]

Within this contemporaneous context, Philo provides a rationale for exclusion. To do this, he relies on the authority of Moses and adopts the basic principle of exclusion from the law of Moses (i.e., Deut 23:1–6). Philo introduces the four groups of people that Moses excluded from "the sacred assembly." He uses the phrase ἱερός σύλλογος ("the sacred assembly"), not the phrase ἐκκλησία κυρίου ("the assembly of the Lord") in Deut 23:1–8 LXX.[116]

112. Philo, *Works of Philo*, 565. Philo, *On the Decalogue*, 288. The perfect participle of ἀποκόπτω ("to cut off"), if it is viewed as the middle voice, will stress the self-imposed act of castration. It seems that Yonge's translation of "all those who have suffered any injury or mutilation" reflects his application of the participle as the passive voice.

113. Korner, *Origin and Meaning of Ekklēsia*, 136.

114. In *Deus* 111, Philo argues that those castrated and mutilated ones are separated from the sacred assembly. Then he refers to "the sacred assembly" (ἐκκλησίας τῆσ ἱερᾶς) as "in which conferences and discussions about virtue are always being practiced." This text is a proof of the view that his interpretation of Deut 23:1–8 takes his situated context of assembly into consideration. Concerning Philo's use of "assembly," Clifford states, "According to a recent study, in some instances Philo uniquely used *ekklēsia* as 'group terminology' for the 'semi-public voluntary association' of Alexandrian Jews: a 'substantial middle' between the public/civic and the private/domestic in expressions of religion in antiquity: i.e. synagogue life." Clifford, "From Exclusion to Inclusion," 180.

115. Philo, *Works of Philo*, 567.

116. Philo uses the phrase ἱερός σύλλογος only twice in his works (*Spec.* 1.325, 344).

In *Leg.* 3.81, however, Philo uses nouns ἐκκλησία and σύλλογος along with the genitive terms θείου ("divine") and κυρίου. Thus, Philo uses ἱερός σύλλογος and ἐκκλησία κυρίου as synonyms.[117] Also, in *Leg.* 3.8, Philo uses Num 5:2–3 and Deut 23:1–2 in a combined format with the subject matter of exclusion from ἐκκλησία θεοῦ ("the assembly of God").[118]

For the eunuch, Philo uses θλαδίας ("eunuch") along with its attributive perfect participle of ἀποκόπτω ("to cut off"), just as in Deut 23:2 LXX.[119] Basically Philo argues that the eunuch's self-castration, which is an act of opposing "the coinage of nature," is an attempt to make himself effeminate. From his theological point of view, Philo interprets the unproductive nature of a eunuch as that of an atheist (*Spec.* 1.330). For the harlot's children, Philo states, "Then he [Moses] forbids not only harlots but also those *from the harlot* (ἐκ πόρνης)" (326). His implication is that the harlot's children cannot know their genetic fathers; Philo applies this notion to polytheists, who do not recognize the absolute true God (332).

Furthermore, Philo states:

> And therefore Moses naturally banished them all from the holy congregation (ἱεροῦ συλλόγου), both those who abolish the Forms, who appear under the name of 'the crushed' [θλαδίας], and those who absolutely deny God, to whom he assigned the suitable title of 'the mutilated' [ἀποκόπων] and those who preach the opposite doctrine of a family of gods, called by him 'the children of the harlot' [ἐκ πόρνης] (*Spec.* 1.344).[120]

As shown, Philo adopts the three Greek expressions (i.e., θλαδίας, ἀποκόπων, and ἐκ πόρνης) from the LXX text of Deut 23:2 and conceptually likens them to an atheist (the eunuch) and a polytheist (the harlot's children). Hence, Philo's introduction of the eunuch and the harlot's children in the section of *Spec.* 1.324–45 is not on a physical level. Instead, he likens

---

117. Philo, *On the Creation*, 354–55.

118. Philo, *On the Creation*, 304–5. In *Leg.* 3.8, Philo uses the phrase "holy soul" (ἅγιος ψυχή) instead of "the camp" (παρεμβολή) in Num 5:2–3 LXX. He also states "unclean" in relation to "soul." It is notable that Philo lists physically incomplete or unclean people, like "leper, discharged one, eunuch, fornicator." His main focus is not on excluding these physically unclean or incomplete beings. Philo uses those characteristics—unclean and incomplete—in relation to "soul." Most probably, Philo uses the phrase "holy soul" to point to his own assembly, which needs to prohibit those unclean "in soul."

119. The only difference is that Philo's text for both words (θλαδίας and ἀποκόπτω) is in plural form, whereas the LXX text is in singular form. Basically, Philo uses three nouns to refer to a eunuch: (1) θλαδίας, (2) σπάδων, and (3) εὐνοῦχος.

120. Philo, *On the Decalogue*, 302–3.

their unique characteristics to the characteristics of ungodly and unvirtuous people. In this regard, Hywel Clifford states that for Philo, "[T]he eunuch, harlot's son, and children of incest, are all likened at a primal and philosophical allegorical level."[121]

Allegorical Interpretation 3.79–81

In *Spec.* 1.324–45, Philo does not mention the Ammonites and the Moabites by name. Instead, he describes them as "all the self-centered; some of them deify reason (λογισμός) but others deify each of the senses (αἴσθησις)" (344).[122] If based on *Leg.* 3.79–81, clearly Philo has both groups in view. In this passage, Philo refers to the Ammonites as those from the mother of "sense" (αἴσθησις) and the Moabites as from the father of "mind" (νοῦς). Philo recalls a historical account related to the Ammonites and the Moabites. The purpose of his recollection is to contrast their inhospitable act to the Israelites with the hospitable act of Melchizedek to Abraham ("bread and water"). Philo emphasizes their inhospitable act as the cause for their exclusion from "the congregation and assembly of God" (ἐκκλησία καὶ σύλλογος θείου). Furthermore, Philo refers to the Ammonites and the Moabites as the descendants of the mother of "sense" (αἴσθησις) and the father of "mind" (νοῦς) respectively; their obsession with "sense" and "mind" results in their devaluation of "the notion of God" (81). Finally, Philo again emphasizes the cause of their exclusion from "the assembly of the Lord" (ἐκκλησία κυρίου). As noticed here, Philo uses the origin of the Ammonites and the Moabites, allegorically conceptualizes them with the philosophical terms, "mind" and "sense," and develops those concepts on a theological level.

On the Virtues 102–8

This passage is in a larger section called "On Humanity" (*Virt.* 51–174). According to Ralph J. Korner, "*Virt.* 108 concludes a topic begun at *Virt.* 80," which contains the phrase "love of people (φιλανθρωπία) of the lawgiver."[123] Hence, *Virt.* 102–8 is part of Philo's introduction of those who are socially marginalized or vulnerable to exclusion.[124]

---

121. Clifford, "From Exclusion to Inclusion?," 179.
122. Philo, *On the Creation*, 352–5.
123. Korner, *Origin and Meaning of Ekklēsia*, 130.
124. Philo, *On the Special Laws*, 224–29.

The section of *Virt.* 102–8 is one of Philo's most comprehensive explanations of proselytes. Philo highlights their sacrificial decision to turn back from their heritage, including their land, ancestors, national customs, temples, and gods (102). He also praises their willing decision to make their new abode in the one true God of Israel (102). Philo uses ἐπηλύτης (102) and ἐπήλυτος (103) for the proselyte.[125] Both terms, etymologically connected to ἔρχομαι, point to the ethnic foreigner's settlement in a new land and among its natives, and even his acceptance of their religion.

By introducing these characteristics of proselytes, Philo emphasizes the need to care for and love them (103–4). Philo bases his rationale for accepting proselytes on Deut 23:7b (106), which addresses the Egyptians and their acceptance into the assembly of the Lord in the third generation.[126] Clearly, his purpose for introducing the Egyptians is to emphasize the need to accept proselytes; in doing so, he again explains the degree of the sacrifice made by the proselytes, along with their turning to "the civic life (πολιτεία) of the Jews" (108).

Philo uses the conditional phrase "in the third generation" in the context of proselytes in his local assembly (Deut 23:9 LXX; *Virt.* 108). He claims that it is necessary to "call [proselytes] in the third generation to the assembly and impart divine words [to them]" through teachings and instructions (108). Hywel Clifford states that *Virt.* 108 "transitions from ancient (cf. 106) to contemporary Egypt."[127] As suggested, Philo has his local assembly, so-called "the disciples of Moses," as his background setting. Philo's mention of the need to call into the assembly and impart the divine words also supports the view that Philo has his own assembly in mind.[128] As Walter T. Wilson states, the text is not clear about how Philo applies the condition "the third generation" for proselytes in his assembly.[129]

Summary

As presented, Philo introduces the entities of people listed in Deut 23:1–8. His purpose is to argue that there exists one absolute God. He highlights

---

125. Philo uses προσήλυτος eight times (*Cher.* 108, 119; *Somn.* 2.273; *Spec.* 1.51, 308; *QE* 1.2.2). In the Greek text of *QE* 1.2.2, προσήλυτος is the one who circumcises not his uncircumcision but his soul; thus, his notion of conversion is not so much on the covenant rite of circumcision.

126. Philo quotes Deut 23:7b from the Greek text (Deut 23:8b LXX); the only change Philo made is from "in his land" to "in Egypt" (106).

127. Clifford, "From Exclusion to Inclusion?," 181.

128. Korner, *Origin and Meaning of Ekklēsia*, 131–36.

129. Wilson, *Philo of Alexandria*, 262.

characteristics unique to each of the entities and utilizes them for his philosophical presentation. Practically, Philo adopts the subject matter of exclusion or inclusion identified in Deut 23:1–8 and applies it to his local assembly in Alexandria. Five features are notable in Philo's use of Deut 23:1–8. First, Deut 23:1–8 has its own textual tradition, thus being recontextualized in a different setting. Second, Philo uses it to distinguish his local assembly from other assemblies. Third, Philo's description about eunuchs reflects a glimpse of unfavorable attitude toward them. Fourth, his usage of Deut 23:1–6 is chiefly for exclusion. Fifth, Philo uses Deut 23:7–8 as a biblical basis for including ethnic others. This is evident in his application of "Egyptians" and "the third generation" for proselytes in his local assembly.

Rabbinic Literature

The Mishnah is "a late second century collection of rulings of oral torah."[130] Using the Mishnah to gain a picture of the Ethiopian in Acts 8:26–40 is anachronistic. However, the Mishnah contains the oral tradition of rabbinic Judaism, so it can reflect what lies behind that tradition.[131] Based on its interpretation of Deut 23:1, the tractate m. Yebam. 8:1–6 deals with the eunuch as its subject matter most thoroughly. The preceding chapter (m. Yebam. 7:1–6) discussed who would be eligible to eat a terumah (תְּרוּמָה "heave offering") in the household of a kohen (כֹּהֵן "priest")—his wife, daughters, and slaves. The following section m. Yebam 8:1–6 continues this subject matter, but with a focus on the kohen's ritual uncleanness at issue. The Mishnah text discusses (1) the kohen who is "uncircumcised" (עָרֵל) or "unclean" (טָמֵא) and (2) the kohen with "mutilated testicles" (פְּצוּעַ דַּכָּא) and "and cut-off penis" (וּכְרוּת שָׁפְכָה). Neither of them is eligible to eat terumah.[132] This ruling appears to indicate that there is no difference between those two kohens.

However, the Mishnah text pronounces different rulings for their wives. The wife of the "uncircumcised" or "unclean" kohen is eligible for terumah. On the other hand, the wife of the kohen with "mutilated testicles" and "cut-off penis" is not eligible. Yet if the kohen does not cohabit with his wife, she is permitted to eat terumah. What is the rationale for this difference? For the former kohen, his "unclean" state—even his "uncircumcised"

---

130. Bock, *Blasphemy and Exaltation in Judaism*, 66.

131. Bock, *Blasphemy and Exaltation in Judaism*, 66.

132. As for the ruling about the latter (i.e., the kohen with mutilated testicles or cut-off penis), the Mishnah does not mention it. Yet this textual absence presupposes his ineligible state, in line with the former.

state—could be temporal.¹³³ However, for the latter kohen, his uncleanness could be permanent, thus indicating his state of incompleteness. Therefore, m. Yebam. 8:1 shows that there are different degrees of uncleanness, and a male like the latter kohen is on the edge of uncleanness. However, this condition does not enact his disqualification from being a kohen.

The tractate m. Yebam. 8:2 introduces a Jewish male with his testicle(s) mutilated or his penis cut off. It discusses (1) his marriage and (2) his ineligibility to enter the congregation.

> Who is [considered] someone with mutilated testicles? Anyone whose testicles were cut, person whose phallus was severed? Anyone whose phallus was cut off; [however,] if even a hairbreadth of the corona remained, he is fit. Persons with mutilated testicles or a severed phallus are permitted to [marry] a convert or an emancipated slave-women; they are forbidden only to enter into the congregation, as it is stated— (Deut 23:1): *A person with mutilated testicles or a severed phallus may not enter the congregation of God* (m. Yebam. 8:2).¹³⁴

There are several characteristics notable in this text. First, it is based on Deut 23:1 [MT 23:2]—in particular, regarding the two descriptive phrases: (1) "mutilated testicles" and (2) "cut-off penis." These phrases describe a kohen in the preceding verse (m. Yebam. 8:1), but here they relate to a Jewish male, not a priest. Second, the Mishnah text makes an analytical description concerning those two phrases and defines each of them from a physiological perspective. It elucidates that losing even one testicle is what the Torah has in view. It also clarifies that the phrase "cut-off penis" in the Torah refers to the complete absence of the corona on the penis. Third, the nature of this interpretive clarification is chiefly concerned with the issue of whether that male can be reproductive or not. Such a damaged state on the testicles or the penis could cause him to be sterile.¹³⁵

Fourth, the Mishnah text applies this notion to the context of marriage. A male, if he fits into either of the cases, is not to have a Jewish woman as his wife. Yet he can have "a female convert (גִּיּוֹרֶת)" or "a freed slave girl."¹³⁶ The

---

133. Rabinowitz, *Yevamos*, 186. Rabinowitz suggests that even a kohen could be forbidden to get circumcised such as "when there is a family history of death from circumcision."

134. Rabinowitz, *Yevamos*, 189. Rabinowitz sees "fit" (כָּשֵׁר) in relation to the marital status of Jews. On the other hand, Jacob Neusner understands it as "valid [to eat heave offering]." Jacob Neusner, *Mishnah*, 355.

135. Rabinowitz, *Yevamos*, 189. See also b. Yebam. 24a:7, which rules that a eunuch is not eligible for the levirate law.

136. Rabinowitz, *Yevamos*, 189. Rabinowitz notes that "emancipated slave-woman"

noun גִּיּוֹרֶת is the feminine noun of גֵּר, which often presupposes the person's converted state in Judaism. This ruling indicates that the Tannaim applied Deut 23:1 to the ethnic Jews, not to the non-Jews. Fifth, the Mishnah ruling, as stipulated in Deut 23:1, forbids a Jewish male of that kind to enter into the congregation of God. Given their juxtaposition, there seems to be a link between his disqualification of marrying a Jewish woman and that of entering into the congregation. That is, the marital status of a Jewish man presupposes his entrance into the congregation. In this regard, Rabinowitz states:

> The prohibition extends only to their marrying a woman who is classified as a member of the *congregation of God*. This is a legal term used to describe the marital status of Jews who were born Jewish and whose lineage is not in any way flawed!! Converts, although fully Jewish in every respect, are not considered part of this *congregation*.[137]

The rationale for disqualifying him from the marital status of Jews and from affiliating with the congregation is to keep "the congregation of the Lord" (Deut 23:1–8) cultically complete and whole—in ethnical and ritual terms. This is done by preventing the ritually incomplete and the ethnically foreign from the congregation.[138] Therefore, disqualifying the ritually incomplete, even though ethnically Jewish, from the marital status of Jews is related to disqualifying him from the congregation.

The text of m. Yebam. 8:4 introduces *saris adam* (סְרִיס אָדָם) and *saris hamah* (סְרִיס חַמָּה). Based on this text, saris adam is a eunuch by a human act. According to Rabbi Aqiba, it refers to a eunuch who used to be "valid" as a husband. In this sense, Rabinowitz states that it refers to "any person who was made sterile after birth, whether by castration or maiming of the reproductive organs, or by illness."[139] As Rabinowitz notes, the phrases ("mutilated testicles" and "cut-off penis") in m. Yebam. 8:2 are an illustration of saris adam in view. This presupposes a human's involvement. On the other hand, saris hamah, according to Rabbi Eliezer, "may be healed." As opposed to saris adam, which is made sterile after his birth, saris hamah is the male born with that condition. Concerning saris hamah, Rabinowitz

---

is a non-Jewish woman. Her freed status makes her to be "a full member of the Jewish community."

137. Rabinowitz, *Yevamos*, 190.

138. m. Yebam. 8:3 introduces the four ethnic groups of people listed in Deut 23:3–8 (Ammonite, Moabite, Edomite, and Egyptian) in relation to their prohibited state from the congregation. Yet its main focus is on their females rather than their males.

139. Rabinowitz, *Yevamos*, 196.

states that it refers to "a man who was born with a defective reproductive system, that is, congenitally sterile."[140]

This distinction is identifiable in y. Yebam. 8.2. This Jerusalem Talmud text uses בִּידֵי אָדָם ("by the hand of man") and בִּידֵי שָׁמַיִם ("by the hand of heaven") to refer to saris adam and saris hamah each.[141] The talmudic text indicates that the Tannaim had a conceptual distinction between a congenital eunuch and an incidental eunuch. For the congenital eunuch, the Tannaim discuss the physiological signs of a male being a eunuch.[142]

For the subject matter of eunuchs, there are six distinctives noticed in the Mishnah. First, its rulings are based on its interpretive exposition and application of Deut 23:1. Second, it deals with the subject matter of eunuchs under the category of ethnic Jewish males. Third, it distinguishes between man-made (i.e., incidental) eunuchs and natural (i.e., born) eunuchs. Fourth, it categorizes eunuchs as belonging to the physically impaired, thus identifying them as incomplete, not just unclean. Fifth, the Mishnah provides various signs to identify eunuchs; among others, lack of beard is most often remarked. Lastly, the Mishnah makes clear that the state of being a eunuch restricts him from the congregation. Yet this does not mean his complete exclusion from God's covenant people.

Luke's Polemic against the Exclusion of the Foreigner and Eunuch

As shown, Deut 23:1–8 had its textual or conceptual tradition in Jewish literature. The main purpose of its usage, particularly in the Old Testament, was to reconstitute the members of the congregation for the setting of worship in the temple. This reconstitution functioned by means of exclusion, by prohibiting the ethnically foreign and the ritually incomplete. Deuteronomy 23:1–8 is not cited nor alluded to in Luke's two-volume work. Yet, it functions as a conceptual basis for understanding the cultic system of the temple. This point of view can be persuasive because of three notable things found in Luke's work.

---

140. Rabinowitz, *Yevamos*, 198.

141. Guggenheimer, *Jerusalem Talmud Third Order*, 341–341.

142. In b. Yebam. 80b. 4–10, those signs are listed: (1) no beard, (2) defective hair, (3) smooth skin, (4) urine not raising foam, (5) dissipating semen, (6) urine not fermenting, (7) giving no steam in the bathing during the rainy season, and (8) defective voice (b. Yebam. 80b. 4–5). See also m. Nid. 5:9 (pubic hair) and b. Šabb. 50b:4 (facial hair).

First, Luke introduces Philip's evangelism of the Samaritans and the Ethiopian in a juxtaposed position (Acts 8:4–40). Given Luke's literary act of collecting, selecting, and arranging multiple episodes (Luke 1:1–4), it is reasonable to assume that Luke intended this arrangement. Second, Luke refers to the Samaritan(s) as "foreigner" (Luke 17:18) and the Ethiopian as "eunuch" (Acts 8:27, 34, 36, 38, 39). The occurrence of the terms "foreigner" and "eunuch" recalls Deut 23:1–8, in which the excluded ones include emasculated males and ethnic others. Third, Isa 56:1–8, which also recalls Deut 23:1–8, refers to the two specific groups, "foreigner" and "eunuch." Luke's reliance on Isa 56:1–8 is also inferable from Jesus' reference to Isa 56:7 ("house of prayer," Luke 19:46; cf. Mark 11:17).

Luke's rhetoric shows a great deal of resemblance to Isaiah's rhetoric. In the section on Isa 56:1–8, this study has dealt with Isaiah's use of the terms "foreigner" and "eunuch" as textual signals in an echoic allusion to Deut 23:1–8. The nature of these signals is provocative enough to retrieve the exclusive idea of Deut 23:1–8. While using these signals as a vehicle, Isaiah's rhetoric is polemical about the idea of exclusiveness and rhetorical about the Lord's demand of justice and righteousness from his covenant people—in anticipation of the Lord's salvation and righteousness. Through this rhetoric, Isaiah projects the eschatological picture of inclusiveness even in the center of the temple, that is, the Lord's house.

Basically, Luke's rhetoric presupposes Christ's eschatological fulfillment. Luke emphasizes the nature of this fulfillment as all-inclusive, regardless of ethnic foreignness and ritual uncleanness or incompleteness. Luke's rhetoric also has a polemical nature, as it challenges the exclusion of the culturally vulnerable based on their ethnic foreignness and ritual uncleanness or incompleteness. Luke's purpose is to make this mindset of exclusion unworkable among Christ's followers, the twelve disciples in particular, — challenging them to embrace others just as Christ did (i.e., ethical). Hence, Luke's rhetoric is eschatological, polemical, and ethical. To demonstrate these characteristics in his rhetoric, Luke uses literary tools such as provocation, comparison, shame, reversal, restoration, and so on.[143] To gain an understanding of how Luke's rhetoric works, this section will investigate two categories of people in Luke's work: (1) the Samaritans (in relation to "foreigner") and (2) the physically unclean or incomplete (in relation to "eunuch"). I will argue that Luke intends to show the reversed status of those most vulnerable to being culturally excluded (that is, the ones prohibited

---

143. Bock suggests that the role of "shame" is to reveal the reversal of the expected pattern. Bock, *Luke*, 1099.

from the benefits of the cultic system in the Jerusalem temple) in the eschatological house of Christ.

Excluding the Ethnically Foreign

In the Gospel of Luke, there are three accounts related to Samaritans: (1) the Samaritans' rejection of Jesus (9:51–56), (2) the parable of the good Samaritan (10:25–37), and (3) the healed Samaritan with leprosy (17:11–19). They share three features, among others. First, all three accounts are unique to the Gospel of Luke.[144] Apart from the account of the Samaritan woman and the Samaritans (John 4:4–42), the other Synoptic Gospels do not deal with the subject matter of Samaritans.[145] Even in Matt 10:5, it is stated, "Go nowhere among the Gentiles and enter no town of the Samaritans."[146] Thus, Luke's concern with the Samaritans—and his intention to reveal their cultural uniqueness and their theological implication in God's eschatological plan for salvation—is what distinguishes the Gospel of Luke from the other Synoptic Gospels.

Second, Luke introduces all three accounts as part of Jesus' travel to Jerusalem (9:51–19:44). Luke mentions this journey six times (9:51; 13:22; 17:11; 19:11, 28, 41). It begins at 9:51. This verse has the Greek phrase ἐγένετο δέ ἐν (plus infinitive), which marks a transition in the narrative, particularly notable in the Gospel of Luke (Luke 1:8; 2:1, 6; 3:21; 5:1; 6:1, 6, 12; 8:22; 9:51; 11:27; 18:35).[147] Thematically, 9:51 anticipates the imminent event of Christ's ascension, thus making a literary connection all the way to Acts 1.[148] Within this literary framework, Luke includes the three accounts

---

144. Luke 10:25–28 has a conceptual parallel to Mark 12:28–34 (par. Matt 22:34–40). Yet, the parable itself is unique to the Gospel of Luke.

145. John 4:4–42 reveals three differences between the Jews and the Samaritans: (1) ethnic (v. 9), (2) cultic (v. 20), and (3) messianic (vs. 22, 25, 29). According to Lidija Novakovic, the main difference between the Jews and the Samaritans is "not their ethnicity or religiosity but the location of their cultic center." Lidija Novakovic, "Jews and Samaritans," in *World of the New Testament*, 215. Bob Becking states, "All inscriptions were found at the same spot [Mount Gerizim] that is qualified within the texts as a בית דבחא, 'house of sacrifice.' External evidence makes clear that this holy ground stands in competition with sanctuaries in Jerusalem, Maqqedah, and probably Lachish." Becking, *Israel's Past Seen from the Present*, 172.

146. The Greek text of Matt 10:5 has the phrases "to the road of the Gentiles [road leading to the Gentiles]" and "to the town of the Samaritans" as a parallel in the middle. Based on this parallel position, Matthew sees the Samaritans more like the gentiles, not the Jews.

147. For Luke 2:1 and 8:22, the preposition ἐν is followed by a noun, not an infinitive.

148. Luke's use of ἀνάλημψις ("ascension") here points to the scene of the risen

related to the Samaritans. This points to Luke's intention to portray Christ's mission as all-inclusive, although its completed form of fulfillment will be in Acts.

Third, one major theme in this travel section is Jesus' rejection. This feature is well-revealed in its chiastic structure, which has 13:31–35 as its center.[149] In this center Jesus prophesies his death at Jerusalem, just as God's prophets died there.

The Samaritans' Rejection of Jesus (Luke 9:51–56)

Luke 9:51–56 records that Jesus sent messengers ahead of him to "a village (κώμη) of the Samaritans" (v. 52). The Samaritans in that village did not welcome him (v. 53a). The ὅτι clause indicates that Luke attributes this rejection not to the Samaritans but to Jesus' ongoing journey to Jerusalem (v. 53b); Luke identifies Jesus' impending arrival at Jerusalem as the time of his ascension. In response to the Samaritans' failure to embrace him, James and John said, "Lord, do you want us to tell fire to come down from heaven and consume them?" (v. 54). The image of "fire down from heaven" recalls the episode of Ahaziah in Samaria and Elijah (2 Kgs 1:2–16), in which the Lord punished Ahaziah's servants through fire from heaven because he inquired of "a god of Ekron" (v. 2). Just as Darrell L. Bock states, James and John's suggestion to Jesus is their demand for an immediate judgment of the Samaritans, reflecting their sense of antagonism toward the Samaritans.[150] Then, Jesus rebukes James and John; the Greek word ἐπιτιμάω ("to rebuke") can denote an act of verbal punishment.[151] Jesus entered "another village" (ἑτέραν κώμην), presumably another village of the Samaritans.

In terms of Luke's literary emphasis, there are three features identified in this account. First, Luke does not emphasize the Samaritans' failure to embrace Jesus. He even attributes their rejection to Jesus' ongoing journey to Jerusalem. Rather, his focus is on Jesus' geographic and ethnic all-inclusive mission. Jesus' visit to "another village" of the Samaritans points to this characteristic. Second, Luke makes note of James and John's antagonistic attitude toward the Samaritans. James and John's use of the image of fire reflects their understanding of the Samaritans as subjects of God's judgment, not subjects of God's mercy. This contrasts with Jesus' continual outreach

---

Christ's ascension in Acts (the passive use of ἀναλαμάνω in 1:2, 11, and 22). Bock, *Luke 9:51–24:53*, 967–68.

149. Puskas and Crump, *Introduction to the Gospels and Acts*, 115.
150. Bock, *Luke 9:51–24:53*, 970.
151. The second meaning of ἐπιτιμάω "to punish" (BDAG, 384).

to the Samaritans. Third, Luke emphasizes that the current time is the time of mercy, not the time of judgment.[152] Jesus' rejection in Samaria appears to result in a failed mission; however, the Christ exalted to the throne of heaven is still working as the One who bestows the gift of salvation, even to the Samaritans who rejected him (Acts 8:4–25).

The Parable of the Good Samaritan (Luke 10:25–37)

Luke 10:25–28 appears like an individual unit. A law expert (νομικός) asks, "What shall I do to inherit eternal life?" (v. 25) Jesus responds, "What is written in the law?" (v. 26). James R. Edwards says the law expert's answer is "a conflation of Deut 6:5 and Lev 19:18" (v. 27).[153] Jesus said, "Do this and you will live" (v. 28). John Nolland maintains that the law expert's question has "an eschatological notion."[154] The phrase "eternal life" is what God will bestow in his eschatological kingdom. Jesus' remark ("you will live") also points to this futuristic aspect.[155] Bock emphasizes this aspect, stating that his question is like, "What must I do to share in the resurrection of the righteous at the end?"[156]

The Greek noun πλησίον functions as a means of further developing the conversation between Jesus and the law expert—the law expert's question (v. 29, "Who is my neighbor [πλησίον]?") to justify himself. This question leads to the parable of the good Samaritan (10:30–35). This parable has three aspects for its understanding. First, there is a ritual aspect of cleanness or uncleanness related to the use of the adjective "half-dead" (ἡμιθανής). Robert H. Stein remarks that the priest's role lies "in the sacrifices and maintenance of the temple, as well as in various purification rites," so it is impermissible to defile himself by touching a dead body (Lev 21:1–4).[157] This is applicable to the Levite to a certain extent. It is assumed that the priest and the Levite passed by partly because of the defilement issue. In contrast, the Samaritan "bound up his wounds, pouring on oil and wine" (v. 34). Ritually, this Samaritan became unclean by touching the almost dead man.

Second, the parable has an ethnic aspect regarding the Jews and the Samaritans. Clearly the priest and the Levite are ethnically Jewish. Right after them, the Samaritan appears as the third character in the parable (v.

---

152. Bock, *Luke 9:51—24:53*, 971.
153. Edwards, *Gospel According to Luke*, 319.
154. John Nolland, *Luke 9:21—18:34*, 583.
155. Cf. Luke 18:18.
156. Bock, *Luke 9:51—24:53*, 1023.
157. Stein, *Luke*, 317.

33). When it comes to the appearance of the Samaritan, Joachim Jeremias describes it as "unexpected and disconcerting."[158] After introducing the priest and the Levite, it would be reasonable to expect another Jew. Also, the law expert "avoids using the hateful term" (i.e., "Samaritan"); instead, he said, "the one who showed him mercy" (37a).[159] This reflects a sense of the Jews' hostility toward the Samaritans.

Third, the parable has a cultic aspect related to the Jerusalem temple, although this aspect is not as textually clear as the other two aspects. Luke describes the priest and Levite as coming down from Jerusalem. Presumably, this points to their role in the cultic system of the temple. On the other hand, the parable describes the Samaritan as "journeying" (ὁδεύω). The verb ὁδεύω denotes "go, travel, make a trip," implicating that this trip is "using an established route."[160] It seems that the Samaritan's use of the road is not related to the cultic worship in the Jerusalem temple. This difference leads to the assumption that Luke has in mind the excluded status of the Samaritans from the cultic system of Jerusalem. Hence, Luke intends to contrast the priest and the Levite with the Samaritan in terms of ethnicity, ritual cleanness, and cultic affiliation.

In addition to these aspects, Luke's rhetoric in this parable can be studied from three perspectives: eschatological, polemical, and ethical. Luke uses the provocative term "Samaritan" to draw immediate attention and response from his literary audience, as it must have originally drawn a similar response from the law expert and Jesus' disciples. This usage is evident in his text. For the "priest," Luke puts the prepositional phrase κατὰ συγκυρίαν δέ ("then by chance") before the noun "priest" (v. 31). For the "Levite," Luke puts the phrase ὁμοίως δὲ καί ("then also likewise") before the noun "Levite" (v. 32). In the mention of the Samaritan, Luke reverses this order and places "Samaritan" at the front with no preceding phrases. This abrupt departure from the pattern points to Luke's intention to emphasize the word "Samaritan." In addition to this position of the word, the word "Samaritan" itself is provocative, reflecting a sense of antagonism that the Jews had toward the Samaritans. For instance, in John 8:48, the Jews refer to Jesus as a "Samaritan." Their use of the noun "Samaritan" is not a reference to Jesus' ethnic background. It is a figurative speech, using the term "Samaritan" as a label, implying hatred toward the Samaritans.

Also, Luke's rhetoric has a polemical nature, using methods such as comparison, shame, and reversal. The parable compares the Jewish religious

---

158. Jeremias, *Parables of Jesus*, 204.
159. Jeremias, *Parables of Jesus*, 205.
160. BDAG, 690.

leaders (i.e., the priest and the Levite) and the Samaritan. While doing so, the parable presents the Samaritan and his practice of mercy as the model to be followed. As implied in the law expert's answer to Jesus' question (v. 36, "Which of these three have been a neighbor to the man who fell among the robbers?"), this presentation intends to create a sense of shame in the law expert by reversing what he considers normal with regard to bestowing mercy and his attitude toward the Samaritans. As N. T. Wright states, it is about recognizing "the hated Samaritan as his [the law expert's] neighbor."[161]

Luke's rhetoric is also eschatological and ethical. The law expert's question about eternal life (v. 25) is by nature eschatological. Now, Jesus said to the law expert, πορεύου καὶ σὺ ποίει ὁμοίως (v. 37, "Go and you do likewise"). Luke's addition of σύ before the imperative ποίει is emphatic. The present tense of that imperative points to the continuous aspect of "mercy" (ἔλος) to be practiced. This command is ethical. To put these two aspects together, it is clear that Luke's rhetoric is about present life in anticipation of eternal life. This framework echoes Isa 56:1, which includes the Lord's demand of justice and righteousness from God's covenant people in anticipation of his salvation and righteousness.[162] Hence, the entire pericope (Luke 10:25–37) reveals Luke's rhetorical use of eschatological, polemical, and ethical language. Practically, Luke's rhetoric implicates that the Jews, including the law expert and the disciples, should embrace the Samaritans as candidates for God's eschatological gift of salvation and mercy.

The Returned Samaritan Leper (Luke 17:11–19)

This account is the last episode in the Gospel of Luke concerning the Samaritans. It illustrates the all-inclusive nature of Jesus' mission, not just ethnically or geographically, but also for the socially marginalized or cultically excluded. Luke identifies the geographic setting as "between Samaria and

---

161. Wright, *Luke for Everyone*, 128. Reich, *Figuring Jesus*, 104. Reich states, "The Lukan Jesus yet again challenges current religious boundary systems. In those systems, Samaritans were unclean and to be excluded from fellowship. The parable radically subverts this view, shattering the carefully constructed boundaries of the Jews." Reich adds, "The priest and the Levite (temple authorities in the current system) will be excluded, while the outcasts (the Samaritans and merchants) will be welcome" (105). In Acts 6:7, however, Luke states that "a great many of the priests became obedient to the faith."

162. Isa 56:1 LXX lists the following four important words: κρίσις, δικαιοσύνη, σωτήριον, and ἔλεος. In Luke 10:25–37, the three words, except for "justice" (κρίσις), appear literally and conceptually. As discussed, "eternal life" is related to God's provision of "salvation" (σωτήριον). The law expert intended to justify himself; this act, although in a reversal way, relates to "righteousness" (δικαιοσύνη). Lastly, Jesus exhorted the law expert to do "mercy" (ἔλεος).

Galilee" (17:11) on Jesus' way to Jerusalem. Jesus enters a village (κώμη) and meets ten lepers. The lepers ask Jesus to "have mercy" (ἐλεέω) on them (v. 13), indicating that Jesus is the provider of "mercy" (ἔλεος). Just as in the preceding Samaritan-related accounts, this account also shows that mercy is a basic theme.

Luke uses three rhetorical methods in this episode. First, Luke again uses the method of comparison between the Jews and the Samaritans by using an authorial note to introduce the returned leper: καὶ αὐτός ἦν Σαμαρίτης (v. 16b, "and he was a Samaritan").[163] This note leads to the assumption that the nine cleansed lepers were Jewish, as Luke makes the same ethnic distinction in the parable of the Good Samaritan.[164] In addition to this ethnic distinction, Luke's rhetoric notes how the returned Samaritan responded: "praising God with a loud voice," "falling on his face at the feet of Jesus," and "giving thanks to Jesus" (vv. 15–16a). Luke's rhetorical method is to put all these God-honoring descriptions at the beginning before adding an authorial note, "And this was a Samaritan" (v. 16b).

This rhetorical method of comparison is evident in Jesus' use of the term "foreigner" (ἀλλογενής) to describe the returned Samaritan (v. 18). Jesus distinguishes the Samaritan's act of returning and honoring God by comparing him with the nine. This is the only place where the Greek noun ἀλλογενής appears in the New Testament. Etymologically, it denotes "another race." This is a social-scientific term designated from the standpoint of ethnic Jewishness.[165] Given the use of its Hebrew equivalent in the Old Testament, as studied in the section of Isa 56:1–8, it is clear that it refers to a person who is ethnically, religiously, and even geographically foreign to

---

163. The phrase καὶ αὐτός [αὐτή] ἦν is often used to add a further piece of information about an introduced person, as evidenced in Luke 7:12 ("and she was a widow") and 19:2 ("and he was a chief tax collector, and he was rich").

164. Bock, *Luke 9:51–24:53*, 1405.

165. Josephus uses the Greek term ἀλλογενής only once in *J.W.* 17.417: "All the forefathers used to receive the sacrifices that were [made] by the foreigners [ἀλλογενής]". There is a similar sentence in *J.W.* 17.412: "Their forefathers had adorned the temple [given] by the foreigners [ἀλλόφυλος] always by receiving the gifts [sent] from the nations." Based on these sentences, it seems that Josephus used ἀλλογενής as a synonym to ἀλλόφυλος. Also, it is stated in *J.W.* 5.194 that there is an inscription in Greek and Roman: "No foreigner (ἀλλόφυλος) should go by within the Sanctuary." Matan Orian translates the inscription in the Herodian Temple as follows: "No foreigner is to enter within the balustrade around the (Inner) Temple and the (Inner) Temple wall. Whoever is caught will have himself to blame for his ensuing death." In this inscription, "foreigner" is used the accusative form of ἀλλογενής. Orian, "Purpose of the Balustrade," 490.

the Israelites. Its implied usage is an expression of hatred by the Israelites toward that person.[166]

What is the intent behind Jesus' use of this provocative term to designate the returned Samaritan? This Samaritan honored the God of Israel. This indicates that he belongs to God's covenant people. In Isa 56:1–8, the Hebrew term "foreigner" (בֶּן־הַנֵּכָר) does not correspond with Isaiah's description about the person's lament, which indicates his post-conversion status. Likewise, Jesus' use of the term "foreigner" does not reflect the returned Samaritan's act of honoring God. It can be viewed as Jesus' objective description about the Samaritan's ethnic otherness. However, given the fact that Luke's authorial note— "And this was a Samaritan" (v. 16b)—points to Luke's rhetorical intent, it is reasonable to assume that Jesus' use of "foreigner" here cannot be treated merely as a neutral connotation of ethnic non-Jewishness. Instead, Jesus' use of "foreigner" implies his intent to reveal the antagonistic mindset of his disciples toward the Samaritans and challenge it.

The second rhetorical method Luke uses is reversal, in this account the implied reversal of the Samaritan's status. Jesus said to the returned Samaritan, "Your faith has saved you" (v. 19b). Luke uses the perfect tense of σῴζω ("to save"). It cannot be denied that this "saved" status refers to the Samaritan's physical healing. Given Luke's rhetorical method of comparison, however, the Samaritan's act of honoring God at the feet of Jesus has an eschatological dimension. Although textually unstated, Jesus' compliment to the Samaritan indicates that Jesus is the bestower of eschatological salvation.

The third level of Luke's rhetoric in this account is the included status of the cultically excluded Samaritan. Presumably, the nine healed Jews showed themselves as "cleansed" to the priests and may have offered a sacrifice in the temple according to Lev 14:1–32. It can be assumed that the Samaritan would show himself to the priest at Mount Gerizim.[167] However, Jesus' original command to the ten lepers does not differentiate the returned Samaritan on an ethnic basis. He gave the command, "Go and show yourselves to the priests" (v. 14), to all ten. Also, if based on Luke 5:14 ("go and show yourself to the priest, and make an offering for your cleansing, as Moses commanded, for a proof to them"), Jesus' command presumes their visit to the priests, most likely in Jerusalem. The fact that the Samaritan returned to

---

166. Kuecker, *Spirit and the "Other,"* 155. Kuecker states, "For Luke, the Samaritans are not quite ἔθνη, but they clearly are not Israelites—they are another form of 'other.' The ambiguity provided by the term ἀλλογενής reflects a sentiment akin to *Kutim* 1, which simultaneously highlights Samaritan similarity and distinction."

167. Bock, *Luke 9:51–24:53*, 1402.

Jesus shows the Samaritan knows he is prohibited from access to the priests and admission to the Jerusalem temple. Hence, Luke's purpose is to show the included status of the Samaritan despite his exclusion from the temple.

In this account, Luke's rhetoric reveals a culture in which Jews had a sense of antagonism toward the Samaritans. In response to this attitude, Luke explicitly compares the returned Samaritan to the nine Jewish healed ones. He presents the returned Samaritan as a perfect model to honor God. In this regard, Darrell L. Bock states, "A 'schismatic' or, at the least, someone distant from covenant promise was the only one to show gratitude."[168] Hence, the episode of the returned Samaritan with leprosy implies the Samaritan's reversed state from exclusion to inclusion.

Excluding the Ritually Incomplete

Luke addresses the Ethiopian in Acts 8:26–40 by "eunuch" (vv. 27, 34, 36, 38, 39). Although the word "eunuch" refers to an addressing title, it would be reasonable to consider that the title indicates the Ethiopian's castrated state (cf. Matt 19:12). The purpose of the eunuch's visit to Jerusalem is "to worship" (the future participle of προσκυνέω).[169] Given his pilgrimage from a distant nation, in which the setting of his worship was most likely a local synagogue, his visit to Jerusalem was to worship within the temple. His physiological features (ex., lack of beard), as a result of his castration, made him noticeable as a eunuch.[170] In addition, his powerful role as a servant of Candace (the Queen of the Ethiopians) and the fact that he was likely in his costumes, made him recognizable. His black skin tone, which can be inferred from the term "Ethiopian," also drew attention.

---

168. Bock, *Luke 9:51–24:53*, 1403–04.

169. There are two issues to be clarified with regard to προσκυνέω. First, its future participle use here does not indicate its unfulfilled expectation. This is evidenced in Paul's pilgrimage to Jerusalem to worship (Acts 21:11). Second, Luke's use of προσκυνέω puts a great deal of emphasis on the act of piety rather than on a physical move. Its meaning is (1) a physical move of prostration and (2) a religious act of worship, although the former could presuppose the latter. Luke uses the word in a restricted manner: the devil (4:7), God (v. 8), and the risen Jesus (24:52). One representative case for this manner is Luke's change of the word in Mark 5:6 to προσπίπτω ("to fall before" in Luke 8:28). In Acts, προσκυνέω occurs four times (7:43 [images of deities]; 8:27 [God] in Jerusalem; 10:25 [Peter]; 24:11 [God] in Jerusalem). It seems odd to see Cornelius's act of falling at the feet of Peter and worshipping him. Yet Luke's use of the term is clearly restricted to the act of worship.

170. Physiological features for a castrated male are notable in Josephus and Philo's descriptions of a eunuch (*Ant.* 4.291; *Spec.* 1.325).

Out of all these notable features, Luke focuses on the Ethiopian's castrated state and his intent to worship in the temple. This is evident in his addressing the Ethiopian as "eunuch" five times and his restrictive use of the term προσκυνέω.[171] Given this focus, it is important to clarify the nature of the Ethiopian's temple worship and understand if Luke's description of this episode has a rhetorical aspect; that is, does it have in view a change in the cultic system of the Jerusalem temple in light of Christ's work? Out of multiple healing accounts in Luke's two volumes, the episode of the healed lame man at the temple gate (Acts 3:1–4:22) shows some resemblances to the Ethiopian account. First, both accounts occur in the temple. Second, both men have a physically incomplete state. Third, both presumably experience a certain degree of restriction in their participation in the cultic worship of the Jerusalem temple.

The Lame Beggar at the Temple Gate (Acts 3:1–4:22)

Acts 3:1–4:22 begins with Peter and John's encounter with a lame beggar at the temple gate (3:2) and ends with a brief description of the healed man's age and the healing's implication as a sign (4:22). Within this broad structure, Peter makes two speeches within the temple, first to the general audience and then to the religious leaders. Peter's focus in these two speeches is God's gift of eschatological salvation in the person of Jesus Christ (4:12). To emphasize this message, Luke uses four literary features.

First, Luke emphasizes the lame man's lifelong condition: "from his mother's womb" (3:2) and his age as "more than forty years old" (4:22). The man's lameness appears incurable. Second, Luke emphasizes the man's healed condition to the fullest. To do so, Luke uses five Greek words to describe the condition (3:8): (1) leaping (ἐξάλλομαι), (2) standing (ἵστημι), (3) walking (περιπατέω), (4) entering (εἰσέρχομαι) into the temple, and (5) praising (αἰνέω) God. In addition, Luke uses the term ὁλοκληρία (3:16), which means "state of soundness or well-being in all parts, wholeness, completeness."[172] Luke also uses the adjective ὑγιής (4:10), which also means "physically well or sound."[173]

Second, Luke highlights this healed state as something noticed by all the people in the temple. The lame man's restoration is indisputable

---

171. The Ethiopian's intent to worship in the temple appears to reverse what is expected from the cultic system of the temple. See Resseguie, "Woman Who Crashed Simon's Party," 10.

172. BDAG, 703.

173. BDAG, 1023.

(3:9–10). To describe this reality, Luke uses perception-related words, as in 3:16 ("to see," "to know," and "before all of you") and 4:10 ("standing before you"). In particular, the undeniable reality of the lame man's healing is clear in 4:14–16; in verse 16, it is stated, "For the fact that indeed a notable sign had occurred through them [Peter and John] is evident to all the inhabitants of Jerusalem, and we cannot deny it."

Third, Luke records Peter's speeches, which argue that this noticeable change in the lame man's status is attributed to "the name of Jesus Christ of Nazareth" (3:6, 16; 4:10). Fourth, Luke illustrates the nature of the healing as the "sign" that God's eschatological program of salvation lies in the rejected but resurrected and risen Lord Jesus Christ (4:22).

It is an open question whether Luke suggests a rhetorical implication, in particular, regarding the cultic system of the temple. The locale of the lame man's healing is "at the gate of the temple," which is called "Beautiful" (Ὡραίαν, 3:2); this gate is referred to again as "the Beautiful Gate of the temple" (3:10).[174] Scholars debate its exact location.[175] Given that the gate is an entrance to ἱερόν, which, according to Luke's usage, refers to the entire complex of the Jerusalem temple rather than the sanctuary proper (cf. ναός, in Luke 1:9, 21, 22, 23:45), it can be assumed that the lame man was sitting at the entrance into the temple complex. Once healed, as a complete man, he entered the temple (3:8).

In addition to the physical setting, Luke describes the cultic setting of this episode. He writes that Peter and John were about to enter the temple "at the ninth hour of prayer" (Acts 3:1). Luke 1:9–10 provides a glimpse into this time of prayer: The priest Zechariah enters the sanctuary to offer incense ("the time of incense offering"), and during this time, "the entire congregation was praying outside" (Luke 1:9–10).[176] According to Craig Keener, Scripture mandates the offering of a sacrifice in the sanctuary "both in the morning and toward dusk," but according to Josephus, it is "in the

---

174. The Greek adjective ὡραῖος means "attractive, beautiful, fair, lovely, pleasant." Thus, it could not be a specific designation to "the gate of the temple." It could be a description generally understood by people as something like a nickname. Concerning the locale of the "Beautiful" Gate of the temple, Craig Keener states, "The events in Acts 3 may fit well the eastern gate and entrance to the Court of Women, near Solomon's Portico." Keener, *Acts*, 1048–49.

175. Dennis Hamm suggests two options for the referent to the Beautiful Gate: (1) "the Shushan Gate, in the eastern *exterior* wall of the temple area" and (2) "the Nicanor Gate, the Gate of Corinthian bronze, "located in the sanctuary proper." Given Luke's use of the Greek term ἱερόν, which Luke refers to as "the temple precincts," the locale of Peter and John's encounter with the lame man is "outside the walls of the temple precincts." Hamm, "Healing of the Temple Beggar as Lucan Theology," 309–10.

176. Keener, *Acts 3:1–14:28*, 1044.

morning and at the ninth hour" (*Ant.* 14.65).[177] Thus, it can be assumed that a priest offers an incense and sacrifice in the sanctuary, while and at the same time people pray outside the sanctuary.

Considering (1) the change in the locale of the lame man from outside the temple to inside the temple and (2) the cultic worship going on inside the temple at the ninth hour of prayer, one can infer that the physically incomplete lame man was not part of the congregation praying outside the sanctuary within the temple. There is no mention of the man's status, that is, if he was prohibited from entering the temple or not. However, this can be suggested based on Luke's intent. In this regard, Dennis Hamm states, "In an author who elsewhere shows a sensitivity to the symbolic possibilities of narrative, the movement from being powerless and paralyzed *outside* the temple area to being healed, active, and praising *within* the temple area might speak more of literary and theological intention than of local topography."[178]

In the episode of the lame beggar, Luke puts a great deal of emphasis on the healed lame man's completeness and wholeness, which suggests his eligibility to participate in the cultic system of the Jerusalem temple. This is suggested in Luke's use of the term ὁλοκληρία (3:16), the only occurrence in the New Testament, although its adjective form occurs two times (ὁλόκληρος, 1 Thess 5:23; Jas 1:4). In the LXX, its adjective ὁλόκληρος occurs nine times. First, it denotes the state of not lacking or omitting anything for "seven weeks" (Lev 23:15; Deut 16:9). Second, it is used to describe the

---

177. Keener, *Acts 3:1–14:28*, 1044–45.

178. Hamm, "Healing of the Temple Beggar as Lucan Theology," 310. Mikael C. Parsons states, "Whether the lame were formally and ritually excluded from the first-century temple is hotly debated and probably irresolvable. In any case, the location of the lame man at 'the gate of the temple' raises a question: would the authorial audience have inferred that the man was socially ostracized, lying, as it were, 'outside' the boundaries of institutional religion?" Parsons, *Body and Character in Luke and Acts*, 115. Second Samuel 5:8 reads, "Therefore it is said, 'The blind and the lame shall not come into the house.'" Shmuel Vargon sees "the house" in 2 Sam 5:8 as "the house of David" rather than "the house of the Lord" (i.e., the temple). Vargon argues that there is no known record about "a prohibition of entry to the Temple by cripples." Vargon, "Blind and the Lame," 500. Le Cornu and Shulam see 2 Sam 5:8 as a regulation related to the temple, although they raise doubt about its literal application (based on a Mishina and the Talmud). Le Cornu and Shulam, *Commentary on the Jewish Roots of Acts*, 1:178. Keener states, "There is some ground for uncertainty about this position [a prohibition of entry to the Temple by a lame person], although some strands of evidence may support it. Biblical law excluded the disabled only from the priesthood (Lev 21:18, but Qumran applied this law to restrict their presence in the community (1QSa II, 5–6)." Keener adds, "The same purity practices that kept women and Gentiles from the Court of Israel perhaps did exclude those unable to walk as well, although they were not ritually 'unclean.'" Keener, *Acts 3:1–14:28*, 1049–50.

"uncut" stones for an altar (Deut 27:6; Josh 8:31; 1 Macc 4:47). Third, it is used to describe a physically healthy state (Ezek 15:5 [vine]; Zech 11:16 [Niphal participle of נצב "to stand"]).[179] Fourth, it refers to completeness regarding piety (4 Macc 15:17) and righteousness (Wis 15:3). Hence, the usage of the noun ὁλοκληρία cannot be restricted to a physically healthy state. It can also refer to the state of wholeness in the cultic setting.[180] Based on this usage, it can at least suggest that the lame man's healing points to the ritual wholeness or completeness, making him eligible to participate in cultic worship in the temple along with other covenant people. In this regard, Ben Witherington states, "The use of the term [ὁλοκληρία] here is telling because formerly the lame man was 'blemished' and could not enter the sanctuary. Now he was whole and seen to be made whole by his Jewish peers, who could testify of his former condition and the change wrought."[181]

Conclusion

In this chapter, this thesis has explored the textual tradition of Deut 23:1–8, in particular, the first four groups of people in the list in relation to their prohibition from the assembly of the Lord. It has suggested that Deut 23:1–8 presupposes the purpose to reconstitute the eligible members of "assembly" in accordance with the setting of cultic worship in the temple by restricting the ritually unclean or incomplete and the ethnically non-Israelite. Its purpose is to manifest God's holiness in that assembly. The entire congregation in the wilderness (i.e., the congregation at Horeb and Moab) was composed of God's covenant people, including the Israelites and the non-Israelites who have joined themselves to God's covenant people through the rite of circumcision. Deuteronomy 23:1–8, however, has in view the setting of the cultic worship in Canaan, most likely in the setting of the temple. This change of setting necessitates the stipulations of Deut 23:1–8. Thus, the assembly of the Lord is defined as an inner circle within a broad circle. According to that stipulation, the ritually incomplete (i.e., a castrated male) and the ethnic non-Israelite (i.e., Ammonite and Moabite) cannot be part of the inner circle, but their status is of God's covenant people. This status

---

179. *HALOT* translates the Niphal participle of נצב (Zech 11:16) as "those who are miserable, exhausted" (715).

180. Bock, *Acts*, 172–73. According to Bock, the noun ὁλοκληρία refers to "an unblemished animal that is qualified for sacrifice because it is sound." Barrett argues that the three Greek words (ὁλοκληρία, ὁλόκληρος, and ὑγιής) are "not technical medical terms." Barrett, *Critical and Exegetical Commentary*, 201.

181. Witherington, *Acts of the Apostles*, 182.

creates ambiguity and causes them to be vulnerable potentially to exclusion. Hence, there are three factors in understanding the application of Deut 23:1–8: (1) the change of cultic setting, (2) the ritually incomplete, and (3) and the ethnically foreign.

This thesis has investigated Ezra-Nehemiah and Isa 56:1–8 with those factors in view. Ezra-Nehemiah is clear about the change of cultic setting to the rebuilt temple in Jerusalem. Both Ezra and Nehemiah use Deut 23:3–4 to prohibit the returned Israelites' intermarriage with local "foreigner" residents and separate them; this application is targeted chiefly at religious leaders such as priests and Levites. Yet both Ezra and Nehemiah accept the non-Israelites who have joined to Yahweh's covenant, which presumes their practice of circumcision as a covenant rite. Ezra-Nehemiah does not deal with the ritually incomplete or eunuchs.

Isaiah 56:1–8 alludes to Deut 23:1–8 conceptually but not textually. The purpose of this allusion is to repudiate the idea of exclusion in Deut 23:1–8. The Isaiah text clearly has in view the following three factors found in Deut 23:1–8: (1) the Lord's house (i.e., the temple) as the new setting of cultic worship, (2) foreigners (i.e., the ethnic others), and (3) eunuchs (i.e., the ritually incomplete). This thesis has discussed Isaiah's rhetoric, which uses the terms "eunuch" and "foreigner" as textual signals to recall Deut 23:1–8. Isaiah 56:1–8 is also a polemic to the idea of exclusion embedded in Deut 23:1–8. This polemic is a result of Isaiah's eschatological vision of God's gathering all his covenant people into his house. Isaiah delivers a rhetorical message to God's covenant people, from whom God demands "justice" and "righteousness" in anticipation of God's salvation. This demand is ethical.

This thesis has studied the Dead Sea Scrolls. The Dead Sea Scrolls distinguish between the Qumran sect of Yahad, and the eschatological temple promised by Yahweh to David (4Q174 III, 1–6). The Qumran sect includes the ethnic others and the ritually unclean or incomplete people in their regional camps, but it excludes them from a special "assembly" (1QSa II, 3–10). 4QMMT lists the entities of people that might be related to the ethnically foreign and the ritually incomplete. Its focus is on the prohibition of intermarriage, which would cause the ethnically foreign and the ritually incomplete to enter the sanctuary. This is the case of Deut 23:1–8 to be used as having in view both intermarriage and entry into the sanctuary, just as suggested in Ezra-Nehemiah.

This thesis has explored Josephus, Philo, and the Mishnah tractate Yebamot. Josephus is not explicit about the setting change for worship. He focuses on the eunuch's act of castration as self-imposed and causing effeminate features; he regards the eunuch as a violator of God's blessing of fruitfulness (giving of life) to humans. Philo uses a eunuch's act of castration to present his philosophical argumentation for the existence of the absolute God. The eunuch's act is likened to that of an atheist. He also likens children of a harlot (cf. Deut 23:2) to a polytheist. Philo describes the Ammonites as obsessed with "sense" and the Moabites with "mind," with their origin in view. It is notable that he relates a word or phrase in Deut 23:1–8 to his philosophical argumentation.

The tractate m. Yebam. 6 is the most thorough expositional application of Deut 23:1, chiefly focused on males whose testicles or penis are damaged or mutilated. Its use of Deut 23:1 is consistently applied to ethnic Jews. It also regards this physical impairment as ritually incomplete, putting it under the category of ritual uncleanness. In addition, it prohibits such a male from being married to a Jewish woman, which is a part of prohibiting him from entering the assembly of the Lord.

This study has explained how Luke portrays the ethnic others (i.e., the Samaritans) and the ritually incomplete people (i.e., the lame man). For this portrayal, Luke has in view "foreigner" and "eunuch" in Deut 23:1–8 and Isa 56:1–8. This conceptual framework is evident in Luke's designation of the Samaritan as a "foreigner" and the Ethiopian as a "eunuch." Luke notably portrays the Samaritans as ethnically foreign and the lame man at the gate of the temple as ritually incomplete; both are cultically excluded in the setting of the temple. Luke clearly portrays them as distant from the temple, yet his focus is not on their excluded state but on their included state as God's eschatological people. This point of view is evident as Luke's rhetoric develops. Luke uses provocation, comparison, shame, reversal, and restoration as rhetorical methods to develop an argument that is eschatological, polemical, and ethical. Yahweh's demand for justice and righteousness from his covenant people (Isa 56:1) is somehow related to those cultically vulnerable to being excluded. This ethical aspect is required of Jesus' disciples, among others.

Concerning the issue of the Ethiopian's ethnic and religious background, the Ethiopian most probably lies in the middle area between the inner circle and the outer circle. According to the textual tradition of Deut 23:1–8, the Ethiopian is regarded as one of God's covenant people in the setting of the local synagogue in Ethiopia but ritually incomplete in the setting of the cultic worship in the temple. His pilgrimage to Jerusalem points to his changed setting of worship. The essential position of circumcision in the Abrahamic covenant for all the Israelite males and non-Israelite proselytes leads to the assumption that the Ethiopian was circumcised. Concerning the Ethiopian's ethnic background, the textual tradition of Deut 23:1–8 indicates that he would be of Jewish descent. This is because Deut 23:1 was used in relation to ethnic Jews. In conclusion, Deut 23:1 is not a legitimate criterion to conclude that the Ethiopian was an uncircumcised gentile.

Chapter 4

Cultural Background of the Ethiopian

THIS STUDY HAS RAISED the issue of cultural gaps that occur in Luke's narrative. For modern readers, those gaps can be filled in through cultural studies. For the original readers, however, those gaps are not gaps at all. Rather, those gaps constitute a common cognitive world shared between the original readers and the author. The Ethiopian episode has two main cultural elements that appear to be gaps in narrative to modern readers: (1) the ancient practice of castration and (2) the Jerusalem pilgrimage. While investigating these areas, this study will also consider the Jewish settlements in Egypt, suggesting the possible presence of the Jews in Ethiopia.

Eunuchs and the Ancient Practice of Castration

Luke's introduction of the Ethiopian (Acts 8:27) has three elements revealed in the text: (1) his castrated state ("eunuch"), (2) his social position ("official"), and (3) his governmental duty ("in charge of all the treasure" of Candace). In general, scholars agree that Luke's usage of "eunuch" for the Ethiopian here is to draw attention to his castrated condition. Thus, this understanding leads to the necessity of studying the ancient practice of castration—in particular, (1) how a male becomes a eunuch, (2) what rationale lies behind this practice, and (3) what roles a castrated eunuch undertakes. The goal of this thesis is to reconstruct the cultural world in which the Ethiopian, as a eunuch, was situated. For this goal, this section will focus on two areas: (1) eunuchs introduced in historical settings and (2) the ancient practice of castration. Based on this reconstructed world of eunuchs, it will be suggested that most probably, the Ethiopian was a war captive, became a slave, and was castrated to be a eunuch before his puberty.

Eunuchs in Jewish Literature

The Old Testament

In the setting of Egypt, there are three servants of Pharaoh, being addressed by "eunuch" (סָרִיס). One of them is Potiphar; he is introduced twice (Gen 37:36 [σπάδων] and 39:1 [εὐνοῦχος] in the LXX).[1] His job is "the captain of the guard." The other two servants are "the chief cupbearer" and "the chief baker" (40:2, 7). It is notable that for each of the three servants, the title "eunuch" has a further description related to what each of them does. Also, there is no clear evidence in the text that those servants were castrated. Lastly, each of the servants is closely related to their master's security and safety.

In the setting of Israel's royal house, סָרִיס is also used to address a king or queen's servant. It first occurs in Samuel's warning to the Israelites about their future kings (1 Sam 8:15). Ahab had one eunuch in his palace (1 Kgs 22:9; 2 Chron 18:8). Jehoram designated one eunuch for a Shunammite woman (2 Kgs 8:6). Jezebel had a few eunuchs serving in proximity to her (2 Kgs 9:32). Jehoiachin—along with his mother, servants, officials, and eunuchs—surrendered to Nebuchadnezzar (24:12). Among the exiled people of Judah in Babylon, Jeconiah's eunuchs are included (Jer 29:2; cf. 34:19). In Jer 34:19, the list of those exiled people reappears. In the MT, it has five groups: (1) rulers (שַׂר) of Judah, (2) rulers (שַׂר) of Jerusalem, (3) eunuchs (סָרִיס), (4) priests, and (5) all the people of the land. In its Greek text (Jer 41:19 LXX), it has four groups: (1) rulers (ἄρχων) of Judah, (2) officials (δυνάστης), (3) priests, and (4) people. The first two groups in the MT are combined into the first one in the LXX. If based on parallelism in translation, it can be suggested that "eunuchs" in the MT can be "officials" (δυνάστης)—"one who is in a position of power."[2] Concerning eunuchs in the setting of Israel, it is notable to see three characteristics: (1) their proximate service to the queen, as in the case of Jezebel, (2) their powerful status, as in Jer 41:19 LXX, and (3) anonymity.

---

1. σπάδων is related to the verb σπάω, which means "to exert force so as to pull or draw" (BDAG, 936). By this etymological connection, σπάδων could refer to a male cut with a knife.

2. *GELS*, 179. Luke uses the Greek noun δυνάστης in connection to the Ethiopian's job description. Fitzmyer refers to the Greek noun as "a term often employed of rulers, chamberlains, or court officials." Fitzmyer, *Acts of the Apostles*, 412.

In the setting of Assyrians, the Assyrian king Sennacherib sends his three officials to Hezekiah: the Tartan, the Rab-saris, and the Rabshakeh (2 Kgs 18:17). "The Rab-saris" is literally a chief eunuch in Hebrew. In the LXX, it is translated into ῥαφίς. According to Cogan and Tadmor, "the *rab-saris* was often dispatched on military duties at the head of Assyrian forces."[3] If "saris" in these cases is literally understood, rather than part of their personal names, Sennacherib's eunuchs were military officials.

In the setting of the Babylonians, the Hebrew term סָרִיס is also used for three occasions. First, Isaiah's prophecy that the descendants of Hezekiah would be "eunuchs (סָרִיסִים) in the palace of the king of Babylon" (2 Kgs 20:18). In the LXX, the Hebrew word is translated into εὐνοῦχος. This account is a parallel in Isa 39:7, in which the LXX uses σπάδων for סָרִיס.[4] This prophecy was made as part of God's judgment. Given this fact, it is more probable that Hezekiah's direct descendants could be exiled to Babylon, be castrated, and serve as eunuchs in the royal palace of the Babylonian king.

Second, when Nebuchadnezzar seized Jerusalem, one of his officials (שַׂר) is addressed as "rab-saris" (Jer 39:3). As noted above, this might not be a personal name but a chief eunuch. Lastly, the book of Daniel uses the term סָרִיס seven times (1:3, 7, 8, 9, 10, 11, 18), introducing Ashpenaz as "the chief of the eunuchs" (שַׂר הַסָּרִיסִים; ἀρχιευνοῦχος in the LXX). Given his status among multiple eunuchs, it is assumed that the royal palace of Babylon had a hierarchical system of eunuchs.

In the setting of Persia, the book of Esther has twelve occurrences of סָרִיס, all of which are associated with the royal court of Persia. Seven names are listed, being introduced as "the eunuchs who served in the presence of King Ahasuerus" (1:10). One eunuch named "Hegai" is introduced as "eunuch of the king who keeps the women" (2:3, 15). "Shaashgaz" is the eunuch of the king who was in charge of the concubines (2:14). "Bigthan and Teresh" are the king's two eunuchs, who guarded the threshold (2:21; 6:2). "Hathach" is introduced as "one of the king's eunuchs, who was appointed to attend her [Esther]" (4:5). "Harbona" is introduced as "one of the eunuchs in attendance on the king" (7:9). There are four notable characteristics of the eunuchs in the book of Esther. First, as in Daniel, it shows a hierarchical system of eunuchs in the Persian palace. Second, their main jobs are related to the king's wives or concubines. Third, as shown in the case of Bigthan and Teresh, eunuchs were powerful enough to rebel against their king. Fourth, all the eunuchs mentioned in the book are introduced also with their real names.

---

3. Cogan and Tadmor, *II Kings*, 229.
4. Cf. Gen 37:36 (σπάδων).

In summary, the Hebrew Bible makes no specific mention about the castrated condition of people addressed by סָרִיס. However, their proximate service for their kings or queens in the royal palace could entail their requirement to be castrated. Also, in the settings of Egypt, Babylon, and Persia, eunuchs are sometimes introduced as their personal names—but not the eunuchs in the setting of Israel. Third, when a male is introduced as eunuch, it entails his job description. Lastly, in the settings of Babylon and Persia, it is notable to see that both Babylon and Persia had a hierarchical structure among eunuchs.

Old Testament Apocrypha

The term "eunuch" appears in four accounts in the Old Testament Apocrypha. In Judith, Bagoas is introduced as "the eunuch who had charge of his [Holofernes] personal affairs" (Jdt 12:11).[5] Bagoas was to bring Judith to Holofernes, who was "the chief general" of the army of Nebuchadnezzar (2:4). In Additions to Esther, eunuchs are introduced as working for Queen Vashti (1:12, 15), King Artaxerxes (2:3, 14, 21; 7:9) and Esther (4:4, 5; 6:14), in charge of keeping a harem for the king (2:14), and the king's security (2:21).[6]

Flavius Josephus

Josephus introduces figures titled "eunuch" chiefly according to their duties or job descriptions. First, he introduces one servant (δοῦλος) as "eunuch" (εὐνοῦχος) and "teacher (παιδαγωγός)" of his child (*Life* 429).[7] Josephus explains how his fellow Jews accused him and Domitian punished them for his defense. This servant was most likely one of those Jews. Second, Herod's eunuchs are in charge of bringing him "drink," "supper," and "putting him to bed." Josephus records that "on account of their beauty" Herod was "fond of them" (*Ant.* 16.230; cf. *J.W.* 1.488). Third, one eunuch is described as "most faithful" to his queen Mariamne (*Ant.* 15.226). This points to his role as an attendant close to his queen. Finally, Josephus records that eunuchs were treated as gifts. On one occasion, Josephus lists the items Herod gave to Archelaus as a present. One of them is "eunuchs" (*J.W.* 1.511). This record

---

5. Wills, "Judith," 47.
6. Mary Joan Winn Leith, "Esther," 53–68.
7. Josephus, *Life*, 156–57.

indicates that becoming a eunuch was related to slavery in the Greco-Roman world.

Philo of Alexandria

Philo's use of the term "eunuch" presupposes that it refers to a castrated male.[8] Furthermore, he uses it as a vehicle by which to make his philosophical argumentation. This aspect is well revealed when he contrasts between Potiphar and Joseph. He introduces Potiphar as "a eunuch and barren of all wisdom" (*Leg.* 3. 236).[9] This point of view is connected to Philo's presupposition that despite his eunuch condition, Potiphar had a woman as his wife, seeking pleasure with her. Philo also uses the term "eunuch" to describe Joseph's act of refusing to seek pleasure with Potiphar's wife. He likens this act to "a most desirable thing to be a eunuch, if our soul, by that means escaping vice." (*Leg.* 3. 236).[10] In line with this usage, Philo states, "It is better to be made a eunuch than to be hurried into wickedness by the fury of illicit passions" (*Det.* 176).[11] Hence, by the term "eunuch," Philo refers to the castrated state of a eunuch, as well as one's determination not to be controlled by senses of mankind. The former usage is physiological, the latter metaphorical.

Eunuchs in the Greco-Roman Material

This section introduces the ancient practice of castration and its characteristics. Its research is restricted to the three regions of Egypt, Persia, and Rome, although it turns chiefly to Greco-Roman materials. This study will elucidate three aspects of the castration practice: (1) its usual pattern, (2) its rationale, and (3) duties of the castrated eunuch.

---

8. Burke, *Queering the Ethiopian Eunuch*, 38. Burke states, "Philo's allegorical readings all depend on the assumption that, in the Septuagint, the word εὐνοῦχος refers to a castrated male."

9. Philo, *Works of Philo*, 77.

10. Cf. *Ebr.* 211–224, *Migr.* 69, and *Her.* 274, *Mut.* 172–173, *Somn.* 2.184, and *Ios.* 58–60, 151–153.

11. The phrase "to be made a eunuch" (*Det.* 175) is from ἐξευνουχίζω, which also appears in *Deus* 111 and *Ebr.* 211. Van Tine, "Castration for the Kingdom," 415–16. According to Van Tine, Philo's use of comparative form here is rhetorical.

Practice of Castration

Defining the usual pattern of castration brings up three questions: Which part of the reproductive organs is removed in castration? When is it practiced—before puberty or after puberty? Who is the most vulnerable candidate for this practice? Just as indicated in the Mishnah, the ancient practice of castration is attributed to the human practice of making a male sterile (i.e., saris adam, by the human hand). So, it is not concerned with a congenital factor. Hence, this ancient practice involves a surgical activity chiefly on the male genital organs—testicle(s) and penis. The question is, which part is more related to a eunuch?

First, the ancient practice of castration could involve a removal of either the testicles or the penis, just as implied in Deut 23:1 and the tractate m. Yebam. 8.2.[12] However, it is commonly agreed among scholars that the ancient practice was mainly related to the removal of the testicles. One main reason is that it can reduce the mortality rate during the surgical process. Vern L. Bullough states, "Sometimes, only the testicles were removed, what we now label as castration, and this was much less life-threatening, particularly if done while young."[13] Bullough adds, "Probably most eunuchs do not have both their testicles and penis removed but only their testicles."[14] Hence, as Bullough suggests, the term "castration"—and its practice—is mainly related to the removal of testicles.

Second, castration was performed on pre-puberty males, rather than on adults. Gary R. Brower lists eleven effects that a castration before puberty could cause. One of them is "a marked lack of body hair"—"beard, mustache, pubic hair and chest hair."[15] In contrast, castration after puberty, according to Brower, makes the eunuch still retain his beard.[16] Just as the Mishnah suggests, a male's lack of beard is one of the physical signs that speak of a congenital eunuch. A castration before puberty would make the eunuch appear more like a congenital eunuch.[17]

Third, ethnic foreign children would be more vulnerable to becoming castrated eunuchs. Burke states, "Most eunuchs in antiquity were slaves or freedmen."[18] That is, becoming a eunuch can be understood within the

---

12. Cheney, *Brief History of Castration*, 6. Removing a male's penis is often practiced as a part of punishment.

13. Bullough, "Eunuchs in History and Society," 2.

14. Bullough, "Eunuchs in History and Society," 3.

15. Brower, "Ambivalent Bodies," 160.

16. Brower, "Ambivalent Bodies," 160.

17. Lev, "Genital Trouble," 81–82. Burke, *Queering the Ethiopian Eunuch*, 108–10.

18. Burke, *Queering the Ethiopian Eunuch*, 98.

structure of slavery.[19] Concerning how a male became a slave, Burke lists four different kinds of occasions behind it: (1) war captives, (2) tribute or gifts, (3) exposure to death, and (4) kidnapping by pirates.[20]

For instance, Herodotus of Halicarnassus (fifth century BC) introduces Hermotimus with a focus on how he became a eunuch (Herodotus, *Hist.* 8.104–6):

> Hermotimus, who came from this place Pedasa, had achieved a fuller vengeance for wrong done to him than had any man within my knowledge. Being taken captive by enemies and exposed for sale, he was bought by one Panionius of Chios, a man that had set himself to earn a livelihood out of most wicked practices; he would procure beautiful boys and castrate and take them to Sardis and Ephesus, where he sold them for a great price; for the foreigners value eunuchs more than perfect men, by reason of the full trust that they have in them. Now among the many whom Panionius had castrated in the way of trade was Hermotimus, who was not in all things unfortunate; for he was brought from Sardis among other gifts to the king, and as time went on he stood higher in Xerxes' favour than any other eunuch (*Hist.* 8.105).[21]

This text provides six main characteristics about Hermotimus. First, he was a captive to ethnic others when he was a child. Second, he became a slave to be sold. Third, he was castrated and became a eunuch. Fourth, he was taken as a gift to the royal house of Xerxes. Fifth, he attained the highest position among eunuchs. Sixth, he became the most trusted servant to the king. It is recorded that Xerxes entrusted all his children to Hermotimus as their "guardian" (*Hist.* 8.104, φύλακος). According to Herodotus, Hermotimus took revenge on Panionius by compelling him to castrate his own children and then his children to castrate their father (8.106).

For another instance, Herodotus introduces the threats made by the Persians to the Ionians. This was the Persians' response to occasional revolts in Ionian cities. Herodotus also records how these threats were put into action. It is stated, "for when they [the Persian generals] had gained the mastery over the cities, they chose out the comeliest boys and castrated them, making them eunuchs instead of men, and they carried the fairest

---

19. Guyot, "Eunuchs," 5:173–74. It is stated that "keeping slaves always meant prestige for the master; eunuchs who were particularly rare and expensive slaves attested to the particularly high social prestige of the owner" (173). Guyot, *Eunuchen als Sklaven*, 28.

20. Burke, *Queering the Ethiopian Eunuch*, 98.

21. Herodotus, *Herodotus*, 104–5.

maidens away to the king; this they did, and burnt the cities, yea, and their temples" (Herodotus, *Hist.* 6.32).²² Herodotus mentions three things that the Persians did to the Ionians: (1) castration of their male children, (2) taking their female children to the king, and (3) burning their cities and temples. Thus, this castration practice is part of punishment in response to rebellion.

Appian (ca. 90s–160s CE), a Greek historian, introduces Pharnaces—and what he had done before—within the context of the battle of Zela between Julius Caesar and Pharnaces (47 BC). According to Appian, Pharnaces had subdued Amisus in Pontus, made its inhabitants into slaves, and "made eunuchs of all their boys (τοὺς παῖδας αὐτῶν τομίας ἐπεποίητο πάντας)" (Appian, *Bell. civ.* 2.91).²³

All these historical data suggest that the ancient practice of castration most likely involved the removal of a male's testicles. Also, it was performed on prepubescent male children—most likely foreign-origin slaves. In this regard, Piotr O. Scholz states, "It was common practice to castrate a vanquished enemy in order both to maintain his 'commercial value' and his capacity for work and not to have to be concerned about the risk of his producing 'alien' offspring who might someday want to avenge their forebear's defeat."²⁴

Rationale of Castration

What is the rationale for castrating males to make them eunuchs in the royal house? One of the main reasons is that a eunuch was perceived as having no source of hindrance to distract his faithfulness to his master. According to Xenophon (ca. 430–354 BC), Cyrus put eunuchs close to him "at meals or at wine, in the bath, or in bed and asleep" (Xenophon, *Cyr.* 7.5.59).²⁵ He selected eunuchs, beginning with the doorkeepers (7.5.58–65). Cyrus put them close to him to protect himself—in particular, during the times when he could be the most vulnerable. This rationale helps explain the roles that eunuchs would undertake for their kings.

---

22. Herodotus, *Herodotus*, 177.

23. Appian, *Roman History*, 414–15. The noun τομίας is etymologically related to τομή "cutting" and τομίς "knife." As the methods of castration, the acts of crushing and cutting were in use. Thus, the use of the term τομίας for "eunuchs" reflects how castration was performed—that is, cutting the testicles.

24. Scholz, *Eunuchs and Castrati*, 24.

25. Xenophon, *Cyropaedia*, 286–7.

Duties of the Castrated Eunuch

The term "eunuch" is used as an addressing title. It is usual to see that it entails the eunuch's job description. This pattern is noticeable in the Greco-Roman material. According to Greco-Roman historians, eunuchs would have such jobs as food taster, treasurer, tutor, and security guard.

Suetonius (ca. 70–130 CE) introduces the death of Claudius (AD 41–54). Claudius was poisoned to death. Concerning who was responsible for his death, Halotus was one of the suspects (Suetonius, *Claud.* 44).[26] He is addressed as a eunuch. His job is Claudius' taster. This role is related to his service close to his emperor. For the same incident, Tacitus (ca. 56–after 118 CE) introduces Halotus as the eunuch "whose regular duty was to bring in and taste the dishes" (Tacitus, *Ann.* 12.66).[27]

In a power struggle between Cleopatra and her brother, Ptolemy, it is known that Ptolemy, a thirteen-year-old boy, was under the protection of Achillas and a eunuch called Pothinus. Pothinus is introduced as in charge of Ptolemy's treasures (Appian, *Bell. civ.* 84). Curtius Rufus Quintus (early first century to second century CE), a Roman historian, introduces a eunuch named Bagoas. Nabarzanes, a Persian military official who surrendered to Alexander the Great, brought gifts to Alexander.[28] It is stated, "Among these [the gifts] was Bagoas, a eunuch of remarkable beauty and in the very flower of boyhood, who had been loved by Darius and was afterwards to be loved by Alexander; and it was especially because of the boy's entreaties that he was led to pardon Nabarzanes" (Curtius, *hist. Alex.* 6.5.22–23).[29] Bagoas was "a eunuch who had won the regard of Alexander through prostitution" (10.1.25). Also, Bagoas was described as one of the influential ones who "filled the king's ears with false charges" (10.1.36).[30]

Eunuchs in the Book of Acts

In the New Testament, there are two individuals most probably regarded as eunuchs. First, Blastus is introduced as "the one in charge of the bedroom of the king [Agrippa I]" (Acts 12:20). This description points to his role as

---

26. Suetonius, *Suetonius*, 79–80.

27. Tacitus, *Annals*, 413.

28. Scholz, *Eunuchs and Castrati*, 115. Scholz states, "Castrati, who more often than not came from outside the empire, were commonly bought or presented as gifts when they were just young boys and so came into the possession of private households or the courts of the nobility at a very early age."

29. Curtius, *History of Alexander*, 47.

30. Scholz, *Eunuchs and Castrati*, 82–83.

"chamberlain." As discussed for the eunuchs in the book of Esther, the chamberlain role for eunuchs is well revealed in the setting of the Persian royal palace. Also, the role of Blastus for Agrippa I is related to the private world of the king—in particular, his wives or concubines. With these elements in view, it is assumed that Blastus should be titled by eunuch. However, Luke does not put the term "eunuch" in the text for Blastus. His failure to use that title disagrees with the general pattern in which the term "eunuch" first appears and then his job description follows it. This being the case, Luke's addressing the Ethiopian by the title "eunuch" (Acts 8:26–40) is assumed to contain his purposeful idea, not just a mere addressing title. That is, most probably Luke puts his theological intentionality into that usage of the title.

In Acts 8:26–40, Luke refers to the Ethiopian as "eunuch" five times. This title is followed by the Ethiopian's position in Ethiopia—"official," which is followed by his job for Candace, the ruling queen of the Ethiopians. There are several features assumed in this introduction. First, Philip's instant recognition of the Ethiopian as eunuch is most probably attributed to the Ethiopian's physiological signs of being a castrated eunuch. One of them, as discussed above, could be his lack of beard, which indicates that he was castrated before his puberty, appearing like a congenital eunuch. Second, the Ethiopian's position as "official" leads to infer that he could be in the highest position among eunuchs in the royal palace of Candace. This recognition makes it reasonable to assume that the Ethiopian served as a eunuch for a long time—most probably since his childhood. Third, his job is to manage the Queen's wealth. As found out, this duty is bestowed to the most trusted eunuch servant by a king or queen. Given these aspects, it is probable that the Ethiopian was castrated as a child before his puberty. Based on this reconstructed picture, it is probable that the Ethiopian was an ethnic foreigner, captured in his childhood and sold as a castrated slave to the royal palace of Ethiopia.

Jewish Exiles in Ancient Egypt and Nubia

The goal of this section is to provide the potential of the diaspora Jews in the land of Ethiopia. First, it will investigate how Ethiopia (i.e., Cush) is depicted in the Old Testament. God's eschatological plan includes Cush; part of it is his ingathering of the exiled Israelites from there. Second, this section will investigate Philo's descriptions about the diaspora Jews in Egypt. Third, it will focus on Elephantine in the land of Egypt, an island at the First Cataract with the Nile from the south. Its topographic, geopolitical, and demographic significance will be suggested in light of the Jewish settlement there. This section suggests the probability that the Ethiopian could be a victim of international affairs between Egypt and Ethiopia—in particular, surrounding the island of Elephantine.

Yahweh's Ingathering of Israel from Cush

The Hebrew word כּוּשׁ ("Cush") appears in the MT 25 times. It is translated in the LXX as (1) "Cush" (Χους) and (2) Ethiopia (Αἰθιοπία) or Ethiopian (Αἰθίοψ).[31] The Greek equivalent Χους occurs only in Gen 10:6 and 1 Chr 1:8, both of which introduce "Cush" as one of Ham's four sons (Cush, Egypt, Put, and Canaan). In its other occurrences, Cush refers to as "Ethiopia(n)" in Greek. In general, the Old Testament describes Cush with its nine aspects in view.[32] Out of them, this thesis will focus on the theme of God's ingathering of his people from Cush.

Isaiah 11:11–12

In Isa 11:11–12, Isaiah makes the prophecy that Yahweh will restore "the remnant of his people" (שְׁאָר עַמּוֹ). This restoration is about Yahweh's ingathering of them from "Assyria, Egypt, Pathros, Cush, Elam, Shinar, Hamath, and the coastlands of the sea" (v. 11). As noted here, Cush is one of the seven listed geographic regions. Isaiah's arrangement of the three nations (Egypt, Pathros, and Cush) suggests that he describes them in the southward direction. Pathros refers to Upper Egypt, which encompasses the area from Memphis in the north down to Aswan and then Elephantine in the south.[33] Cush is the land south of Egypt. It is not clear whether Egypt in v. 11 refers to Lower Egypt or the entire land of Egypt, including Pathros. In terms of their direction and scope, Isaiah has in view the entire land of Egypt and its southern border neighboring Cush (cf. Ezek 29:10).[34]

Isaiah 11:12 reads,

---

31. Ezek 30:5 and Esth 1:1 have no Greek-translated word for כּוּשׁ.

32. In the Old Testament, Cush is described in relation to the following nine aspects: (1) land (Gen 2:13), (2) a son of Ham (Gen 10:6; 1 Chr 1:8), (3) Tirhakah as its king (2 Kgs 19:9; Isa 37:9), (4) God's ingathering of the exiled Israelites (Isa 11:11; 43:3; Zeph 3:10), (5) God's judgment (Isa 18:1; 20:3–5; 45:14; Jer 46:9; Ezek 30:4–5, 9; 38:5; Nah 3:9), (6) Egypt's territory and its border with Cush (Ezek 29:10), (7) its turning to Yahweh (Pss 68:31 [MT 32]; 87:4), (8) topaz of Ethiopia (Job 28:19), and (9) Cush under Persia's control (Esth 1:1; 8:9).

33. Williamson, *Critical and Exegetical Commentary*, 2:693.

34. Burrell, *Cushites in the Hebrew Bible*, 265.

וְנָשָׂא נֵס לַגּוֹיִם
וְאָסַף נִדְחֵי יִשְׂרָאֵל
וּנְפֻצוֹת יְהוּדָה יְקַבֵּץ מֵאַרְבַּע כַּנְפוֹת הָאָרֶץ

> He will raise a signal for the nations,
> and he will assemble the banished of Israel,
> and he will gather the dispersed of Judah from the four corners of the earth.

In this text, Isaiah uses the verbs "assemble" (אסף) and "gather" (קבץ). Their direct objects are "the banished of Israel" and "and the scattered of Judah."³⁵ This text itself seems to be presupposing the exiled status of both Israel and Judah. Their ingathering to the land is "from the four corners of the earth." This prepositional phrase is all-inclusive, indicating that those banished and scattered of Yahweh's people are present in all the earth. Yahweh's promise to restore his covenant people is traced back to Deut 30:3, in which the two words, "gather" (קבץ) and "scatter" (פוץ), are used from that aspect.³⁶ In this sense, the two Hebrew words (קבץ and פוץ) in Isa 11:12 point to God's ingathering plan for his people. The three lands (Egypt, Pathros, and Cush), according to H. G. M. Williamson, were "areas of refuge at more or less any time once the eastern powers of Assyria and Babylon became dominant in the Levant."³⁷ Hence, Isa 11:11–12 points to the probability that the exiled Israelites were in the land of Cush.

Isaiah 43:1–7

Isaiah 43:1–7 also indicates Yahweh's ingathering of his people from Cush. Just as in Isa 11:11–12, Isaiah refers to Yahweh's people as "Jacob" and "Israel" (v. 1). It also alludes to the exodus of the Israelites from the land of Egypt; their exodus is illustrated with the image of their passing through the waters (v. 2). Also, Yahweh promises the nations of Egypt, Cush, and Seba as a ransom to redeem his people of Israel, just as Yahweh did to the Egyptians to redeem the Israelites.³⁸ As in Isa 11:11–12, Isaiah's description of

---

35. The Hebrew phrase נִדְחֵי יִשְׂרָאֵל ("the banished of Israel") appears three times (Isa 11:12; 56:8; Ps 147:2). Its usage here, in a broad sense, refers to God's covenant people who used to settle in the land of Israel. In this sense, eunuchs and foreigners in Isa 56:1–8 could belong to "the banished of Israel."

36. Widengren, "Yahweh's Gathering of the Dispersed," 228.

37. Williamson, *Isaiah 1–27*, 2:693.

38. Smith, *Isaiah 40–66*, 194. Burrell, *Cushites in the Hebrew Bible*, 266–67. For the use of "ransom," Burrell states, "The image of Yahweh giving Egypt, Cush and Seba in Israel's stead evokes Exodus 13:15 where the firstborn males are redeemed by a

the three nations—Egypt, Cush, and Seba—has in view the direction from north to south. According to Geoffrey W. Grogan, in the Isaiah text here it is "primarily the return from exile that is in view."³⁹

Zephaniah 3:10

The prophet Zephaniah is introduced as "Zephaniah, the son of Cushi" (בֶּן־כּוּשִׁי), which is the Greek text as τὸν τοῦ Χουσι υἱὸν (Zeph 1:1). The term "Cushi" in Hebrew also appears in Zeph 2:12. This occurrence is Yahweh's utterance for the destruction of "Cushites" (כּוּשִׁים).⁴⁰ Yet its Greek translation is "Ethiopians" (Αἰθίοπες). The LXX distinguishes between "Cushi" (1:1) and "Cushites" (2:12). With this in view, it looks appropriate to see "Cushi" here as a personal name, not necessarily relating to the ethnic or geographic origin of Zephaniah's father from the land of Cush.⁴¹

As in Isa 11:11–12 and 43:1–7, Zeph 3:10 also indicates the probability that Cush would be the land from which Yahweh would gather his exiled people, although its textual corruption would cause this argument to be weak. Zephaniah 3:10 reads,

מֵעֵבֶר לְנַהֲרֵי־כוּשׁ
עֲתָרַי בַּת־פּוּצַי יוֹבִלוּן מִנְחָתִי

From beyond the rivers of Cush
those who pray to me, the daughter of my dispersed ones, will bring me tribute.

When it comes to the geographic locale of "the rivers of Cush" (3:10), it is usually identified as the Blue Nile and the White Nile in the land of Nubia.⁴² Both of the rivers get combined into the Nile right after Khartoum, which is located before the Sixth Cataract. This being the case, Zephaniah had knowledge about the land of Cush even down to the Sixth Cataract in

---

substitute animal. Israel is thus Yahweh's firstborn and where his life is required, again evoking the Exodus motif, Egypt, Cush, and Seba are given in exchange for Israel." The Hebrew word סְבָא (Seba) appears along with Cush in the Hebrew Bible (Gen 10:7 [1 Chr 1:9]; Isa 43:3; 45:14 [the Sabeans]) except Ps 72:10. With this juxtaposition in view, Seba is "presumably in the same general area." Goldingay and Payne, *Critical and Exegetical Commentary on Isaiah 40–55*, 1:275–76.

39. Grogan, "Isaiah," in *Proverbs-Isaiah*, 747.

40. Berlin, *Zephaniah*, 134.

41. Berlin, *Zephaniah*, 67. Cf. Duguid and Harmon, *Zephaniah, Haggai, Malachi*, 2. Duguid does not negate the possibility that "Cushi" for Zephaniah's father could be his ethnic background from ancient Ethiopia.

42. Cf. Isa 18:1.

the south. Also, the Greek text of the LXX translates "Cush" as "Ethiopia." This indicates that at the least, the LXX translator understood "Cush" in Zeph 3:10 as the land of Ethiopia south of the entire land of Egypt.[43]

The Hebrew phrase בַּת־פּוּצַי ("the daughter of my dispersed ones") is believed to have a textual corruption. This phrase is not found in the Greek text of the LXX. Adele Berlin suggests views possible to solve this issue, but she asserts that there is "no possibility of solving the problem."[44] Berlin asserts that Zeph 3:10 is not a reference to "Judean exiles but foreign nations who will recognize the Lord."[45] Marvin A. Sweeney agrees with Berlin's view, referring to Zeph 3:8–10 as more related to Yahweh's actions to the nations. That is, Yahweh's wrath would change the heart of the nations, and in response, they would bring their offerings to Jerusalem.[46] Thomas Renz suggests that the picture of Jewish exiles in Cush offering worship in Jerusalem without returning from exile would be awkward—"that would be unique within the prophetic literature."[47]

Does Zeph 3:10 refer to an ingathering of the Israelites in exile or a turn of the non-Israelite nations to Yahweh? In general, from an eschatological perspective, Yahweh's plan for the restoration of Israel includes both aspects. It involves the recognition of Yahweh by the nations and the return of his exiled people whom he dispersed as part of his punishment.[48] Hence, even if Zeph 3:10 itself does not textually prove Yahweh's ingathering of his exiled people from the land of Cush, the theme—God's restoration of Israel—does not negate this aspect. Also, Zephaniah's geographic knowledge of Cush, particularly its rivers, points to the probability that the exiled Israelites would live in the land.

In summary, Yahweh's plan for restoration includes the ingathering of the Israelites in exile to be in Jerusalem. One of the nations referred to in this regard is Cush. Hence, it is inferable that, according to the three texts (Isa 11:11–12; 43:1–7; Zeph 3:10), in the land of Cush, there were diaspora Israelites to be gathered as part of God's restoration program.

---

43. Cf. Berlin, *Zephaniah*, 134. Berlin sees "Cush" as a reference to the Mesopotamian Cush.

44. Berlin, *Zephaniah*, 134–35.

45. Berlin, *Zephaniah*, 135.

46. Sweeney, *Zephaniah*, 171.

47. Renz, *Books of Nahum, Habakkuk, and Zephaniah*, 611. Cf. Johannes Vlaardingerbroek, *Zephaniah*, 199. Vlaardingerbroek suggests that Zeph 3:10 could be "a reference to the restoration of Judah in the form of a return of the dispersed."

48. Duguid and Harmon, *Zephaniah, Haggai, Malachi*, 39. Duguid emphasizes both aspects in terms of God's restoration program.

Jews in the Land of Egypt

Flavius Josephus

Josephus introduces Moses in the setting of a series of struggles occurring between the Egyptians and the Ethiopians (Josephus, *Ant.* 2.238–53). His rationale for using this setting is to describe Moses as such a heroic figure for the purpose of bringing down the Egyptians and raising the Israelites (2.238). Josephus introduces the Ethiopians as "neighbors to the Egyptians" (2.239). The Ethiopians invaded the Egyptians "as far as Memphis and the sea itself" (2.241). Moses joined the battle against the Ethiopians and proceed to Saba (Σαβά), "a royal city of Ethiopia, which Cambyses afterwards named Meroë (Μερόη) after the name of his own sister" (2.249). Meroë was "encompassed by the Nile, quite round, and the other rivers, Astapus and Astaboras" and it was like "an island" (250). Moses had Tharbis, the daughter of the king of the Ethiopians, as his wife (253). The general motif behind this account is Josephus' introducing Moses as such a heroic person to be able to subdue the Ethiopians (2.282).

Philo of Alexandria

Philo (ca. 20 BC–50 CE) introduces Flaccus as "Flaccus Avillius," whom Tiberius Caesar appointed "viceroy of Alexandria and the country around about" (Philo, *Flacc.* 1–2). Flaccus was the governor of Egypt for six years—for the first five years under Tiberius (AD 14–37) and for the last year under Caligula (AD 37–41; *Flacc.* 8–9). It is known that around 42 CE, Philo worked on this writing about the things that Flaccus had done to the Jewish settlers in Alexandria. According to Philo, Flaccus planned to erect images in the synagogues, an act that was impermissible to the Jews (*Flacc.* 42). In response, Philo illustrates that this issue would not be restricted to Alexandria; it would impact the Jews in other places.

In this context, Philo illustrates demographic information about the Jews, in Alexandria as well as in the other regions of the Greco-Roman world. Philo states, "Jews who inhabited Alexandria and the rest of the country from the Catabathmos on the side of Libya to the boundaries of Ethiopia were not less than a million of men; and that the attempts which were being made were directed against the whole nation" (*Flacc.* 43).

Basically, this statement indicates two geographical references: (1) Alexandria and (2) the entire land of Egypt. In the north, the land of Egypt has Catabathmos neighboring with Libya. In the south, it has a border with

Ethiopia. This geographical information is about the land of Egypt, where Jews were dwelling. Philo also states:

> for it was sufficiently evident that the report about the destruction of the synagogues, which took its rise in Alexandria would be immediately spread over all the districts of Egypt, and would extend from that country to the east and to the oriental nations, and from the borders of the land in the other direction, and from the Mareotic district which is the frontier of Libya, towards the setting of the sun and the western nations. For no one country can contain the whole Jewish nation, by reason of its populousness (*Flacc.* 45).

Philo's main point here is that Jews were dwelling not just in the land of Egypt, but also in the other areas neighboring Egypt in the north, in the west, and in the east. He also indicates the presence of Jews in the countries of Europe and Asia (*Flacc.* 46). When it comes to the population of the Jews in Alexandria, Philo states that out of five districts in Alexandria, two of them are called "the quarters of the Jews, because the chief portion of the Jews lives in them" (*Flacc.* 55).

In addition to this demographic information about the diaspora Jews, Philo illustrates their settlement in those places and their heart toward Jerusalem:

> looking indeed upon the holy city as their metropolis in which is erected the sacred temple of the most high God, but accounting those regions which have been occupied by their fathers, and grandfathers, and great grandfathers, and still more remote ancestors, in which they have been born and brought up, as their country; and there are even some regions to which they came the very moment that they were originally settled, sending a colony of their people to do a pleasure to the founders of the colony (*Flacc.* 46).

There are three points to be discussed here. First, the diaspora Jews consider Jerusalem as their "metropolis," not losing heart toward the Jerusalem temple as Yahweh's presence. Second, the diaspora Jews understand their settled lands from a perspective of their fatherland. Third, their settlement traces itself back to more than a couple of generations, even to the beginning of the colony. This aspect makes it realistic to see that the concept of ethnic Jewishness is more inclusive or even trans-ethnic among the diaspora Jews. At the same time, this realistic point of view leads to the need of understanding Jewishness from an ancestral aspect—that is, descent. Philo makes no specific mention about the presence of Jews in Ethiopia.

Both Josephus and Philo make no mention about the presence of Jews in ancient Ethiopia. Their main focus is on Ethiopia's geographic location—Ethiopia is south of Egypt. Josephus introduces Ethiopia in relation to its capital Meroë.

Jews in Elephantine

Craig S. Keener states, "There had been Semitic-speaking Jews in Elephantine, near Aswan, at least as early as the fifth century B.E.C. (cf. also Jer 44:1), and at least some in Ethiopia as well."[49] In Jer 44:1, it is indicated that Jews lived "in the land of Egypt, at Migdol, at Memphis, and in the land of Pathros." The Greek name for Pathros is Παθουρης. It refers to Upper Egypt, which encompasses the area from Memphis in the north down to Aswan and then Elephantine in the south.

Herodotus of Halicarnassus (fifth century BC) traveled from Elephantine down to Meroë. He mentions three things, among others, about Elephantine. First, he states that the land of Egypt is "down from the Cataracts and the city Elephantine" (*Hist.* 2.17).[50] There are six cataracts along the Nile from the land of Ethiopia down north to the land of Egypt. He understands Elephantine as the edge of Egypt in its south.

In addition to this geographic information, Herodotus introduces Elephantine in terms of its demography. He states that "all who dwelt lower down than the city Elephantine and drank of that river's water were Egyptians" (*Hist.* 2.17). He states, "Above Elephantine the country now begins to be inhabited by Ethiopians, and half the people of the island are Ethiopians and half Egyptians" (*Hist.* 2.29). For Herodotus, Elephantine functions as a geographic and demographic demarcation between Egypt and Ethiopia.

Lastly, Herodotus states, "In the reign of Psammetichus there were garrisons posted at Elephantine on the side of Ethiopia" (*Hist.* 2.30). Psammetichus was Psamtik I, who restored Egypt from the Ethiopians and their rule (the Twenty-fifth Dynasty of Egypt). It can be inferred that Psamtik I used Elephantine as the frontier to protect Egypt from the Ethiopians. Also, Herodotus states that Persian guards are posted at Elephantine (*His.* 2.30). In this regard, Salima Ikram and Christian Knoblauch state, "The main function of the island [Elephantine] was to act as a frontier garrison."[51]

---

49. Keener, *Acts*, 1566.
50. Herodotus, *Herodotus*, 295.
51. Ikram and Knoblauch, "Elephantine and Aswan," 406.

It is generally acknowledged among scholars that Jews settled at Elephantine as mercenary garrisons during the Persian period.[52] According to Ikram and Knoblauch, "Aramaic-Jewish mercenaries and colonists were stationed on the island and in Syene (Aswan). Their remains include a temple to Yahweh and a significant deposit of papyrus texts pertaining to the daily lives of the local inhabitants, recovered from houses of the period."[53] According to Karel van der Toorn, the Babylonians put Syria, Samaria, and Judah under their control through Nebuchadnezzar II. As a result, people from those nations migrated to Egypt and obtained a paid job for their service at military colonies.[54] Toorn suggests that the garrison of Syene (i.e., Aswan), which is located next to Elephantine, was one of those colonies.[55]

According to Bob Becking, during the Persian period, Elephantine Island—and its neighboring settlement—hosted four major ethnic groups: (1) Persians, (2) Egyptians, (3) Yehudites, and (4) Syrians/Arameans.[56] When it comes to the Yehudites, Becking analyzes them based on the remains found at Elephantine. His conclusion is that "the Yehudites can be construed as an ethnic group with some self-awareness, but they did not live in isolation from the greater community."[57]

To a certain extent, the Yehudites showed a sense of commonality regarding their ancestral descent, although not being so explicit as Philo described (*Flacc.* 46).[58] According to Becking, the Yehudites addressed each other by "brother" and "sister" or "our fathers." However, it is not clear how this commonality was expressed in relation to the Jerusalem temple. Yet, it is clear that the Yehudites at Elephantine showed a great bond with the temple at Elephantine.

In addition to their common ancestral-descent awareness, however, it is also identified that their intermarriage with the other ethnic groups was common at Elephantine.[59] This trend appears to be opposed to Deut 23:3–8 and Ezra-Nehemiah's prohibition of intermarriage. Just as Philo's statement about the diaspora Jews and their long-history settlement in the land of

52. Yamauchi, *Africa and the Bible*, 47.
53. Ikram and Knoblauch, "Elephantine and Aswan," 409.
54. van der Toorn, *Becoming Diaspora Jews*, 87.
55. Toorn, *Becoming Diaspora Jews*, 87.
56. Becking, "Identity of the People at Elephantine," 106. Becking sees the Aramaic term "*yhwdy* (pl. *yhwdyn*) as "Yehudites" instead of "Jews." His basic reason is that "Jewish" is for Judaism in Hellenistic times. The Persian period, according to him, was "the time of transition from Yahwism to Judaism."
57. Becking, "Identity of the People at Elephantine," 111.
58. Becking, "Identity of the People at Elephantine," 107–11.
59. Nutkowicz, "Some Aspects of Family Bonds," 24–25.

Egypt indicates (*Flacc.* 46), it is necessary to take into consideration both of the aspects for the Yehudites—their common ancestral descent as well as their interaction with other ethnic groups in reality, which includes their intermarriage with them. Hence, the diaspora Jews had a sense of openness and inclusiveness toward trans-ethnic identity. Despite this, their mutual bond is their common shared ancestry—ancestral descent.

Ethiopians in the Land of Nubia

Nubia is a geographic term that refers to the land south of Egypt. The land of Nubia encompasses the area around six cataracts along the Nile that flows down from the south to the north. More specifically, it lies south of Aswan and Elephantine, where the First Cataract, the last one of the six cataracts along the Nile, is located. It extends further down from the Sixth Cataract.[60] The name "Nubia" originated from the Egyptian word *nub*, which means "gold." Part of the reason is that the land was known as the richest supply of gold in the ancient world.[61] "Cush" was often in use among the Egyptians, Assyrians, Persians, and Hebrews. To the Greco-Roman world, "Ethiopia [Aethiopia]" was used, although it often referred to other parts of Africa.[62]

It is known that the New Kingdom of Egypt (1532–1070 BC) ruled the entire land of Nubia. Tuthmosis I (1504–1492 BC) invaded Nubia as far as the Fifth Cataract of the Nile.[63] Also, the Cushites invaded Egypt, put it under their rule, and annexed it as part of Cush. This period is called the Twenty-fifth Dynasty (ca. 722–655/53 BC).[64] In 663 BC, the Egyptians expelled the Cushites from the land of Egypt. In 591 BC, the Egyptian pharaoh Psammetichus II invaded the land of Nubia as far as Napata, which is located before the Fourth Cataract.[65] This compelled the Cushites to move to Meroë, which is located in the middle between the Fifth and Sixth Cataract. This settlement can be understood as a prelude leading to the Kingdom of Meroë (c. 590 BC—AD 350).[66]

60. O'Connor, *Ancient Nubia*, 73.
61. Lacovara, "Land of Nubia," 6.
62. O'Connor, *Ancient Nubia*, 3. Lacovara, "Land of Nubia," 6–7.
63. Haywood, *Penguin Historical Atlas of Ancient Civilizations*, 64–65.
64. Fisher, "History of Nubia" in *ANAKN*, 34. The Cushite King Piankhi (Piye) (ca. 753–722 BC) invaded Egypt as far as "the Memphite region and Western Delta." The Twenty-fifth Dynasty by the Cushite kings were Shebitqo, Taharqo, and Tanwetamani. Taharqo appears in the Old Testament in the historical context of Sennacherib and Hezekiah (2 Kgs 19:9; Isa 37:9).
65. Jackson, *At Empire's Edge*, 130.
66. Snowden, *Blacks in Antiquity*, 4. Snowden assigns the Meroitic Period to 542

One notable characteristic of the Kingdom of Meroë was the existence of its ruling queens. The Meroitics developed their own script in the pattern of the Egyptian script. According to Yamauchi, only twenty-six words in the script are identifiable in terms of translation; two of them are (1) the word (the variants *kdke*, *ktke*, and *kdwe*), which refers to the Greek *Kandake*, and (2) *qore* ("ruler").[67] Haynes and Santini-Ritt state:

> Michal Zach has listed seven *kandakes* for this period. Three of these were also called *qore*, or ruler, namely Amanirenas, Amanishakheto, and likely Amanitore. This title, *qore*, was definitive proof that the queen had taken the throne. However, it is possible that a given queen lacks the title *qore* due to poor preservation or archaeological accident. In these cases, iconography could demonstrate that she was a ruling queen. Such features would include sitting on the lion throne, wearing or carrying the other kingly insignia . . . or having kingly titles such the Son of Re preceding her cartouche. However, the queen's name in a cartouche alone does not necessarily mean that she was a ruling queen.[68]

From 50 BC to AD 40, there were four ruling queens archaeologically identified, with the first three in succession: (1) Nawidemak, (2) Amanirenas, (3) Amanishakheto, and (4) Amanitore.[69] One temple found in Naqa, which is located in the region of Butana, east of the Sixth Cataract, depicts King Natakamani (on the left) and Queen Amanitore (on the right) as smiting enemies by holding their hair (second half of the first century AD).[70] Haynes and Santini-Ritt state, "In this scene, the queen is depicted in an unusual role as fierce protector of the country and upholder of *maat*, a role traditionally reserved for the king."[71] Hence, Amanitore could be the Candace, the Queen of the Ethiopians that Luke introduces in Acts 8:27.

BC–AD 339/350. Fisher, "History of Nubia," 10. Fisher regards that period as "midthird century BC to mid-fourth century AD."

67. Yamauchi, *Africa and the Bible*, 169.

68. Hayes and Santini-Ritt, "Women in Ancient Nubia," in *ANAKN*, 180.

69. Hayes and Santini-Ritt, "Women in Ancient Nubia," 182.

70. Yellin, "Naqa," in *ANAKN*, 231. Fisher, "History of Nubia," 38. This archaeological record indicates that the Meroë Kingdom expanded its territory not to the north toward Egypt but to the south and east.

71. Hayes and Santini-Ritt, "Women in Ancient Nubia," 184.

Summary

This section has discussed the probability of Jewish settlements in the land of Ethiopia in three ways. First, it has suggested that the Old Testament, particularly in Isaiah, indicates the presence of the exiled Jews in the land of Cush (i.e., Ethiopia). Second, Elephantine, which functions as a border between Egypt and Ethiopia, hosted Jews as its inhabitants. Given its geopolitical significance, between the Egyptians and the Ethiopians, the fact that Jews settled in Elephantine leads to the likelihood that they would have been further exiled to Ethiopia. Third, the three-consecutive rulership of the Meroë Kingdom by its queens indicates that the episode of the Ethiopian eunuch has a specific historical setting. Although it is not conclusive, this section contributes to setting a historical context for the Ethiopian and his episode in Acts 8. Hence, it increases the probability that the Ethiopian was a Jewish-descent Ethiopian.

Pilgrimage

Luke states that the purpose of the Ethiopian's travel to Jerusalem was "to worship" (v. 27). Luke's use of the pluperfect tense of ἔρχομαι, along with the purposeful idea of the future participle of προσκυνέω, indicates that Luke's intent here is to provide the Ethiopian's pilgrimage as background information about the Ethiopian. To construct the Ethiopian as a pilgrim in the cultural setting of pilgrimage to Jerusalem, this section will investigate Josephus, Philo, the Greco-Roman writers, and one Mishnah tractate, Šeqalim. This investigation will be made from three perspectives: (1) three annual Jewish festivals, (2) Jewish and gentile pilgrims to Jerusalem, and (3) half-shekel contribution by the diaspora Jews. It will be suggested that the nature of the Ethiopian's pilgrimage and temple worship would be more like what is depicted about the ritually unclean or incomplete Jews.

Three Annual Festivals of Pilgrimage

In Exod 23:13–17, it is stipulated that all the males of Israel should appear before the Lord on an annual basis: (1) the Feast of Unleavened Bread, (2) the Feast of Harvest (i.e., the Feast of Weeks), and (3) the Feast of Ingathering (i.e., the Feast of Booths).[72] Their appearance before the Lord is obligated to "all the males" (Exod 23:17).

---

72. Deut 16:1–16 refers to (1) Passover (vv. 1–8), (2) the Feast of Weeks (vv. 9–12), and the Feast of Tabernacles (vv. 13–15).

Tobit and 2 Maccabees

The book of Tobit is about Tobit, who lived as a diaspora Jew after becoming a captive in Assyria (Tob 1:1). Tobit elucidates his life before the Assyrian captivity.[73] Despite the fact that his ancestral origin is from Naphtali, Tobit states, "But I alone went often to Jerusalem for the festivals, as it is prescribed for all Israel by an everlasting decree" (Tob 1:6).[74] Based on the Torah, the festivals for his pilgrimage would be (1) Booths (Sukkot), (2) Passover (Pesach), and (3) Weeks (Shavuot/Pentecost). The list of his offerings, according to Tobit, are "the first fruits of the crops and the firstlings of the flock, the tithes of the cattle, and the first shearings of the sheep" (1:6). Tobit emphasizes his life as "in the ways of truth and righteousness" (1:3).

Judas Maccabeus was in the midst of conquest in the region of Transjordan (2 Macc 12:1–28). The writer of 2 Maccabees introduces a pilgrimage by Jews to Jerusalem, stating, "Then they went up to Jerusalem, as the festival of Weeks was close at hand. After the festival called Pentecost, they harried against Gorgias, the governor of Idumea" (2 Macc 12:31–32).[75] According to this record, the Jews celebrated Pentecost at Jerusalem, even during their military campaign.

Flavius Josephus

Josephus indicates that pilgrims to Jerusalem were not just Jews but also gentiles. He introduces people "from the parts beyond Euphrates" who traveled to Jerusalem "to honor the Temple" (*Ant.* 3.318). Then, Josephus provides a brief explanation about the nature of their worship in the temple:

> when they had offered their oblations, could not partake of their own sacrifices, because Moses had forbidden it, by somewhat in the law that did not permit them, or somewhat that had befallen them, which our ancient customs made inconsistent therewith; some of these did not sacrifice at all, and others left their sacrifices in an imperfect condition; nay, many were not able, even at first, so much as to enter into the temple (318–319).[76]

There are three main rituals the gentile pilgrims intended to do: (1) to offer sacrifices (θύω), (2) to partake in their sacrifices (μεταλαμβάω), and

---

73. In Kgs 15:29, it is stated that Tiglath-pileser king of Assyria captured all the land of Naphtali and carried its people to Assyria.

74. Levine, "Tobit," in *NOAA*, 11.

75. Schwartz, "2 Maccabees," in *NOAA*, 268.

76. Josephus, *Complete Works*, 119.

(3) to enter the temple.⁷⁷ The nature of those rituals is the cultic worship in the temple. However, just as Josephus indicates, they could not gain access to the fullest degree of the cultic worship that Jews had. Concerning the basis of this exclusion, Josephus states, "Moses forbade it" (318).

Josephus seems to make a distinction between the act of offering sacrifices and the act of partaking in them (318, θύσαντες οὐκ ἴσχυσαν τῶν ἱερῶν μεταλαβεῖν). There were gentiles who offered their sacrifices but could not partake them. This fact indicates that the cultic act of partaking was regarded as the fullest degree of worship in the temple.⁷⁸ Then, Josephus makes a further note about gentiles who could not even offer their sacrifices nor enter the temple.⁷⁹

In *J.W.* 6.420–428, Josephus introduces the gathering of Jews at Jerusalem to celebrate the Feast of Unleavened Bread (421) and the Feast of Passover (423). The context of this introduction is about how Jews ended up being confined in Jerusalem by the Romans (428). Josephus states:

> which, upon the allowance of no more than ten that feast together, amounts to two million seven hundred thousand and two hundred persons that were pure and holy; for as to those that have the leprosy, or the gonorrhea, or women that have their monthly courses, or such as are otherwise polluted, it is not lawful for them to be partakers of this sacrifice; nor indeed for any foreigners either, who come hither to worship (425–27).⁸⁰

The cultic setting of this occasion is the Feast of Passover, specifically the ritual of eating the offered sacrifices. Concerning who is not eligible for this partaking ritual, Josephus has two groups in general: (1) the ritually unclean ("those that have the leprosy, or the gonorrhea, or women that have their month courses, or such as are otherwise polluted") and (2) the ethnically foreign ("any foreigner either, who come hither to worship"). In

---

77. Josephus, *Jewish Antiquities*, 472.

78. The ritual of eating the offered meat most probably points to peace offering (Lev 3; 7:11–34). Averbeck, "Sacrifices and Offerings," in *DOTP*, 715. Averbeck states, "The distinctive nature of this offering was the communal celebration of the worshipers occasioned by the sharing in the meat of the offering."

79. *Ant.* 15.417 ("an inscription, which forbade any foreigner to go in, under pain of death"). The entire inscription reads, "No foreigner is to enter within the balustrade and forecourt around the sacred precinct. Whoever is caught will himself be responsible for (his) consequent death." It is the warning sign found in the stone balustrade, which separates "the outermost court of the Temple Mount, where Gentiles were allowed, from the inner courts and sanctuary (here ἱερόν), where they were not." Price, "Greek Warning Sign on Temple Mount," 43.

80. Josephus, *Complete Works*, 898.

this statement, Josephus has in view the ritually unclean Jews and the ethnic non-Jews regarding their ineligibility of partaking the offered sacrifice.

Hence, the two accounts of Josephus suggest three notable things. First, he distinguishes between the ritual of offering sacrifices and that of partaking. Second, he tends to regard the ritual of partaking as the fullest degree of worship. Third, there are people who offer their sacrifices but cannot partake them—the ritually unclean or incomplete and the ethnically non-Jewish. To put these three points together, it can be suggested that the notion of Deut 23:1–8, as discussed in chapter 3, is valid in the cultic setting of the temple during the time of Josephus—that is, God's covenant people but the excluded ones because of their ritual uncleanness and ethnic foreignness, in particular, regarding the partaking ritual of the sacrificed animal.

Of the three annual festivals, Josephus often refers to Pentecost (*Ant.* 17.254, *J.W.* 1.253; 2.42). There are three features identified according to his descriptions about Pentecost. First, Josephus states that Pentecost is a gathering for a multitude of Jews at Jerusalem. Second, he also makes plain that their gathering was not purely religious. Their purpose was to express a sense of resistance or participate in their protest. He states that "the people got together, but not on account of the accustomed divine worship, but of the indignation they had" (*J.W.* 2.42). Third, he often refers to the geographic origins of those gathered people, most of which are confined to the land of Palestine (Galilee, Idumea, Jericho, the Trans-Jordan region), although he does not exclude other areas (*Ant.* 17.254). In general, Josephus describes the three annual festivals and their related pilgrims (1) from a cultic perspective of the temple and (2) from a political perspective of the situations where the Judeans were facing.

Philo of Alexandria

Philo describes the pilgrimage of Jews from a perspective of the diaspora. This feature is well revealed in *Spec.* 1.68–70. In this text, five notable characteristics are identified. First, the diaspora Jews travel to Jerusalem because the temple is the only place for sacrifices. Philo states that "he [God] does not permit those who desire to perform sacrifices in their own houses to do so" (*Spec.* 1.68).[81] In this respect, Safrai states, "There were synagogues at this period in all places where Jews had settled. But divine worship in the form of sacrifice, one of the main religious rites among the nations and in

---

81. Philo, *Works of Philo*, 540.

Israel, was impossible in the synagogues. All that could be done was to send a sacrifice to Jerusalem or to bring it there personally."[82]

Second, Philo's geographic portrayal is an expanded, all-inclusive picture of pilgrimage—"even from the furthest boundaries of the earth" (68) and "a countless variety of cities" (69). Third, Philo emphasizes a sense of attachment among the diaspora Jews toward their friends in the motherland (68). Fourth, Philo implies that the three annual festivals are the occasions for pilgrimage (69). Fifth, their pilgrimage to Jerusalem is a time of relief and tranquility (69). That is, their pilgrimage to Jerusalem and their participation in its cultic worship would lead the Jewish diaspora pilgrims to comfort and peace.

In *Spec.* 1.77–78, Philo provides a more detailed and practical description about the contribution of first fruits among the diaspora Jews. This account is not so much focused on their pilgrimage to Jerusalem. Instead, it describes how the diaspora Jews practice the obligation to offer their first fruits in foreign lands. Philo describes the rationale for their first fruit offering. First, their contribution is based on the law—"all men shall every year bring their first fruits to the temple" (77).[83] Second, their contribution has the aspect of atonement—"ransom" (77). Third, this contribution is an expression of their wish—"a relaxation from slavery," "a relief from disease," and "freedom and safety for the future" (77).

In addition to this rationale, Philo elucidates how the diaspora Jews contribute their first fruits as an offering to Jerusalem (78). He states, "Accordingly there is in almost every city a storehouse for the sacred things to which it is customary for the people to come and there to deposit their first fruits, and at certain seasons there are sacred ambassadors selected on account of their virtue, who convey the offerings to the temple" (78).[84]

In this statement, the diaspora Jews select their ambassadors to carry their offerings to Jerusalem. It is stated that for this job, "the most eminent men of each tribe are elected" (78). Those agents are the ones who "conduct the hopes of each individual safe to their destination (i.e., the temple)" (78). This account shows the case of pilgrimage in which the diaspora Jews perform their first fruit duty through their elected agents, rather than their personal visit to Jerusalem. This practice reflects the reality of the diaspora Jews in foreign lands.

---

82. Safrai, "Relations between the Diaspora and the Land of Israel," 1:187.
83. Philo, *Works of Philo*, 541.
84. Philo, *Works of Philo*, 541.

Half Shekel

The half shekel is another form of contribution made by the diaspora Jews. Giving half a shekel as an offering to the Lord is traced back to Exod 30:11–16. According to J. Liver, the Exodus text regulates three characteristics about the half-shekel offering: (1) its relation to the census, (2) its binding obligation to all the adult Israelites, and (3) its function as a ransom to the Lord.[85] There is an issue of how the collected atonement money was used. It is stated, "You shall take the atonement money from the people of Israel and shall give it for the service of the tent of meeting" (v. 16). According to J. Liver, the phrase "the service of the tent of meeting" is about constructing the tent of meeting and its appurtenances.[86] To run its cultic functions, the Jerusalem temple used the revenue attributed to the half shekel that all the Israelites were obligated to contribute.[87]

Flavius Josephus

Josephus makes no specific remarks about the half-shekel offering as a regulation to the diaspora Jews. Instead, he focuses on how faithful they were to this offering. In *Ant.* 18.311–313, he refers to the half shekel as something that "everyone, by the custom of our country, offers unto God."[88] This is the only occurrence of the term "half-shekel" (δίδραχμον) in the works of Josephus. Instead of the term "half-shekel," Josephus uses the terms like "sacred money that is carried to the temple at Jerusalem" (*Ant.* 16.167) or "sacred money of the Jews" (168). According to Josephus, the Jews used "Neerda" (*Ant.* 18.311) and "Nisibis" (312) as the cities for the deposit of their collected half-shekel fund. He also notes that a multitude of men were in charge of this fund to be carried to Jerusalem.

In *Ant.* 16.171–173, Josephus mentions three things that the diaspora Jews do: (1) assemble together, (2) send money to Jerusalem, and (3) carry the first fruits to Jerusalem. His mention of these is in the context of arguing that Caesar Augustus permitted the Jews to do those things. As noted, Josephus uses the term "money" to refer to the collected half-shekel fund.

---

85. Liver, "Half-Shekel Offering," 174.

86. Liver, "Half-Shekel Offering," 176. In 2 Chr 24:4–14, Josiah refers to the half-shekel donation as "the tax that Moses the servant of God laid on Israel in the wilderness" (v. 9). He also indicates the usage of that donation—"to repair the house of your God from year to year" (v. 5).

87. Safrai, "Relations between the Diaspora and the Land of Israel," 188.

88. Josephus, *Complete Works*, 596.

This being the case, Josephus distinguishes between the half-shekel and the first fruits.

Philo of Alexandria

Philo does not mention the term "half-shekel" but uses the terms "sacred money" or "money" to refer to it. Philo elucidates the life of the Jews in Rome, who settled down on the other side of the river Tiber. According to him, their life began there as captives (*Legat.* 155–157). He states, "And they were mostly Roman citizens, having been emancipated; for, having been brought as captives into Italy, they were manumitted by those who had bought them for slaves, without ever having been compelled to alter any of their hereditary or national observances" (155).[89] Philo also explains their commitment to their religious life: (1) their Sabbath gathering at the synagogue, (2) their collection of "sacred sums of money" from their first fruits, and (3) their donation of them to Jerusalem. Just as Josephus did, Philo recalls Caesar's policy not to prohibit the Jews from doing them (*Legat.* 157; 315).

Marcus Tullius Cicero (106–43 BC) is known as the author of "numerous letters as well as speeches and treatises."[90] One of them is *Pro Flacco*. Flacco was the Roman governor of Asia. He issued an edict to forbid the gold collected by the diaspora Jews in Asia to be sent to the Jerusalem temple.[91] Flacco confiscated the collected gold through his subordinate agents in the following four cities: (1) Apamea, (2) Laodicea, (3) Adramyttium, and (4) Pergamum (62–61 BC). Regarding the collected gold, Cicero states, "It was the practice each year to send gold to Jerusalem on the Jews' account from Italy and all our provinces" (Cicero, *Flac.* 67).[92]

Mishnah Šeqalim 1.3

The Mishnah text states:

> From whom did they seize collateral? [From] Levites and Israelites, proselytes and freed slaves, but not from women, slaves nor minors. [In the case of] a minor whose father has commenced to contribute the half shekel on his behalf, [the father] may not

---

89. Philo, *Works of Philo*, 771.
90. Evans, *Ancient Texts for New Testament Studies*, 289.
91. Marshall, "Flaccus and the Jews of Asia," 140.
92. Cicero, *Cicero in Twenty-Eight Volumes*, 515.

cease to do so. For the sake of peace, they do not seize collateral from the *Kohanim* (m. Šeqal. 1.3).[93]

In the context of the half-shekel contribution, the term "collateral" refers to some valuable items that can be seized "to assure eventual payment of the debt."[94] The two entities here, "proselytes" and "freed slaves," are ethnically non-Jewish. According to Goldwurm, "In the event he [a slave] is subsequently freed, he automatically attains the status of a proselyte, and becomes obligated in the performance of all *mitzvos*."[95] In terms of God's covenant, the proselytes and the freed slaves belong to God's covenant people, and they are obligated to perform all the religious duties required by the law.

When it comes to a contribution by a gentile and a Cuthean, the ruling states, "[However,] if a Gentile or a Cuthean contributed, we do not accept [it] from them. Nor do we accept from the bird offerings of *zavim*, *zavos* and women after childbirth; nor sin offerings and guilt offerings. But we accept vow offerings and gift offerings from them" (m. Šeqal. 1.5).[96] Goldwurm sees the Cutheans as those non-Jewish settlers in the land of Samaria because the Assyrians forced them to settle there (i.e., Samaritans).[97] This ruling forbids the gentiles or Samaritans to give the half shekel as an offering to God. This is most likely because of their status as non-covenantal people. Based on the Mishnah rulings about the half-shekel contribution, this offering is just for God's covenant people, including ethnically non-Jewish proselytes.

Conclusion

This chapter has covered three areas: (1) the ancient culture of castration, (2) the Jewish settlement in Elephantine, and (3) the Jerusalem pilgrimage. Its purpose is to reconstruct the cultural setting in which the Ethiopian might have been situated. First, Luke's introduction of the Ethiopian as "eunuch" and "official" (Acts 8:27) indicates that the Ethiopian became a castrated eunuch before his puberty and grew up to be in such a high position as to oversee the treasure of his ruling queen. This means that his castration was not a voluntary act but a forced one. Given the characteristic of foreignness that the ancient practice of castration has, it is probable that the Ethiopian

---

93. Goldwurm, "Tractate Shekalim," 11–13.
94. Goldwurm, "Tractate Shekalim," 11.
95. Goldwurm, "Tractate Shekalim," 11.
96. The word *zavim* is related to the man's discharge (זָב), as described in Lev 15:1–15. The word *zavos* is related to the woman's blood flow (זָבָה), as described in Lev 15:25.
97. Goldwurm, "Tractate Shekalim," 17.

had been a war captive or a slave. Second, Elephantine was one of the major Jewish settlements in the land of Egypt. Geopolitically, for the Egyptians, this island functioned as a frontier in the southern border with the Ethiopians. With these two facts in view, it is probable that Jews in Elephantine had become captives carried to Ethiopia. Third, this chapter has introduced the practice of the Jerusalem pilgrimage. The nature of the Ethiopian's worship in the temple could be a restricted form for those ethnic Jews who had physical blemishes, being regarded as unclean or incomplete. The Ethiopian most likely fulfilled the obligations required of ethnic Jews but could not participate in the fullest degree of benefits that are allowed for Jews.

In conclusion, the Jewish conceptual world about a castrated eunuch in the setting of cultic worship is consistent: his affiliation with God's covenant and his exclusion from the cultic system of the temple to a certain degree. The next chapter will discuss how this characteristic is embedded in Luke's harmonizing or synthesizing development of narrative in Acts.

Chapter 5

Literary Approach to the Ethiopian

LUKE USES HIS "ORDERLY" arrangement of individual episodes to provide a sense of "assurance" to Theophilus (Luke 1:3–4). An analysis of how Luke did so is critical in understanding the position of the Ethiopian's ethnic origin and religious status. Three trajectories are notable in Acts. First, the geographic progression is a visible portrayal in Luke's narrative development. Second, the gentile inclusion flows in tension throughout the entire narrative. Third, both trajectories are projecting themselves amid the ethnoreligious culture of Judaism, and both center around the work of Christ. This chapter will examine the position of the Ethiopian in each of those trajectories.

Luke's Geographic Progression and the Ethiopian's Position

Luke provides multiple geographic locales in Acts. How does each of the locales contribute to Luke's literary work? There are a few features to be identified in Luke's usage of those locales. First, Luke uses them to describe the gradual fulfillment of the Acts 1:8 mandate, chiefly with a focus on the gospel's geographic expansion. Second, Luke uses each of the locales as a demarcation that subdivides his work into literary units. That is, each locale works as a means by which Luke frames his narrative.[1] For instance, "all

---

1. Witherington, 34. Witherington argues that Luke's arrangement of all the episodes in Acts agrees with "the Greek κατα γενος of arranging one's history, whereby the work proceeds along geographical as well as chronological lines." Witherington's

Judea and Samaria" is what Luke uses as a literary framework to introduce Philip's outreach (8:5–40) and Peter's ministerial work (9:32–43) before the Cornelius episode in the locale of Caesarea.

Third, each of the locales—from a Jewish perspective of perception—retains its own cultural convention or conception. In this regard, Joel B. Green states:

> Geography—and especially such geographical markers as 'Judea' and 'Samaria'—is not a 'naively given container' but rather a social production that both reflects and configures being in the world. Note, for example, the identification of 'Jerusalem' as the location of the temple and abode of God in Jewish and Lukan perspective and the religious sensibilities that would have been transgressed by this juxtaposition of 'Judea' (land of Jews) and 'Samaria' (land of the Samaritans).[2]

In addition to Jerusalem, Judea, and Samaria, Luke is also conscious of how Jews culturally perceived Gaza and Caesarea. This section will briefly introduce the locales of Gaza and Caesarea. It will also scrutinize how Luke understands each of them from a Jewish perspective. Then, in terms of the Ethiopian's ethnic identity and religious status, it will illuminate Luke's purpose of designating the locale of the Ethiopian's conversion as "the road to Gaza." Luke's introduction of Philip's outreach is contextualized in the land of Judea. This geographic contextualization, although not in an absolute sense, would serve at least as a boundary marker within which the Ethiopian's ethnic and religious background could be categorized.

Contextualization of Gaza

Acts 8:4–40 introduces Philip's outreach to (1) the Samaritans (vv. 5–25) and (2) the Ethiopian (26–40). For the latter, Luke attributes it to the Lord's direct guidance. Philip was commanded to take "the road going down from Jerusalem to Gaza" (v. 26). According to Craig S. Keener, there were two routes of travel from Jerusalem to Gaza: (1) to Bethlehem, Hebron, and then the main road of Gaza along the coastline and (2) to the west, and then the coastal road before Gaza.[3] In favor of the latter, Keener states, "Since the angel specifies that the road goes as far as Gaza, Philip may not expect to

---

emphasis is on Luke's use of geographic locales as the basic flow of his narrative development. Yet Witherington emphasizes the Ethiopian episode on the Ethiopian's geographic origin—Ethiopia.

2. Green, "Acts of the Apostles," in *DLNT*, 15.
3. Keener, *Acts*, 1548.

travel beyond this."[4] This view is also contextually more appropriate. First, Philip's outreach was originally directed toward the north—in Samaria (vv. 5–25). Second, Philip's return to Caesarea after his outreach to the Ethiopian (8:40)—most probably, his hometown—indicates that he was heading to the far north of Judea. Third, just as Keener indicates, the angel's description of the route supports the view that Philip encountered the Ethiopian on the road before Gaza. It is clear that Gaza was not Philip's destination.

How is Gaza perceived by the Jews? In the MT, Gaza (עַזָּה) occurs twenty times[5]. In general, the Old Testament describes Gaza as one of the five cities—Gaza, Ashkelon, Ashdod, Ekron, and Gath—that belonged to the Philistines, although "Gaza" in Gen 10:19 (the Canaanites) and Deut 2:23 (the Avvim) does not identify the Philistines as its residents.[6] Occasionally the Israelites gained Gaza as their territory (Josh 10:41; Judg 1:18), but it did not remain as their territory for long. According to Martin Hengel, Gaza is "the first Gentile city, which Luke mentions in Acts in connection with the process of the mission before the calling of Paul at Damascus."[7] Concerning the geographic setting of the Ethiopian's conversion, in particular, Luke's note about it as "desert," Matthew Sleeman sees it as "a gateway to the peoples of the south" that Luke's narrative did not touch.[8]

Contextualization of the Road to Gaza

How is this aspect of Gaza embedded in Luke's illustration of the Ethiopian episode? Clearly, Philip's witnessing occurred on the road before Gaza. Luke's authorial note added about this road ("this is a desert," v. 26) reflects his intent to draw attention to this locale.[9] Philip's outreaching evangelism (Acts 8:5–40) occurred in "all Judea and Samaria." So, Luke's reference to the locale ("the road to Gaza") can be viewed as his literary intent to develop Philip's evangelism in accordance with the geographic framework of Acts 1:8. Also, Luke makes a brief note about Philip's outreach in Azotus and all the cities before Caesarea (v. 40).[10] Most presumably, all those cities here,

4. Keener, *Acts 3:1–14:28*, 1548.
5. Gen 10:19; Deut 2:23; Josh 10:41; 11:22; 15:47; Judg 1:18; 6:4; 16:1, 21; 1 Sam 6:17; 1 Kgs 5:4; 2 Kgs 18:8; Jer 25:20 [LXX 32:20]; 47:1, 5; Amos 1:6, 7; Zeph 2:4; Zech 9:5 [x2]. In LXX, "Gaza" also occurs in Josh 13:4 and 1 Macc 11:61–62.
6. Jost, "Abimelech," in *DOTP*, 6–7.
7. Hengel, *Between Jesus and Paul*, 112.
8. Sleeman, *Geography and the Ascension Narrative*, 187.
9. Roloff, *Apostelgeschichte*, 294. Witherington suggests that Gaza is the desert.
10. Azotus is referred to as Ashdod (אַשְׁדּוֹד) in the Hebrew Bible (1 Sam 5:1; Isa

including Azotus ("Ashdod"), belong to the land of Judea, although their demographics do not indicate the dominance of Jews there.[11]

Contextualization of Caesarea

Philip initiated the outreach to the Samaritans, and then Peter and John administered an official confirmation of their faith by the work of the Spirit (Acts 8:5–25). As forementioned, Luke's brief note about Philip's outreach in Azotus and all the cities before Caesarea points to the pioneering nature of Philip's evangelism. In addition, the fact that Luke's narrative makes no further illustration of Philip's evangelism in Caesarea indicates that the locale of Caesarea could be another instance of Luke's literary contextualization of geographic locales.

Acts 9:32–43 is Luke's brief description of Peter's ministry in the coastal plain of Judea—most likely the area that Philip traveled (8:40); this description appears prior to Peter's visit to Caesarea (10:23–24). There are two elements notable about this travel. First, his travel was not evangelistic but ministerial.[12] It is stated that Peter visited "the saints" in Lydda (9:32) and "the disciples" (v. 38) and "the saints" (v. 41) in Joppa.[13] Second, it is believed that Peter visited ethnic Jews. For instance, Aeneas, a paralyzed one healed by Peter, is in support of this view. Margaret H. Williams states, "The name Aeneas had entered the Palestinian Jewish onomastikon early—it first occurs in the reign of Hyrcanus I (135/4–104 BC)—and was still part of it at the time of the First Jewish War (AD 66–73). It continued in use among Palestinian Jews until at least the 4th century AD."[14] According to Martin Hengel, "Peter's activity as 'inspector' of the Jewish-Christian communities in the coastal plain is primarily limited, in contrast to Philip, to expressly Jewish cities."[15]

Historically, Caesarea belonged to the control of the Hasmoneans through Alexander Jannaeus, the second king in the Hasmonean dynasty

---

20:1). Azotus ("Ashdod") was one of the five chief cities of the Philistines. Avi-Yonah, however, states that "From the time of the Hasmoneans until the second century C.E., Ashdod appears to have been a Jewish town" (557). Avi-Yonah and Dothan, "Ashdod," 2:557. Cf. Hengel, "Geography of Palestine in Acts," 53–55. Hengel sees Azotus and Caesarea both as ethnically mixed areas.

11. Cf. Keener, *Acts 3:1–14:28*, 1596. Keener suggests that Azotus was a city like Gaza and Caesarea in terms of its large gentile populations.

12. Bock, *Acts*, 376.

13. Luke uses ἅγιος in the plural to refer to Christians.

14. Williams, "Palestinian Jewish Personal Names in Acts," 110.

15. Hengel, *Between Jesus and Paul*, 117.

(96 BC). Augustus captured it from Cleopatra and returned it to Herod. Archelaus, a son of Herod's, ruled it until his banishment to Gaul (6 CE). During the reign of Agrippa I (41–44 CE), it belonged to the territory of Judea. Since then, Caesarea remained as "the capital of Roman and Byzantine Palestine."[16] The population of Caesarea was half gentile and half Jewish. According to Michael Avi-Yonah, this demographic tension between Jews and gentiles in Caesarea often caused frequent disputes between them, eventually working as the beginning of the Jewish war against Rome (66 CE).[17]

How does Luke depict Caesarea in his usage of geographic locales for the progression of the gospel? Peter's travel to the north stops at Joppa. In fact, Peter is often identified as an apostle who lags behind, as shown in his visits to the Samaritans (Acts 8:14), to Joppa (9:38), and to Caesarea (10:23–24). From a perspective of Luke's literary contextualization of geographic locales, Peter's travel to Caesarea is significant in that God's direct guidance was the ultimate cause of his visit there. This characteristic, among others, intensifies Luke's intent to contextualize Caesarea, at least from a Jewish perspective, for his literary purpose. This divine initiative is well revealed in Peter's explanation of how he came to Cornelius in Caesarea. Although it is not attributed completely to Caesarea and its Jewish understanding of Caesarea, Peter's statement to Cornelius reflects this aspect (10:27). In this sense, as Martin Hengel points out, Luke seems to be depicting Caesarea as "a predominantly pagan city."[18] This aspect is most presumably reflected on Luke's most dramatized illustration of Peter's travel to Cornelius in Caesarea.

It has been suggested that Gaza and Caesarea are the locales that Luke contextualizes in his literary work to describe the geographic progression of the gospel in accordance with Acts 1:8. Based on this contextualization, Luke's designation of the Ethiopian's conversion at "the road to Gaza" is meaningful. First, this indicates that Philip's witnessing to the Ethiopian occurred within the boundary of Judea, not in Gaza. This agrees with the second part of Act 1:8—"all Judea and Samaria." This aspect of his literary demarcation is evident in his usage of Caesarea. Luke makes no further description about Philip's evangelism in Caesarea. And he depicts Peter's visit to Caesarea as the incident purely attributed to God's revelation and guidance, rather than his volition.

Second, it is often argued among scholars that the Ethiopian episode is an initial fulfillment of Acts 1:8c ("to the end of the earth"). This is because

16. Avi-Yonah, "Caesarea: From Ancient Times to the Mamluks," in *EncJud*, 4:333.
17. Avi-Yonah, "Caesarea: From Ancient Times to the Mamluks," 4:333.
18. Hengel, *Between Jesus and Paul*, 114.

of the Ethiopian's geographic origin from Ethiopia, which the Greco-Roman world often referred to as the end of the earth.[19] However, Luke's literary contextualization of geographic locales draws attention to the actual site of Philip's witnessing, "the road to Gaza." In this regard, E. Earle Ellis states:

> (1) At most, Luke portrays only a prospective evangelization of Ethiopia by an otherwise insignificant representative figure. (2) He places the episode in the midst of the Christian missionary enterprise in 'Judea and Samaria' and (3) gives no further attention to the movement of Christianity southward. (4) On the whole he structures the latter half of his work around the mission of Paul and that means, geographically, the movement of Christianity westward.[20]

Third, Luke's literary contextualization of the locale "the road to Gaza" for the Ethiopian's conversion within the land of Judea does not necessarily indicate the Ethiopian's ethnic and religious background. However, it seems that it can work as a broad boundary within which to understand the Ethiopian. As noted above, Peter ministered to ethnic Jews in Lydda and Joppa before his visit to Cornelius, an uncircumcised gentile. With this aspect in view, Luke's locating the Ethiopian within the boundary of Judea might indicate that the Ethiopian is distinct from gentiles, but approximate to Jews—in terms of ethnic background and religious affiliation.[21]

Luke's Ethnic Progression and the Ethiopian's Position

Luke's narrative development deals with the ethnic expansion of the gospel as critical. To clarify the position of the Ethiopian account in this trajectory, it is essential to understand Luke's use of the term "Ethiopian" and Luke's differentiation of the Ethiopian from Cornelius in terms of ethnicity. For this, this section will analyze (1) the characteristics of how Luke uses regional-name adjectives and (2) the methods which Luke utilizes to make

---

19. Tannehill, *Narrative Unity of Luke-Acts*, 107. Karl Matthias Schmidt, "Bekehrung zur Zerstreuung," 200.

20. Ellis, "'End of the Earth,'" 128. Pao, *Acts and the Isaianic New Exodus*, 94. Pao sees the phrase "the end of the earth" as gentiles, based on Paul's use of it in his reference to Isa 13:47 (Acts 13:47). Niccum, "One Ethiopian Eunuch," in *Teacher for All Generations*, 2:889.

21. Cf. Kollmann, "Philippus der Evangelist," 564–65. Kollmann states, "Bei Philippus hat es sich, soweit das spärliche Quellenmaterial ein Urteil darüber zuläßt, um den ersten namhaften Heidenmissionar gehandelt." He sees Philip's outreach to the Samaritans and the Ethiopian as something that transgressed the geographic, ethnic, and ritual bounds of Jews.

the Cornelius episode significant. This analysis leads to the understanding that the Ethiopian episode is distinct from the Cornelius one.

Regional-Name Adjectives

Use of τῷ γένει for Individuals

Luke attaches the phrase τῷ γένει ("by birth") to an adjectival form of a people in a certain region in his introduction of three individuals (Acts 4:36 [Cypriot for Barnabas]; 18:2 [Pontian for Aquila], 24 [Alexandrian for Apollos]; cf. Mark 7:26 [Syrophoenician]).[22]

First, in Acts 4:36, Luke introduces Barnabas, and this introduction has four components about him: (1) his name ("Joseph"), (2) his nickname ("Barnabas") and its meaning, (3) his tribal descent ("Levite"), and (4) his geographic origin ("Cypriot"). Κύπριος ("Cypriot") is an adjective form of Cyprus, indicating that Barnabas was a citizen of Cyprus.[23] According to C. K. Barrett, the phrase τῷ γένει attached to "Cypriot" denotes his place of birth.[24] Based on this, it is clear that Barnabas was born as a citizen of Cyprus. Also, Barnabas has his ancestral descent traced back to the tribe of Levites; thus, most probably, he is ethnically Jewish.

In Acts 18:2, Luke introduces Aquila with two elements: (1) his ethnic Jewishness ("a certain Jew"), and (2) his geographic origin (Ποντικός). Luke's mention of "a certain Jew" here is related to his intent to explain the background against which Aquila and his wife Priscilla left Pontus and settled in Corinth—the edict of Claudius (AD 49). Ποντικός is the adjectival form, denoting a native of Pontus. For Aquila, Luke mentions his Jewish origin. Also, his use of "by birth" for him indicates Aquila's birth in Pontus. In Acts 18:24, lastly, Luke uses the phrase τῷ γένει to introduce Apollos. This introduction is identical to that of Aquila. That is, Apollos is ethnically Jewish, and his place of birth is Alexandria. Thus, Apollos was born as an "Alexandrian" (Ἀλεξανδρεύς). In conclusion, Luke's usage of the phrase τῷ γένει attached to an adjectival form of a regional name stresses the place of birth for each of the characters mentioned.

---

22. The γένος appears in Acts nine times: (1) the place of birth (4:36; 18:2, 24), (2) the ancestral descent in a broad sense (4:6; 7:19; 13:26; 17:28, 29), and (3) the direct family in a narrow sense (17:13).

23. Κύπριος occurs three times only in Acts (4:36; 11:20; 21:16). In Acts 11:20, Luke introduces some of the dispersed Hellenist evangelists as Cypriots and Cyrenians, who preached the Lord Jesus to even the Greeks, not just to Jews in Antioch. In Acts 21:16, Mnason is a Cypriot, who hosted Paul and his companions on the road to Jerusalem.

24. Barrett, *Critical and Exegetical Commentary*, 260.

Use of Regional-Name Adjectives

What if a character is described just with an adjectival form of a regional name without the phrase τῷ γένει? This section will investigate (1) the Hellenist or diaspora Jews (Acts 2:9–11), (2) the tribune's mention of "Egyptian" (21:37–38), and (3) Paul's self-introduction (21:39; 22:3).

First, Acts 2:9–11 lists fifteen entities of people who witnessed the outpouring of the Spirit on Pentecost.[25] In terms of their designation, there are two different ways identified in the list: (1) regional-name adjectives, and (2) regional-name nouns. The former includes Parthians, Medes, Elamites, and Romans. The "Romans" in the list has the participle of ἐπιδημέω attached to it, indicating their temporal dwelling in Jerusalem. It also has an additional note, "Jews and proselytes" (Ἰουδαῖοί τε καὶ προσήλυτοι) in juxtaposition. This is because of their common belief in Judaism despite their ethnic differences.[26] Craig S. Keener states, "Luke's term for 'proselyte' here could mean 'resident alien' (as often in the LXX), but its contrast with 'Jews' in the same line indicates the more technical sense of 'convert' here."[27]

For the latter (Mesopotamia, Judea, Cappadocia, Pontus, Asia, Phrygia, Pamphylia, Egypt, the parts of Libya belonging to Cyrene), the present participle of κατοικέω is used to modify those regional names. "Pontus" (Πόντος) here is a regional name. As noted above, for Aquila, its adjectival form (Ποντικός) is used. Hence, Luke's use of Πόντος and Ποντικός makes no significant difference.

In this list, Luke uses Ἰουδαία (v. 9) and Ἰουδαῖος (v. 10). Clearly, Ἰουδαία denotes the regional-name noun for Judea because it occurs along with the other regional nouns in the list. Ἰουδαῖος appears to be the regional-name adjective "Judean," that is, a resident in the land of Judea. In this text, however, it occurs in juxtaposition with the term "proselyte," which is ethnically foreign to the Jews but religiously and even geographically attached to the Jews. Hence, at least in this list, Luke uses Ἰουδαῖος in an ethnic sense. In a broad sense, this fact points to Luke's consciousness of Jewishness and Judaism in his narrative development of the gospel's progression.[28]

---

25. Craig S. Keener introduces each of the listed nations in detail. Keener, *Acts 3:1–14:28*, 845–51.

26. It is often suggested that the Greek term Ἰουδαῖος is a geographic term, indicating a Jew living in the land of Judea. However, Luke's use of that term is more inclined toward the ethnic nature of Jewishness, which presupposes the person's affiliated status in Judaism.

27. Keener, *Acts 3:1–14:28*, 850. In Acts 6:5, Nicolaus introduced as "a proselyte Antiochene."

28. In his speech at the synagogue of Pisidian Antioch (13:13–52), Paul categorizes his audience ethnically into Jews and gentiles. For the Jews, he uses "men of Israel" (v.

For the other entities in this list, however, as shown in Πόντος and Ποντικός, Luke's use of their adjectival forms and nominal forms in Acts 2:9-11 makes no significant difference between them. Also, this view is supported by what the people witnessing the outpouring of the Spirit said before this listing: "And how is it that we hear, each of us in his own native language? (ἕκαστος τῇ ἰδίᾳ διαλέκτῳ ἡμῶν ἐν ᾗ ἐγεννήθημεν)" (2:8). The verb ἐγεννήθημεν indicates that all those people were born in those regions.

Second, the tribune of the Roman troops stationed at the Jerusalem temple mistook Paul for an Egyptian rebel (21:37-38). He used the Greek term σικαρίων ("the Assassins"), which recalls a series of Jewish rebels against Rome and its political leaders in Jerusalem. These rebels were called "sicarii" in Latin (σικάριος in Greek), which is the term used for the small, crooked swords used by the rebels (*Ant.* 20.186). Josephus introduces one of those rebellion leaders as follows:

> an Egyptian false prophet that did the Jews more mischief than the former; for he was a cheat, and pretended to be a prophet also, and got together thirty thousand men that were deluded by him; these he led round about from the wilderness to the mount which was called the Mount of Olives, and was ready to break into Jerusalem by force from that place; and if he could but once conquer the Roman garrison and the people, he intended to domineer over them by the assistance of those guards of his that were to break into the city with him (*J.W.* 2.261-262).[29]

Josephus records that Felix subdued this revolt and the Egyptian leader escaped (263). Provided that Felix became procurator of Palestine in AD 52/53, it is estimated that that revolt occurred in AD 54.[30] Acknowledging that Paul was able to speak in Greek, the tribune admitted that Paul was not the Egyptian rebellion leader (Acts 21:37-38). Probably, the tribune had expected that the Egyptian rebellion leader would not speak Greek.[31] What is

---

16), "people Israel" (v. 17), "all the people of Israel" (v. 24), and "brothers, sons of the family [γένος] of Abraham (v. 26). For the gentiles, "those who fear God" (v. 26). As a result of his speech, it is stated that "many of the Jews and the devout proselytes followed Paul and Barnabas" (v. 42). For those gentiles, Luke refers to both God-fearers and proselytes. Hence, the setting of a local synagogue seems to be not so strict in terms of distinguishing between the God-fearers and the proselytes—probably interchangeable.

29. Josephus, *Complete Works*, 737. Le Cornu and Shulam make an extensive discussion of this incident. Le Cornu and Shulam, *Commentary on the Jewish Roots of Acts*, 2:1205-207.

30. Witherington, *Acts*, 662.

31. Jervell, *Apostelgeschichte*, 538. In contrast, Witherington sees that Paul's fluent Greek speaking led the tribune to believe that Paul could be a rebel. Witherington, *Acts*, 661. The function of οὐκ in the interrogative question presupposes to expect the

notable here is that both the tribune and Josephus used the word "Egyptian" not as an ethnic designation but as a geographic origin. Given that both had in mind a Jewish revolt and its leader, it is most likely that the Egyptian rebellion leader was an Egyptian Jew. That is, his ethnic origin was from Jewishness but his geographic origin—most likely his place of birth—was from the land of Egypt.

Lastly, Paul introduces himself both ethnically and geographically. In Acts 21:39, he states, "I am a Jew, a Tarsean of Cilicia" (21:39). "Tarsean" (Ταρσεύς) is the adjective form of the regional name, Tarsus (Ταρσός). In 22:3, he states, "I am a Jew, born in Tarsus in Cilicia" (22:3). Here, Paul uses the regional-name noun, "Tarsus." In both accounts, Paul emphasizes his ethnic origin from Jewishness.

Use of Trans-ethnic Marriage

Luke introduces Timothy from his awareness of trans-ethnic marriage from a Jewish perspective. This introduction (16:1b) has five elements describing Timothy: (1) his status as "disciple," (2) his name, (3) his mother's ethnic "Jew," (4) his father's ethnic "Greek," and (5) his uncircumcised state. Here, Luke does not use an ethnic designation for Timothy, apart from his ancestral descent to Jewishness through his mother. Also, Luke implies that Paul's circumcision of Timothy was part of his evangelistic purpose to reach out to ethnic Jews (16:3).

A few characteristics in Luke's usage of regional-name adjectival forms in Acts are notable. First, Luke introduces multiple figures in Acts, and if they are ethnically Jewish, he often adds this ethnic note. At the same time, he refers to their geographical origins. This pattern is identified in Luke's introduction of the Hellenistic or diaspora Jews (Acts 2:9–11), Barnabas (4:36), Aquila (18:2), Apollos (18:4), and Paul (21:39; 22:3). Second, Luke does not use the ethnic note of "Jew" for a person like Timothy (16:2); so, he does not designate children of trans-ethnic marriages as ethnically Jewish. Given that Luke does not use the ethnic note "Jew" for the Ethiopian in Acts 8, the Ethiopian can be viewed at least as similar to Timothy.

Third, the tribune's use of "Egyptian" for Paul indicates that the regional-name adjective "Ethiopian" in Acts 8:27 could refer to an Ethiopian Jew, ethnically from Jewishness and geographically from the land of Ethiopia. In conclusion, Luke uses those regional-name adjectives primarily to indicate their geographic origins, thus not necessarily their ethnic backgrounds.

---

affirmative answer. Yet the context does not agree with this answer. Hence, the question made by the tribune indicates his indecisive attitude.

Luke's Signification of the Cornelius Episode

Luke regards the inclusion of gentiles into God's eschatological people as significant. In Luke 4:24–27, Jesus refers to the Elijah-Elisha outreach to the gentiles: (1) a widow in the land of Sidon, and (2) Naaman the Syrian. His mention of them is the very reason Jesus was rejected in Nazareth. That is, at the beginning of his Gospel, Luke has in view the gentile-inclusive mission. Yet Luke postpones its actual fulfillment until the risen Christ's exaltation to the heavenly throne and the outpouring of the Spirit.

Luke utilizes the Cornelius episode to inaugurate the inclusion of the gentiles in God's eschatological program in the person of Jesus. To maximize the episode's dramatic effect, Luke adopts multiple methods. Out of them, the followings are evident: (1) omission of the gentile mission by Philip and Paul, (2) characterization of Peter and Cornelius, (3) repetition of the Cornelius episode and Paul's calling, (4) God's direct involvement, and (5) narrative synthesizing harmonization. These literary methods reveal Luke's intentional signification of the Cornelius episode and its thematic significance in Acts. In other words, this is the way Luke is doing theology. This being the case, Luke's authorial intent in the episode of the Ethiopian is not something like foreshadowing what is to come—the Cornelius episode. Instead, the Ethiopian episode should be studied as an independent one, with a focus on how it contributes to the whole projection of Luke's theology in Acts.

Omission of the Gentile Mission

The angel of the Lord led Philip, one of the seven deacons (Acts 6:5), to the road down to Gaza to evangelize the Ethiopian (8:26–40). After this witnessing, according to the text, Philip did an evangelistic outreach to "Azotus" and "all the cities" until he arrived at Caesarea (v. 40). Luke's mention of this itinerary has in view Philip's continual evangelistic outreach. Given Philip's pioneering missional characteristic, most likely he continued in Caesarea. Also, in Caesarea, Philip reappears later in the narrative of Acts (21:8–16), in which Luke is one of Paul's companions. It is likely that Luke obtained information here from Philip, not just about the Samaritans and the Ethiopian (Acts 8:4–40) but also about others. However, Luke is silent about it. In this regard, Martin Hengel states, "Presumably—despite Luke's silence on the matter—he [Philip] carried on the mission to the Gentiles as well in mixed Jewish and Gentile cities like Azotus or Caesarea."[32] This

---

32. Hengel, *Between Jesus and Paul*, 115.

being the case, Luke did not put into his text Philip's plausible mission to the gentiles, and this absence is probably due to his intent to regard the conversion of Cornelius as the first uncircumcised gentile.

Paul encountered the resurrected Christ, who revealed his calling through Ananias, a disciple in Caesarea. According to this mandate, Paul's mission is toward "the Gentiles," as well as "the children of Israel" (9:15). Given their contrast with "the children of Israel," "the Gentiles" here are ethnically non-Jewish. After this incident, Paul was with the disciples in Damascus (v. 19b). Luke explains about Paul's ministry in Damascus: "Saul increased all the more in strength, and confounded the Jews who lived in Damascus by proving that Jesus was the Christ" (v. 22). This explanation indicates that Paul's mission after his calling appears to be limited to Jews, even in Damascus. Despite his gentile-missional mandate, Luke does not depict Paul's ministry toward the gentiles in Damascus. From a literary perspective, Luke intentionally does not include in his text the gentile mission that Philip and Paul presumably did. This intentional omission is a literary technique to dramatize the event of Cornelius' conversion and its thematic significance.

Characterization of Peter and Cornelius

Luke also dramatizes the Cornelius episode by the means of characterization, particularly Peter and Cornelius. For Peter, Luke's characterization is twofold, that is, ignorance and transition. First, Peter is portrayed as ignorant, particularly about the inclusion of gentiles. For instance, God revealed the animal vision three times (Acts 10:9–16); Peter did not gain an understanding about its meaning. Second, Peter is portrayed as transitional. At his meeting with Cornelius, Peter recalled the animal vision and explained it to Cornelius. Then he said, "God has shown me that I should not call any person common or unclean" (v. 28). In Jerusalem, Peter explains to the Christians there about the animal vision again and how he gained an understanding about its meaning (11:4–10). Hence, Luke portrays Peter as a round character—transitional from ignorance to knowledge. By this means, Luke dramatizes the Cornelius episode and emphasizes its thematic significance. This is the way Luke is doing his theology.

For Cornelius, Luke's introduction about him even before his conversion is notable (Acts 10:1–2). It has two main categories: (1) his job-related information, and (2) his piety and its related information. In the Gospel of Luke, there are two individual characters identified as "centurion" (Luke 7:1–10; 23:47). One of them was the nearest witness to the death of Jesus, who announced Christ's innocent death (23:47). Oleksandr Kyrychenko argues that "at key points in Luke-Acts, the Roman centurion plays the role of the prototypical Gentile coming to Christ, foreshadowing the following mission of expansion of the Christian gospel from Palestine throughout the Empire and to its capital."[33] In Acts 10, Cornelius, the uncircumcised gentile centurion, also contributes another phase of narrative in Luke's work—that is, the inclusion of gentiles in God's eschatological salvation program.

In terms of Cornelius' piety, Luke presents him as an undeniable gentile model to be affirmed, presumably by Jews. The Greek adjective εὐσεβής is etymologically related to the combined form of εὖ and σέβομι, denoting "devout, pious."[34] This adjective entails a further description about his piety—God-fearing, alms giving, and prayerful life (v. 2).[35] Witherington argues that Cornelius is "depicted as performing most of the typical duties of Jew (prayer, fasting, almsgiving)."[36] Luke's emphasis on Cornelius' piety is evident—as affirmed by the Lord (v. 4), by the three men sent by Cornelius (v. 22), and by Peter (v. 35).[37] According to Shaye J. D. Cohen, a gentile could be acknowledged by Jews as showing respect or affection toward Judaism. Fearing the God of Israel and giving alms to Jews are two of the seven ways that Cohen suggests.[38] From a perspective of Luke's characterization, Luke intends to present Cornelius as such a gentile figure to be worthy of acknowledgement even by Jews. The ultimate goal that Luke

---

33. See Luke 7:1–10, 23:47, Acts 21–23, and 27 for the centurions in Luke's Gospel and Acts. Kyrychenko, "Role of the Centurion in Luke-Acts," 187.

34. Zerwick and Grosvenor, *Grammatical Analysis of the Greek New Testament*, 382. The adjective εὐσεβής is also used to refer to a solider sent by Cornelius to Peter in Joppa, along with the other two servants (10:7). The servants used the adjective δίκαιος, instead of εὐσεβής, to describe their master, Cornelius.

35. Cornelius' almsgiving might be his care for Jews in Caesarea. The Greek phrase τῷ λαῷ ("to the people") refer to Jews, as seen in Luke's usage of the noun λαός, although it can denote "people in a general sense" (BDAG, 586–7). This view is supported in what the three servants of Cornelius spoke about Cornelius to Peter: ἀνὴρ δίκαιος καὶ φοβούμενος τὸν θεόν, μαρτυρούμενός τε ὑπὸ ὅλου τοῦ ἔθνους τῶν Ἰουδαίων (10:22). Instead of λαός, the text refers to "the entire nation of Jews."

36. Witherington, *Acts*, 347.

37. Peter's remark in 10:34–35 is for gentiles as a whole, but its content is also related to Cornelius. It is reasonable to see that Peter had in mind Cornelius—and his piousness in terms of his relationship with God.

38. Cohen, "Crossing the Boundary," 14–15. Cohen's seven ways are "(1) admiring some aspect of Judaism, (2) acknowledging the power of the god of the Jews or incorporating him into the pagan pantheon, (3) benefiting the Jews or being consciously friendly to Jews, (4) practicing some or many of the rituals of the Jews, (5) venerating the god of the Jews and denying or ignoring the pagan gods, (6) joining the Jewish community, and (7) converting to Judaism and 'becoming a Jew.'"

intends to achieve by this is to make the gentile inclusion more appealing and persuasive to his audience.

Repetition of the Cornelius Episode and Paul's Calling

According to James L. Resseguie, repetition is "a stylistic device that reiterates words, phrases, themes, situations, and actions for emphasis."[39] In Acts this literary method is evident in two incidents: (1) the conversion of Cornelius and (2) the calling of Paul. Its function surrounding these two incidents is to indicate that the gentile inclusion is the dominant theme that flows through the entire book.

First, Peter reiterates the Cornelius episode. In Acts 11, the sect of circumcision in the Jerusalem church accuses Peter of his table fellowship with the "uncircumcised" gentiles (Acts 11:3). In response, Peter explains to them the things that surrounded his visit to Caesarea and what happened to Cornelius and his household. Peter's explanation here is focused on God's revelatory guidance of him and Cornelius alike, and on God's outpouring of the Spirit—as promised by John the Baptist (Luke 3:16; Acts 1:5) and actualized on Pentecost (Acts 2:1–4). In Acts 15:7–11, Peter does not address Cornelius, but he has the Cornelius episode in view. He states, "God who knows the heart, bore witness to them [the Gentiles], by giving them the Holy Spirit, just as he did to us, and he made no distinction between us and them, having cleansed their hearts by faith" (15:8). Luke's repetition of the Cornelius episode points to his emphasis on its theological significance. Ernest Haenchen states, "This technique of repetition is one to which Luke always resorts when he wants to impress something specially upon the reader."[40]

Second, Luke introduces Paul's calling three times (Acts 9:1–19a; 22:6–16; 26:12–18).[41] The first one is more focused on the historical setting of what happened to Paul. The second one is Paul's testimony before a Jewish crowd. The last one is before Agrippa II. These different settings would cause variations in terms of wording and emphasis.[42] Yet, one common ele-

---

39. Resseguie, *Narrative Criticism of the New Testament*, 42.

40. Haenchen, *Acts of the Apostles*, 357.

41. Clouston, *How Ancient Narratives Persuade*, 32. Clouston defines "Gentle Steps" as a literary technique: "The hearer is led, ideally unaware, through a cumulative series of minor developments in their attitude or thinking." He argues that Paul's calling in Acts is one of the instances in which Luke uses this technqiue; Luke describes it "in more and more detail" and "being communicated more and more directly by Jesus to Paul" (161).

42. Marguerat, "Saul's Conversion," 132. Marguerat states, "The repetition of

ment among them is Paul's calling for the gentile mission, which is chiefly related to his rejection by the Jews.

In Acts 22:6–16, Luke puts Paul's Damascus calling (Acts 9) into his text from the perspective of Paul, particularly in the setting of his speech to the Jews. Paul's emphasis here is on God's initiative in his calling. First, this calling here is explained on Paul's personal level. God's choice of him is "to know his will," "to see the Righteous One," and "to hear a voice from his mouth" (v. 14). Second, this calling is Paul's missional level—witnessing for the "Righteous One" to all humans about the things that Paul has seen and heard (v. 15). The phrase "to all humans" is ethnically all-inclusive.

In this account, Luke adds what is not included in Acts 9. That is, while Paul was in Jerusalem after his calling on the Damascus road, the Lord said to him, "Go, for I will send you far away to the Gentiles" (v. 21). The phrase "far away to the Gentiles" (εἰς ἔθνη μακρὰν) is Paul's mandate from the Lord toward the gentiles. Based on Paul's explanation, it seems that Paul intended to remain in Jerusalem. However, the Lord's will for Paul in terms of witnessing is not confined to the Jews in Jerusalem but expanded to the gentiles in the nations.

Luke introduces the crowd's response on the spot. The phrase "until this word" (ἄχρι τούτου τοῦ λόγου, v. 22) refers to the preceding sentence, which is the Lord's command to Paul—"Go, for I will send you far away to the Gentiles" (v. 21). According to Luke's description, Paul's reference to this command caused the Jewish crowd to get agitated about Paul and thus demanded his death from the tribune (v. 22). The rejection of Paul by those Jews is related to Paul's reference to the gentile mission. Hence, from an authorial perspective, the gentile mission is treated as the most significant theme in the second account of Paul's calling.

Acts 26:12–18 is the third account of Paul's calling—this time to Agrippa II. Just as shown in the second account, in this account, Paul's calling is explained on two levels: (1) personal and (2) missional. On the personal level, the purpose of the Lord's self-revelation to Paul is to appoint him to be a servant and witness to the Lord's revelation in the past (Acts 9 and 22), as well as the Lord's continual revelation in the future (26:16).[43] The Lord's

---

narrative, with its play of similarity and dissimilarity, allows one to signify *both* continuity *and* displacement, change *and* identity." He adds, "The three accounts do not work together according to the principle of a 'coinciding of narrative point of view', but according to the principle of a differentiation of points of view, since the narrative apparatus distinguishes the objective and earlier point of view of the omniscient narrator (Acts 9) from the subjective and later point of view of the speaker Paul in Acts 22 and 26" (137).

43. Zerwick and Grosvenor, *Grammatical Analysis*, 445. Zerwick states, "The general sense seems to be that Paul is to be a witness equally to what he has already seen of

revelation—in the past and in the future—is about his protection of Paul "from the people and from the Gentiles" (v. 17). The "people" here refers to the Jews, in contrast to "the Gentiles." On the personal level of Paul's calling, the Lord's continual revelation will be with Paul, and this will be evidenced in the Lord's rescuing Paul from the Jews and gentiles. The missional level of Paul's calling is "to open their [Jews and Gentiles] eyes" (v. 18).

Paul explains to Agrippa II about his missional witnessing in obedience to his calling. Paul makes a brief presentation as part of his defense. This has four elements. First, Paul recalls the Lord's appearance to him on the Damascus road (Acts 9). His use of the phrase "the heavenly vision" (v. 19) points to it. Second, Paul describes how he obeyed the calling he had received. This description includes (1) his preaching in "Damascus," "Jerusalem," "all the region of Judea," and to "the Gentiles" and (2) his preaching about "repentance" (v. 20). This is a brief summary of all the missional work that Paul did until he returned to Jerusalem (21:17). Third, Paul retells Agrippa II about the incident when the Jews seized him in the temple. Fourth, Paul emphasizes that his preaching about Christ's death and resurrection is what "the prophets and Moses said," and Christ would be proclaimed as light "both to the people (i.e., the Jews) and to the Gentiles" (v. 23). As seen, Paul's calling in Acts 26 also includes Paul's mission to the gentiles.

Hence, all three accounts of Paul's calling (Acts 9, 22, 26) show that Paul's mention of the gentile mission caused a sense of agitation among the Jews—that is, the Messiah is not just for Jews but also for gentiles.

Narrative Synthesizing Harmonization

Luke's signification of the gentile inclusion in God's eschatological salvation program is identified in Luke's narrative-synthesizing harmonization surrounding the text of Acts 11:18–26. Recognizing this feature will make it more reasonable to conclude that Luke has the gentile inclusion as critical in his narrative development. The issue to be dealt with in this section is how Luke synthesizes all the components found in Acts 11:18–26 in order to make his narrative development gradual and harmonious about the gentile inclusion and the birth of the church in Antioch.

In a broad context, Acts 11:18–26 has two functions: (1) recalling the dispersed Hellenist Christians and their evangelism ("scattered because of the persecution that arose over Stephen," v. 19; cf. 8:4) and (2) anticipating what is to come, that is, the birth of the Antioch church (11:20–26). Bruce

---

Christ and to what he will be shown in time to come."

W. Longenecker introduces a structuring model that Luke uses—"chain-link interlock."[44] His basic illustration of this model is the construction of A-b-a-B. Unit A contains an element that belongs to Unit B—that is, "b." Unit B contains an element that belongs to Unit A—that is, "a." The "a" and "b" both combined function as an interlock connecting the units "A" and "B." In addition, the function of "b" is to foreshadow what is to come in "B." On the other hand, the function of "a" is to recall what is in "A." Hence, this model has two functions: (1) anticipatory and (2) retrospective.[45] Based on this model, it can be suggested that Acts 11:19 recalls 8:4—retrospective, whereas 11:20 is anticipatory—in regard to the birth of the Antioch church.

In terms of Luke's narrative development, there are things to be clarified in Acts 11:18–26. This text contains four elements: (1) the official confirmation of the gentile inclusion by the Jerusalem church, (2) the Jewish-confined outreach by the Hellenists, and (3) the ethno-transgressing outreach by the Cyprians and Cyrenians, and (4) the birth of the Antioch church.

First, it seems that the Jerusalem church's gentile-mission endorsement makes no direct contribution to the birth of the Antioch church. As shown, the Jerusalem church sent Barnabas to Antioch because of what was happening in Antioch (v. 22). Second, in a form of summary, Luke introduces the outreach by the dispersed Hellenists in Phoenicia, Cyprus, and Antioch—in general, as confined to Jews alone (v. 19). In the participle phrase (μηδενὶ λαλοῦντες τὸν λόγον εἰ μὴ μόνον Ἰουδαίοις), "no one," "alone," and "except Jews" combined implicate the ethnocentric characteristic of their mission. In terms of narrative flow, this aspect of their mission disagrees with the Jerusalem church's gentile-mission endorsement. Third, Luke introduces some of those Hellenists (i.e., Cyprians and Cyrenians) as the ones who reached out to the Greeks (i.e., gentiles).[46] Their ethno-transgressing mission is not the result of the Jerusalem church's endorsement. All four elements in the text of Acts 11:18–26 appear to be somehow discontinuous or contradictory. How does Luke synthesize them?

First, Acts 11:18–20 shows Luke's literary intent to consider the Cornelius incident in light of the gentile inclusion. In 11:18, Luke portrays the

---

44. Longenecker, *Rhetoric at the Boundaries*, 165–205.

45. Longenecker, *Rhetoric at the Boundaries*, 229. Based on this model, Longenecker proposes four main textual units in Acts: (1) 1:1–8:3, (2) 8:4–12:25, (3) 13:1–19:41, and (4) 20:1–28:31.

46. There is a textual variation: (1) Ἑλληνιστὰς "Hellenists" (text reading), and (2) Ἕλληνας "Greeks" (variant reading). Metzger, *Textual Commentary on the Greek New Testament*, 342. Metzger sees "Greeks" as original, defining the Hellenists here as "the mixed population of Antioch in contrast to the Ἰουδαῖοι in v. 19."

Jerusalem church as submissive to God's salvific grace given to the gentiles. The Greek verb ἡσυχάζω appears four times in Luke's work (Luke 14:4; 23:56; Acts 11:18; 21:14). It means "to refrain from saying anything"—an absolute sense of submission.[47] Also, the ascensive use of the conjunction καί ("even") indicates that this is a new phase in the progression of the gospel. In response, all the church in Jerusalem glorified God. This act reflects the recognition that the gentile inclusion is attributed to God alone, not to humans.

Second, Acts 11:18–20 shows Luke's intent to depict the issue of gentile inclusion as a gradual progression—his literary attempt to harmonize and synthesize (1) the ethnocentric mission before the Cornelius episode and (2) the ethno-transgressing mission by the Hellenists. This aspect is well revealed in the construction of μέν οὖν plus δέ in 11:19–20. Jenny Read-Heimerdinger analyzes the construction of μέν οὖν plus δέ in Acts, and states:

> μέν is prospective, causing the sentence that it adds to the narrative to look forward to a further sentence introduced with δέ. It is this δέ sentence that moves the narrative forward, the first one being of secondary importance for the development of the story. In the firm text of Acts, μέν always occurs accompanied by οὖν, which produces an interesting two-directional movement—οὖν looking back to tie the new events or actions to the previous sentences, and μέν anticipating a further event or action after the initial sentence, one that will advance the story[48]

The particle μέν points to the conjunction δέ. By the means of this construction, Luke's main intent is to show that the ethno-transgressing mission by the Cypriots and Cyrenians as a progress in his narrative development. This is Luke's main point of view here. The content introduced with μέν is regarded as less significant—that is, the ethnocentric outreach to Jews alone.[49] Luke's use of the conjunction οὖν points to what precedes it—that is, the Jerusalem church's confirmation of the gentile inclusion. By doing so, Luke intends to create a textual interaction between the Jerusalem church's endorsement of gentiles and the ethno-transgressing outreach by the Cypriots and Cyrenians, at least on the literary level of Luke's working.

---

47. BDAG, 440.

48. Read-Heimerdinger, "Acts," 169. See also Levinsohn, *Discourse Features of New Testament Greek*, 170.

49. Levinsohn, *Discourse Features of New Testament Greek*, 171. Levinsohn regards 11:19 as a case in which the material introduced with μέν is of secondary importance in comparison with the following material introduced with δέ.

This discourse analysis provides three implications about Acts 11:18–20. First, Luke's main focus is on the gentile-inclusive outreach by the Cyprians and Cyrenians in Antioch. Second, on the literary level here, Luke treats the ethnocentric outreach of the Hellenists as less significant. Third, Luke's intent is to create a certain degree of contextual interaction. That is, the decision of the Jerusalem church to confirm the gentile inclusion—in terms of narrative flow—is related to the gentile outreach in Antioch. This does not mean that the former caused the latter. Hence, Luke's purpose in the construction of μέν οὖν plus δέ is to show the gradual flow of narrative development, narratively harmonizing and synthesizing between the Jerusalem church's gentile-mission endorsement and the actual gentile mission in Antioch, although there is no contextual interrelationship between them.

What is the rationale that Luke has for this literary attempt? According to Luke, this gradual development is not attributed to the official affirmation of the gentile inclusion by the Jerusalem church. It is made possible by God's direct involvement. It is stated, "And the hand of the Lord was with them [those Cyprians and Cyrenians]" (11:21). In this respect, Witherington states:

> Taking Acts 8–11 together, one gains the rather clear impression that Luke is presenting a complex picture of the origins of the proclamation of the good news to Gentiles. It was not a mission originated by the leadership of either the Jerusalem or Antioch church but by God through a variety of means including Peter, Paul, these anonymous men from Cyprus and Cyrene, and perhaps even Philip.[50]

Hence, the gentile inclusion is the tallest obstacle to the progression of the gospel. This obstacle has now been removed because of God's direct involvement with Peter as well as the Cyprian and Cyrenian Hellenists.

If so, what is the purpose of Luke's ethno-exclusive note about the outreach by the Hellenists ("no one," "alone," and "except Jews" in v. 19)? As noted, in terms of Luke's narrative development in Acts 11:18–26, this note is not so significant. However, this note is another piece of evidence that Luke portrays the gentile inclusion as being treated unacceptable even among the dispersed Hellenists. This being the case, Luke's intent is to provide the impression that the gentile mission has not been inaugurated or activated until the Cornelius episode and its subsequent endorsement by the Jerusalem church. This is the way Luke considers the Cornelius episode. With this aspect in view, it seems inappropriate to argue that Luke thought of the Ethiopian as the first gentile convert.

50. Witherington, *Acts*, 369.

Luke's Religious Progression and the Ethiopian's Position

Luke uses the speeches of Peter, Stephen, and Paul to reveal that Jesus is the servant, the exalted Davidic king of the throne of heaven, and the bestower of eschatological salvation. This proclamation, along with its theological implications, has become an inevitable challenge to the ethno-religious identity of Jewishness and Judaism. This struggle rises to the surface on the issues of the Jerusalem temple, the food laws, circumcision, and the law of Moses. Luke's mode of dealing with them is sometimes explicit and other times implicit, but it is gradual. The Ethiopian episode is a part of Luke's progressive development of Christ's event and its theological implications amid that struggle.

For the purpose of locating the Ethiopian's ethnic origin and religious status in this narrative progression, this section will investigate Peter's Pentecost speech, Stephen's speech, and Peter's illustration of the Cornelius episode. Five components will be introduced that constitute Christ's work (death, exaltation, bestowing of the Spirit, building of God's house, and cleansing). It will be suggested that the episode of the Ethiopian makes its own contribution to revealing theological implications surrounding Christ's work.

Peter's Pentecost Speech

Acts 2 consists of four main parts: (1) the outpouring of the Spirit, (2) Peter's scripture-based expositional speech, (3) Peter's invitation of faith, and (4) Luke's description of the new Christians in Jerusalem.

Christ's Heavenly Enthronement

At Pentecost, Peter's speech (2:14–36) is chiefly toward the diaspora or Hellenist Jews (v. 5) and gentile proselytes (v. 11) who have witnessed the outpouring of the Spirit. Clearly, this speech is focused on Peter's explanation of what lies behind this phenomenal incident—that is, the risen Christ's enthronement in heaven (v. 33). Hence, Peter's aim by this speech is to elucidate the interrelatedness of the Christ's heavenly enthronement with his outpouring of the Spirit. While doing this, Peter explains Christ's crucifixion (v. 23) and his resurrection (vv. 24–32). In other words, Peter illustrates Christ's work in his four stages of life: (1) his death, (2) his resurrection, (3) his enthronement, and (4) his outpouring of the Spirit. With all these stages in view, Peter now proclaims that Jesus is "both Lord and Christ" (v. 36).

This speech contains three citations and one allusion to the Old Testament: (1) Joel 2:28–32, (2) Ps 16:8–11, (3) Ps 132:11 or 2 Sam 7:12–13, and (4) Ps 110:1. Peter's citation of the Joel text, while adding the phrase "in the last days," is to indicate that this is eschatological (Acts 2:17).[51] Basically, Peter's point is that all those messianic promises are fulfilled in the person of Jesus. For Christ's resurrection, Peter cites Ps 16:8–11 (Acts 2:25–28). He defines the role of David as a prophet, thus suggesting that this psalm is pointing to a future Messiah. He also illustrates David's death to his audience (v. 29), emphasizing the unfulfilled nature of the psalm—still awaiting its fulfillment in Messiah.[52] Peter announces that Christ's resurrection is the fulfillment of this psalm.

Then Peter further develops his argumentation by connecting Christ's resurrection to Christ's enthronement. For this, Peter alludes to Ps 132:11 or 2 Sam 7:12–13.[53] In this allusion, Peter introduces David as a prophet who foreknew God's determined or unconditional promise—to make a descendant (lit., [one] from the fruit of his loins) sit on his throne. The context of Ps 132:11–12 puts an emphasis on the perpetual reign of David's multiple descendants on his throne. Yet, Peter sees this alluded text as messianic, to be culminated in the Messiah, the Davidic Son. What is the basis of this hermeneutical approach? In particular, 2 Sam 7:12–13 itself has room for its ultimate fulfillment to be made by Messiah. In this regard, Gordon H. Johnston states, "The threefold repetition of the expression עַד־עוֹלָם 'forever' (vv. 13, 16a, 16b) certainly points to the open-ended nature of the duration of the kingdom which the reign of David and his son would inaugurate."[54]

Lastly, Peter cites Ps 110:1 (Acts 2:34–35) to argue that this prophecy has been fulfilled in the person of Jesus. Historically, this psalm might be related to the Davidic kings and their enthronement. However, as seen in the other OT references here, Peter sees it as messianic. For him, Christ's heavenly enthronement is what Ps 110:1 is ultimately about. Hence, Peter refers to these Old Testament texts to argue that all those messianic promises have been fulfilled in the person of Jesus. For him, the outpouring of

---

51. The cited text of Joel indicates the universal availability of the Spirit (Acts 2:17, "upon all flesh"). This characteristic of the Spirit will be discussed in Stephen's speech, in his citation of Isa 66:1–2.

52. Marshall, *Luke*, 162.

53. The Greek phrase ἐκ καρποῦ appears in Acts 2:30 and Ps 131:11 LXX (132:11 MT). For what follows the phrase, the former has the genitive phrase τῆς ὀσφύος αὐτοῦ, whereas the latter τῆς κοιλίας σου. Second Samuel 7:12 LXX does not have the phrase, ἐκ καρποῦ; instead, it has ἐκ τῆς κοιλίας σου. Evidently, Acts 2:30 alludes to Ps 131:11 LXX more directly and 2 Sam 7:12 LXX less directly, while at the same time referring to the Davidic covenant.

54. Johnston, "Nature of the Davidic Covenant," 3.

the Spirit, as the result of Christ's exaltation to the throne in heaven, is the undeniable evidence that leads to this interpretation.[55]

Christ's Spiritual Temple Building

Peter's Pentecost speech puts a great deal of emphasis on the exalted Christ's heavenly enthronement. The exalted Christ reigns as the Davidic king in heaven. However, there is something undiscussed in this speech—that is, the exalted Christ's role in building the eschatological temple of God. The Davidic king's temple building is what is expected. As noted above, the text of 2 Sam 7:12b–13a itself creates a sense of linguistic openness in terms of its ultimate fulfillment. If based on the chiastic structure of the Old Testament text, God's promise—"he [son] shall build a house for my name" (v. 13a)—is pivotal. Prophetically, this text indicates that the Davidic Son's enthronement entails his role in building "a house" for God's name (v. 13a). Michael P. Barber suggests that the connection between the Son of God and the role of temple building is evident in 2 Sam 7:12–13.[56]

Psalm 132:11–12 also has in view the Davidic king's enthronement.[57] What follows is the Lord's dwelling place: "For the Lord has chosen Zion; he has desired it for his dwelling place: This is my resting place forever; here I will dwell, for I have desired it" (vv. 13, 14). This relatedness—between the Davidic Son's enthronement and his construction of Yahweh's dwelling place—is clear. However, it appears that based on Luke's cited or alluded texts, Peter's Pentecost speech does not deal with this role. Does this mean that Luke has no concern with this role? It seems that Luke's description of the first Christians in Jerusalem, in an implicit manner, points to this reality—Christ who has built the eschatological temple among Christians.

Reality of Christ's Temple

After this speech, Peter invites his audience to put their trust in Jesus (2:38). This invitation of faith has four elements: (1) repentance, (2) baptism, (3)

---

55. Bock, "Book of Acts and Jewish Evangelism," 65. Bock asserts that "it is Jesus' exaltation in resurrection that tells us where he went, where he is, what he is doing, and, most especially, who he is."

56. Barber, "Jesus as the Davidic Temple Builder," 940. Fitzmyer introduces New Testament texts that indicate Christ's ascension. Fitzmyer, "Ascension of Christ and Pentecost," 410–21.

57. Cf. Beale, "Descent of the Eschatological Temple," 69. Beale sees that the allusion to Ps 132:11 itself is about an eschatological temple construction.

forgiveness, and (4) the gift of the Holy Spirit. The phrase "in the name of Jesus Christ" here contains all the elements of Christ's work that Peter has proclaimed in his speech. Luke's authorial note ("those who received his [Peter] word were baptized," v. 41) indicates that baptism is what entails all the other three. That is, baptism presumes repentance as a human responsibility, and the spiritual realities of forgiveness and the gift of the Spirit.

Furthermore, Luke describes how the two spiritual realities—forgiveness and the gift of the Spirit—are manifested among the new believers (vv. 42–47)—teaching, preaching, miracles, meals, sharing of goods, and worship. This is a picture of "the Spirit-filled life of the church."[58] One of the habits going on among those Christians is their daily attendance of the temple and breaking bread in their houses (v. 46). Regarding their habit of temple attendance, C. K. Barrett states, "There are passages in Acts that assume that Jewish Christians will naturally continue to use the Temple as they did in their pre-Christian lives."[59] Given the fact that Luke uses "the temple" and "house" (v. 46), it is not clear whether Luke implies some sort of dichotomy between them.

Implication of Luke's Unincluded Text

Here, Luke's pattern of citing or alluding to the Old Testament is recognized. First, he interprets those passages as messianic, thus being fulfilled in Christ. Second, his choice of citation or allusion is thematically confined. That is, his included text contains its own specific theme in terms of fulfillment by Christ. This means that Luke is explicit in that regard. Third, Luke's unincluded text from the Old Testament text does not agree with the theme that Luke intends to show. Yet Luke describes the fulfillment of this unincluded text as what comes because of the included text's fulfillment—that is, contextually implied in his narrative. Hence, this pattern is evident, based on Acts 2, about Christ's heavenly enthronement and Christ's building of the eschatological temple; the former is textually evident in Luke's citations, whereas the latter is contextually implied in Luke's descriptions.

---

58. Booth, *Tabernacling Presence of God*, 136. Shepherd, *Narrative Function of the Holy Spirit*, 167. Shepherd argues that the Spirit initiated this ideal community.

59. Barrett, "Attitudes to the Temple in the Acts of the Apostles," 54.

Stephen's Speech

Stephen made a long speech before the Sanhedrin (Acts 7:2–53). This speech is known as the longest in Acts.[60] Instead of studying the entire speech, this section will focus on the last part of the speech (vv. 45–53), for it contains Stephen's understanding of the Jerusalem temple in light of Christ's temple-building work.

Man-Made Nature of the Jerusalem Temple

The temple has been the main setting of Peter and John in their ministry, as indicated in the imperfect tense (ἐπαύοντο) in the summary statement of Acts 5:42. However, this pattern is not so evident in Stephen's engagement with his non-Christian Hellenists (6:8–15). These Hellenists charged Stephen with speaking words against the temple and the law (6:13). Luke describes this charge as a result of their instigation (v. 11), and yet it should not be treated as a pure falsehood.

How did Stephen view the temple? How did Christ's work affect his understanding about the temple? First, Stephen understands the temple in light of Christ's eschatological temple. For the Jerusalem temple, Stephen regards it as χειροποίητος ("made by human hands"). This adjective often occurs in relation to buildings, specifically temples.[61] In the New Testament, this adjective appears six times, and almost all of its occurrences are in the context of comparison—between the Jewish ethno-religious system (temple [Mark 14:58; Acts 7:48; 17:24; Heb 9:11, 24] and circumcision [Eph 2:11]) and Christ's work.[62] In this regard, Stephen uses that word to describe the temple in light of Christ's work—in particular, Christ's temple building work.[63]

---

60. Polhill, *Acts*, 187.
61. BDAG, 1083.
62. Sweeney, "Stephen's Speech," 205.
63. Rebell, "χειροποίητος," 3:464. Rebell states, "Neither occurrence [Acts 7:48; 17:24] expresses any fundamental criticism of the temple; rather, both pick up the idea of the limitation of the temple's significance." Walker, *Jesus and the Holy City*, 66–67. Regarding Stephen's use of χειροποίητος, Walker states, "The Temple has lost its former status and is now *in his* [God] *sight too* merely a human construct (χειροποίητος), void of significance." Walton, "Tale of Two Perspectives?," 143. Walton states, "Overall, then, the material in Stephen's speech related to the Temple should be seen as highlighting the transcendence of God over against the universal human temptation to localize the deity, and specifically against the common Jewish belief that Yahweh was locally present in the Temple in a way that was not regularly or predictably true of other locations on earth." Walton sees Stephen's use of χειροποίητος in light of Stephen's citation of Isa

Second, Stephen alludes to the Davidic covenant in 2 Sam 7:12–14. The Greek term οἶκος, in addition to his reference to David and Solomon, recalls 2 Sam 7:12–14.⁶⁴ If based on the chiastic structure of the Old Testament text, God's promise—"he [son] shall build a house for my name" (v. 13a)—is pivotal. The promise was originally applied to Solomon. However, this promise was ultimately for the Messiah, the Davidic Son of God, who would build οἶκος for God's name. The mutual relatedness of (1) the enthronement of the Davidic Son and (2) the restoration of God's altar in the temple is evident, as discussed above.⁶⁵ That is, the enthronement of the Davidic Son entails his building of the eschatological temple. In this sense, James Dunn states, "This promise (2 Sam 7:13–14; 1 Chron 17:11–14) was very much at the heart of Israel's self-understanding as a dynasty under God and became central also in the eschatological hope of a restored or renewed temple."⁶⁶

Third, Stephen's confession emphasizes the exalted Christ's heavenly enthronement—"Behold, I see the heavens opened, and the Son of Man standing at the right hand of God" (Acts 7:55). This is a vivid portrayal of the exalted Christ's heavenly enthronement. This characteristic has been identified in Peter's speech at Pentecost (Acts 2:14–36).

Universal Nature of Christ's Temple

Stephen's speech caused the Jewish religious leaders to get agitated, ultimately leading him to death. It also ignited persecution against the Hellenist Jewish Christians, not the apostles (Acts 8:1). What elements in Stephen's speech make it distinct from Peter's Pentecost speech? Regarding Stephen's speech, Darrell L. Bock suggests that "something Stephen is teaching appears to have triggered a hostile reaction and an opportunity to examine him for claiming things the apostles' preaching has not."⁶⁷

Stephen's citation of Isa 66:1–2 needs to be illumined from Stephen's regained thought about the theme of God's dwelling. God's dwelling is not

---

66:1–2. Sweet, "House Not Made with Hands," 386–87. Sweet notes the adjective as "not so much idolatry as the refusal to acknowledge God." According to him, Stephen's accusation is "not the Temple but the Jews who reject the work of God's hand and resist the Holy Spirit."

64. Walton, "Place of the Temple in Acts," 141. Walton regards this textual reference as an allusion.

65. See Jer 33:17–18, Ps 132:12–13, and 4Q174 III. Psalm 131:13 LXX uses the Greek term κατασκία for the "dwelling place" of God.

66. Dunn, *Acts of the Apostles*, 96.

67. Bock, *Acts*, 272.

limited to man-made temples. From a Christological point of view, the Spirit is the manifestation of God's dwelling and dwells among Christians. What is the nature of Luke's citation of the Isaiah text? According to Nicolas Fox, it is the decentralized nature of God's dwelling house. He states, "In fact, verse 48 and following may be the climax of Stephen's defense, bringing home his point about decentralization of God's people and the move of God's presence to all who would seek him, rather than a building and a Jewish traditional religion."[68]

Luke suggests that Christ's role as the Builder of God's house is evident among Christians in Jerusalem. Now Luke further develops this role not as confined to Jerusalem but as expanded to other regions. God's universal presence, although conceptually embedded in the Old Testament, is now fulfilled, and actualized through Christ's fulfillment of building God's universal dwelling house—as a result of Christ's heavenly enthronement. God's universal dwelling house is no longer a conceptual notion, which is attributed chiefly to the view that God is the Creator of the universe. God's universal dwelling is now actualized as reality, being experienced by those who recognize Christ's enthronement in heaven.[69] Christ's building of God's eschatological house is in Peter's speech. Yet Stephen's speech further develops this reality to another level. This aspect will be discussed in the Ethiopian episode.

Philip's Exposition to the Ethiopian

Philip's evangelistic approach to the Ethiopian begins with his question— "Do you understand what you are reading?" (v. 30). Luke's referencing method here is a quotation, as indicated in his use of a citation formula (v. 32a, "Now the passage [περιοχή] of the Scripture that he was reading

---

68. Fox, *Hermeneutics of Social Identity*, 217.

69. Yahweh's attribute of transcendence is evident in the Old Testament (Deut 4:12–18; 1 Kgs 8:27; 2 Chr 6:18; Isa 66:1–2). As he cites Isa 66:1–2, Stephen rejects the idea that God can be confined to the temple. Regev, *Temple in Early Christianity: Experiencing the Sacred*, 178. Rhodes, "Tabernacle and Temple," in *Contemporary Studies in Acts*, 126–27. Rhodes states, "[T]heir [tabernacle and temple] humanly constructed or material quality was not an issue as long as one did not lose sight of the divine transcendence" (127). Smith, *Fate of the Jerusalem Temple in Luke–Acts*, 168. Smith argues that Stephen's citation here is the attitude and practice that the religious leaders had toward the temple. Regev, Rhodes, and Smith view Stephen's citation of Isa 66:1–2 as intending to recall the notion that God is transcendent. However, Stephen's citation here is not just a reminder of God's transcendence, but also its actuality by the exalted Christ's enthronement. This aspect is what is intended in Stephen's citation here.

was this"). The noun περιοχή denotes "portion of written text."⁷⁰ With this meaning in view, Luke's cited text here is the result of his careful choice. By this, Luke intends to prove that the cited text is what Christ has fulfilled—one of the elements that constitute Christ's work.

This characteristic is well revealed in his included portion and unincluded portion from Isa 56:7–8 LXX.⁷¹ First, Luke did not include Isa 53:7a ("And he, because he has been ill-treated, does not open his mouth"). Semantically, Isa 53:7a is identical to the included portion of 53:7b. Both point to the servant's silence.

Second, Luke also did not include Isa 53:6c ("and the Lord gave him over to our sins") and 53:8d ("he was led to death on account of the acts of lawlessness of my people"). Both point to the atoning work of the servant's death. This theme is theologically significant in terms of understanding Christ's death and its theological implication, but Luke did not include this theme in his cited text.

Third, Luke's included portion is confined to the theme of Christ's death—humiliation and injustice. It is often suggested that Luke's cited text points to the servant's resurrection; this view is related to αἴρω (v. 33). However, Luke's usage of the word is limited to death.⁷² In Acts 22:22, the Jewish mob accused Paul and said, "Away with such a fellow from the earth" (αἶρε ἀπὸ τῆς γῆς τὸν τοιοῦτον). Hence, this being the case, Luke's citation of the Isaiah text is thematically confined to Christ's suffering and death—one of the elements in Christ's work.

Luke's Unincluded Text of Isaiah

Does that mean that Luke has no concern with the theological implication of Christ's death, based on his uncited Isaiah text? As noted in Peter's Pentecost speech and Stephen's speech, Luke's cited portion of text contains what he intends to emphasize in terms of Christ's fulfillment. However, his uncited portion of text that lies in the immediate context of his source text, although not cited, is thematically provoked, that is, revealed not textually but contextually in Luke's illustration. In this regard, Luke would not negate Christ's death and its atonement nature.⁷³ This aspect is also found in Luke's

---

70. BDAG, 803.

71. The English translation is based on NETS.

72. Acts 20:9; 21:36; 22:22.

73. When it comes to Luke's description of Jesus' death, his primary focus, based on his text, is on Christ's innocence: (1) Luke's citation of Isa 53:12 (Luke 22:37), (2) Pilate's declaration (Luke 23:4, 14–15, 22), (3) a criminal's confession at crucifixion

description of Philip's exposition on Scripture—"beginning from this scripture, he [Philip] preached Jesus to him [the Ethiopian]" (Acts 8:35). This means that Luke has in view more than Isa 56:7a–8b concerning Philip's scriptural exposition.[74]

Luke's primary focus here is on the servant's death in humiliation and injustice and Christ's fulfillment of it. In this regard, David M. Moffitt states, "Luke has not stressed the sacrificial aspects of Jesus' death, but has highlighted the atoning benefits of Jesus' exaltation because he understands Jesus to have offered his atoning sacrifice as part of his exaltation to the right hand of God."[75]

As explained, Peter's Pentecost speech contains four main elements about Christ's work: (1) death, (2) resurrection, (3) enthronement, and (4) outpouring of the Spirit. Philip's evangelism here for the Ethiopian, certainly, begins with Christ's death, which is what Luke's cited portion thematically deals with. Furthermore, Philip's witnessing, most probably, included the other three elements also, which are not textually cited but contextually implied.[76]

The Ethiopian's Baptism

To Philip's expositional witnessing, the Ethiopian responds with an acclamation: "See, here is water! What prevents me from being baptized?" (Acts 8:36). Luke makes no specific remarks about the Ethiopian's confession of faith or repentance.[77] Luke focuses on the Ethiopian's active desire of baptism. As discussed above, Peter's invitation of faith had four elements: (1) repentance, (2) baptism, (3) forgiveness of sins, and (4) the gift of the Spirit

---

(23:40–41), and (4) a gentile centurion's proclamation (23:47). In his citation of Isa 53:12, Luke does not include the servant's atoning death. This aspect is identified in Luke's citation of Isa 53:7b–8a in Acts 8:32–33. Luke's primary basis for forgiveness is found in Christ's exaltation, shown in Paul's speech in Pisidian Antioch—his citation of Pss 2:7 and 16:10. Kimbell, *Atonement in Lukan Theology*, 121. Also, Mark 10:45 is not included in the Gospel of Luke. However, Luke's emphasis on innocence in relation of Jesus' death should not be interpreted as Luke's negation of its atonement nature. This point of view is evidenced in the Last Supper (Luke 22:19–20) and Paul's speech to the Ephesian elders at Miletus (Acts 20:28). Most likely, Luke assumes that his audience is already aware of Christ's death for atonement.

74. Bock, "Isaiah 53 in Acts 8," 139.

75. Moffitt, "Atonement at the Right Hand," 549.

76. von Dobbeler, *Evangelist Philippus*, 147.

77. Metzger, *Textual Commentary on the Greek New Testament*, 315. Metzger sees Acts 8:37 as a Western addition, not in the original text.

(2:38). Baptism presumes all the other three elements. This is true of the Ethiopian.

Luke describes the Ethiopian's returning journey to his homeland Ethiopia: "he [the Ethiopian] went on his way rejoicing" (v. 39). The present participle of χαίρω denotes a continuous aspect of joy. Hence, although it is not textually illustrated, this can be the spiritual reality of the Spirit bestowed as the gift by the enthroned Son in heaven. In this regard, A. Andrew Das states, "This indication of rejoicing may very well be a Lukan indication of the possession of the Spirit."[78] This being the case, the spiritual reality of God's bestowing him the forgiveness of sins is now manifested in his uplifted heart on his journey to Ethiopia.

This aspect of the Spirit's movement along with the Ethiopian is conceptually identical to what Stephen understands about Christ's role as the builder of the universal house of God's dwelling. In this respect, the Ethiopian's return to Ethiopia, his faraway homeland, could be implicit evidence of God's universal dwelling among his eschatological people because of Christ's enthronement in heaven.

Peter's Speech to Cornelius

The episode of Cornelius reveals Christ's work with a focus on the exalted Christ's cleansing work. Although textually not explicit, this cleansing work is culminated in God's declaration for the uncircumcised gentile Christians; it is a declaration of what has been actualized. This characteristic is well revealed by (1) Peter's vision, (2) Peter's retrospective confession, and (3) Peter's explanation of the Cornelius episode to the Jewish Christians in Jerusalem. The most essential element in this discussion is the uncircumcision of the gentiles.

Peter's Animal Vision

Luke's description of Peter's animal vision has four characteristics. First, its origin is from heaven (10:11), an implication that the exalted Christ in heaven continues his ministry. Second, Luke indicates that this vision is by nature all-inclusive and universal. His illustration of the vision uses the phrases "a great sheet" with "four corners upon the earth" and "all kinds of animals and reptiles and birds of the air" (v. 11). This aspect is not yet clear until Peter's retrospectively gained lesson. Third, this vision reflects the

---

78. Das, "Acts 8: Water, Baptism, and the Spirit," 120. See Acts 13:52 and 16:34.

Jewish mindset of uncleanness—food laws. To the command to eat those animals, Peter responds, "By no means, Lord; for I have never eaten anything that is common (κοινός) or unclean (ἀκάθαρτος)" (v. 14). His use of "by no means" (μηδαμῶς) and "never" (οὐδέποτε) indicates his absolute sense of refraining from those unclean animals. In Jewish culture, eating what is common and unclean is detestable, even choosing to die.[79]

Fourth, Peter's vision from heaven indicates a new phase of God's eschatological program. For Peter's reluctance to eat those animals, the heavenly voice proclaims in a prohibitive manner: ἃ ὁ θεὸς ἐκαθάρισεν, σὺ μὴ κοίνου ("What God has made clean, do not call common," v. 15). The Greek word καθαρίζω denotes "to make clean" or "declare clean" in the sense of a Levitical cleansing.[80] In the Gospel of Luke, this word occurs seven times (4:27; 5:12, 13; 7:22; 11:39; 17:14, 17). Four of the occurrences are related to Jesus' cleansing ministry (5:13; 7:22; 17:14, 17). Based on this usage in the Gospel of Luke, the Greek word, when it is used for Jesus, points to his act of making clean. Also, its use in the aorist tense here most probably conveys the ingressive idea—"to stress the beginning of an action or the entrance into a state."[81] That is, what is unclean is now in the state of cleanness.

Peter's Retrospective Confession

Peter's animal vision is a little clearer in the statement he made to Cornelius and his relatives and friends (10:28):

> You know how unlawful it is for a Jew to *associate with* (κολλάω) or to visit *foreigner* (ἀλλόφυλος), but God has shown me that I should not call any person common or unclean.

Here, Peter refers to Cornelius and his relatives and friends as ἀλλόφυλος, which adjective denotes "alien, foreign."[82] This word occurs only here in the New Testament. This definition itself does not imply much about its conceptual meaning. The context of how it is being used tells what it implicates. Here, the word is contextualized to refer to an unclean, uncircumcised gentile (10:28a; 11:3); thus, for Jews, their association with that kind of gentile is inappropriate. The Greek word κολλάω denotes an intimate

---

79. Keener, *Acts 3:1–14:28*, 1769–771.
80. BDAG, 488.
81. Wallace, *Greek Grammar Beyond the Basics*, 558. καθαρίζω appears with the third-person singular aorist active indicative form in Lev 8:15; 2 Chr 34:5; 1 Macc 13:47, 50; 2 Macc 2:18 in the LXX. All these connotate the idea of ingression.
82. BDAG, 48.

association. This aspect is more revealed by the accusers of Peter. The members of the circumcision party said, "You went to uncircumcised men and ate with them" (11:3). According to this accusation, Peter's table fellowship with the uncircumcised gentiles caused the circumcision party to see Peter's act as unacceptable.

Also, Peter's new understanding of what the animal vision was meant to be clarifies what is embedded in that designation ἀλλόφυλος ("foreigner"). He states, "God has shown me that I should not call any person common or unclean" (10:28). He uses the adjectives κοινός ("common") and ἀκάθαρτος ("unclean"), the words that he used to refer to the animals in the vision. The difference is that the referent of those adjectives here is not the animals but Cornelius. It is an issue among scholars how to understand this connection of the two different referents. Yet according to the context, it is about a table fellowship with the uncircumcised gentiles, which could involve "unclean" and "common" food.

Peter's Explanation before the Jerusalem Council

Peter recalls the episode of Cornelius and his conversion before the council of the apostles and the elders, stating,

> καὶ ὁ καρδιογνώστης θεὸς ἐμαρτύρησεν αὐτοῖς δοὺς τὸ πνεῦμα τὸ ἅγιον καθὼς καὶ ἡμῖν καὶ οὐθὲν διέκρινεν μεταξὺ ἡμῶν τε καὶ αὐτῶν τῇ πίστει καθαρίσας τὰς καρδίας αὐτῶν
>
> And the heart-knowing God witnessed to them by giving the Holy Spirit just as to us and he made no discrimination between us and them by cleansing their heart by faith (15:8–9).

In this account, Peter illustrates the phenomenal outpouring of the Spirit to the gentiles as the sign identical to that which occurred on Pentecost (Acts 2). Based on Peter's Pentecost speech, this sign presumes the exalted Christ's enthronement at the Father's side. Also, Peter uses the word καθαρίζω here. At the scene of Peter's animal vision, the heavenly voice made an effectuating declaration—"God has cleansed" (10:15). Before the council, Peter emphasizes that it is God who cleansed the hearts of the gentiles (15:9). The means of this purification is their faith (τῇ πίστει). Furthermore, in view of the fact that the Jerusalem council is dealing with the issue of circumcision for the gentiles, it is clear that God's act of cleansing the gentiles by faith negates the necessity of their circumcision.

To put all these pieces of information together, there are three Jewish elements identified in the text surrounding the Cornelius episode: (1) food laws, (2) uncleanness, and (3) uncircumcision. All the texts related to the Cornelius episode (Acts 10–11:18; 15:7–11) reveal the Jewish culture based on the Mosaic ceremonial laws in relation to gentiles. Through Peter, the circumcision party, and the council of the apostles and elders in the Jerusalem church, Luke shows how this culture collides with God's new phase of salvation program through the exalted Son. Hence, the issue is no longer the physical circumcision but the circumcised heart, which is enabled by God through faith in the exalted Christ.

There are multiple elements that could make the Cornelius episode distinct from the Ethiopian episode, but among others, circumcision is essential. Hence, based on the Abrahamic covenant and its circumcision law, Cornelius represents the inclusion of the unincluded in the Abrahamic covenant. That is, the uncircumcised gentiles were not part of God's covenant people, but now through their faith in the gospel of Christ, they are now among God's eschatological people. This aspect is a clear-cut distinction between the Ethiopian and Cornelius.

Conclusion

This study has investigated the position of the Ethiopian episode in light of Luke's geographic, ethnic, and religious projection of the gospel's expansion in accordance with Acts 1:8. First, it has been suggested that Luke uses geographic locales as the means of dividing his narrative development. Luke puts an emphasis on the locale of Philip's witnessing, that is, "on the road to Gaza" (Acts 8:27), rather than on the Ethiopian's geographic origin from Ethiopia. This witnessing locale suggests that the Ethiopian cannot be regarded as a gentile like Cornelius. Most probably, the Ethiopian was ethnically related to Jewishness. This view is also supported by Luke's illustration about Philip's evangelism within the land of Judea and Peter's ministry toward ethnic Jews in that land.

Also, this study has investigated Luke's use of regional-name adjectives and concluded that the Ethiopian cannot be regarded as a gentile because of Luke's introduction of him as "Ethiopian." The term "Ethiopian" is primarily related to the Ethiopian's geographic origin, not to his ethnic background. Along with this, Luke's use of literary techniques, in relation to the Cornelius episode and Paul's gentile mission, proves that Luke treats the inclusion of gentiles into God's eschatological people as the most significant in the entire narrative of Acts. With this understanding in view, the Ethiopian cannot be identified as a gentile like Cornelius, nor can the Ethiopian episode be treated as foreshadowing the Cornelius episode.

Lastly, this study has suggested that Luke puts an emphasis on the role of Christ, as the exalted Davidic king, in establishing the eschatological dwelling house of God. In terms of Luke's textual citations, this role is not explicit, but in terms of Luke's contextual illustrations in narrative, it is apparently revealed. Peter's Pentecost speech and Stephen's speech both have this role in view, but what sets them apart is that the latter points to the universal nature of God's eschatological dwelling house, a notion that is retained in Stephen's cited text of Isa 66:1–2. This notion is actualized by the exalted Christ in heaven. Luke portrays this reality in his description of the Ethiopian's returning to the land of Ethiopia ("rejoicing," Acts 8:39). Thus, the Ethiopian's pilgrimage to Jerusalem to worship, most likely in the temple, goes parallel with the Ethiopian's realized reality of God's presence in his returning home.

In conclusion, the Ethiopian episode itself is unique, meaningful enough to contribute to Luke's narrative development. This understanding makes it necessary to treat the Ethiopian as distinct from Cornelius, who was an uncircumcised gentile. In other words, the Ethiopian is ethnically and religiously approximate to Jews.

Conclusion

To CONTINUE THE SCHOLARLY discussion about the ethnic and religious identity of the Ethiopian in Acts 8:26–40, this dissertation raised three questions, among others. The first question was, "Is it legitimate to use Deut 23:1 as a criterion to conclude that the Ethiopian was an uncircumcised God-fearing Gentile?" With this question in view, this dissertation explored the textual tradition of Deut 23:1–8 in Neh 13:1–3 and Isa 56:1–8, and other Jewish materials, including the Dead Sea Scrolls, Josephus, Philo, and the Mishnah. This exploration led this dissertation to five conclusions.

First, Deut 23:1–8 functioned, as a scriptural basis, to reconstitute the participants of the cultic worship in the temple. It worked so by restricting the ritually incomplete and the ethnically foreign. The transition of the worship setting from the wilderness to the temple in Jerusalem made their exclusion legitimate. Its purpose was to manifest God's holiness in the temple. Second, this exclusion did not mean that the ritually incomplete and the ethnically foreign were not part of God's covenant people. The stipulation was to define an inner circle within the broad circle of God's covenant people. Based on the Abrahamic covenant and the significance of circumcision in it, it is theoretically reasonable to regard those excluded ones as circumcised. Third, Deut 23:1 had its application solely in relation to ethnic Jews with their reproductive organs damaged or mutilated, not to ethnic others. This was a general pattern identifiable in its textual tradition, but most notable in the tractate m. Yebam. 6:1–8.

Fourth, Isa 56:1–8 showed how the exclusive idea of Deut 23:1–8 was affecting God's covenant people in its literary context. Yet its intent was to present the inclusive idea of God's eschatological program. Isaiah did so by echoic allusion. He used "foreigners" and "eunuchs" to allude to Deut 23:1–8 and retrieve the idea of exclusivity in it. His purpose by this allusion, however, was to oppose this idea and offer the ideal of "justice" and "righteousness" (Isa 56:1). This attitude is what God's covenant people, in anticipation of the Lord's salvation, need toward "foreigners" and "eunuchs," the most vulnerable to exclusion in the cultic system of the temple. Thus, by its rhetorical nature, Isa 56:1–8 has eschatological, polemical, and ethical characteristics.

Fifth, in the Gospel and Acts, Luke recontextualized Isa 56:1–8 ("foreigners" and "eunuchs") in relation to Samaritans and the Ethiopian. This is clear in three ways. First, Luke addresses the returned Samarian with leprosy as "foreigner" (ἀλλογενής, Luke 17:18) and juxtaposes the Samaritans (Acts 8:5–25) and the Ethiopian ("eunuch," vv. 26–40) under Philip's evangelism. Second, Luke portrays both the Samaritans and the Ethiopian as part of God's covenant people but excluded from the cultic system of the Jerusalem temple. The exclusion of the Samaritans was due to their ethnic foreignness, whereas the exclusion of the Ethiopian was due to his ritual incompleteness. Third, Luke utilizes the characteristics identified in Isa 56:1–8 (i.e., eschatological, polemical, and ethical) as his rhetorical methods. He does so for the purpose of rejecting the culture of exclusivity and promoting the all-inclusive nature of Christ's people.

Hence, Deut 23:1 cannot be a criterion to regard the Ethiopian as an uncircumcised God-fearing gentile. Rather, the textual tradition of Deut 23:1–8 points to the view that the Ethiopian was ethnically and religiously proximate to Jewishness and Judaism. Based on this tradition, the Ethiopian, as a circumcised Jew, belonged to God's covenant but not to the cultic system of the Jerusalem temple.

The second question was, "Can it be possible that the Ethiopian was an Ethiopian of Jewish descent?" This dissertation dealt with this question by reconstructing the cultural setting in which the Ethiopian was situated. It explored the ancient practice of castration, the Old Testament's implication of Jewish exiles in Ethiopia (i.e., Cush), the archaeological records of Jews in Elephantine, and the pilgrimage of the diaspora Jews to Jerusalem.

First, the ancient practice of castration led this dissertation to disagree with the view that the Ethiopian would not have been circumcised. This practice occurred, most likely, to foreign, pre-pubescent males. It also involved the removal of the child's testicles, not his penis. A castrated eunuch would undertake tasks related to a king or queen's safety and wealth. In fact, the Ethiopian undertook the wealth of his ruling queen (Acts 8:27). In light of this ancient practice, the Ethiopian was not a native Ethiopian. After being a war captive and slave, he became a physical eunuch, gained trust from his ruling queen, and reached such a prominent position.

Second, Isaiah presumed the presence of Jews in Ethiopia (11:11–12). In fact, Elephantine hosted Jewish exiles and mercenaries there. Geographically, it is at the bottom of Egypt, bordering Ethiopia. Politically,

Elephantine was significant in terms of conflicts between Egyptians and Ethiopians. Third, not just the Jewish materials but also the Greco-Roman world testified about the attachment of the diaspora Jews to the Jerusalem temple. This attachment is identifiable in their pilgrimage to Jerusalem for the annual festivals and their contribution of the first fruits and half shekels to the temple. In fact, the Ethiopian's pilgrimage to Jerusalem reflects the customs practiced by the diaspora Jews. This reconstructed ancient culture led this dissertation to the view that the Ethiopian was at least a man of Jewish descent.

The third question was, "Is the Ethiopian episode, as an individual episode, meaningful?" Its role is often viewed as foreshadowing the Cornelius episode. To evaluate this view, this dissertation explored three trajectories that Luke is drawing in his narrative development of Acts: (1) geographic, (2) ethnic, and (3) religious.

Geographically, Luke uses each of the locales in Acts 1:8 to demarcate his narrative units. While doing so, Luke also implicates common notions that each locale holds in terms of Jewishness and Judaism. This characteristic is clear, as shown in Peter's ministerial work in Judea (Acts 9:32–43) and his visit to Cornelius in Caesarea (10:23–29). This fact redirects our attention from the Ethiopian's geographic origin (i.e., Ethiopia) to his actual witnessing locale by Philip ("the road to Gaza," Acts 8:26). This locale belongs to "Judea," not to "the end of the earth." Thus, the Ethiopian was within the category of ethnicity and religion conceptually embedded in the land of Judea. That is, he was proximate to Jewishness and Judaism, distinct from Cornelius, who was an uncircumcised gentile.

Ethnically, Luke's use of the adjective "Ethiopian" (8:27) is not what denotes his ethnic identity. Primarily, Luke has in view the Ethiopian's geographic origin. This is clear, as shown in the tribune's use of "Egyptian" for Paul (21:37–38). As one of the most significant themes in Acts, Luke deals with the inclusion of gentiles as God's eschatological people. For this, Luke uses multiple literary techniques, such as omission, characterization, repetition, and synthesizing harmonization. Given Luke's signification of Cornelius and his conversion as the uncircumcised gentile, it is unreasonable to argue that Luke introduces the Ethiopian episode to foreshadow what is to come, that is, the Cornelius episode.

Luke's gradual development of the gospel's expansion is not just geographic and ethnic, but also religious. Luke presents Christ's work, including its theological implications, amid its conflicts with Judaism. According to Judaism, the Ethiopian episode has the setting of the cultic worship in the Jerusalem temple, as shown in the purpose of his pilgrimage (Acts 8:27). On the other hand, the Cornelius episode deals with the food laws and circumcision in relation to gentiles. Based on Judaism, the Ethiopian episode is distinct from the Cornelius episode.

According to Christ's work, the episodes are also distinct from each other. Stephen's citation of Isa 66:1–2, in light of Christ's heavenly enthronement as the Davidic Son of God, points to the actualization of God's universal presence among his eschatological people (Acts 7:49–50). This characteristic is most notable in Stephen's speech. Luke's portrayal of the Ethiopian's returning home ("rejoicing," 8:39) emphasizes this aspect of God's presence, even to the faraway land of Ethiopia. On the other hand, the Cornelius episode focuses on Christ's purification work for gentiles, as clear in Peter's explanation to the Jerusalem church (15:8–9). These are the ways the Ethiopian episode is distinct from the Cornelius episode. These distinctives are how the Ethiopian episode uniquely contributes to Luke's gradual narrative development of the gospel's expansion.

In conclusion, the Ethiopian belonged to God's covenant people but not to the cultic setting of the Jerusalem temple. This is because of his physical incompleteness due to his castration. The Ethiopian was at least an Ethiopian of Jewish descent. This is based on the dissertation's cultural reconstruction of the Ethiopian. The Ethiopian was distinct from Cornelius in light of Luke's gradual narrative development of the gospel's geographic, ethnic, and religious expansion. Hence, the Ethiopian was an African of Jewish descent, the episode itself is uniquely meaningful, and fits well into the entire narrative of Acts.

Bibliography

Abernethy, Andrew T. *Eating in Isaiah: Approaching the Role of Food and Drink in Isaiah's Structure and Message*. Biblical Interpretation Series 131. Leiden: Brill, 2014.
Allen, W. C. "On the Meaning of ΠΡΟΣΗΛΥΤΟΣ in the Septuagint." *The Expositor* 10.4 (1894) 264–75.
Alter, Robert. *The World of Biblical Literature*. New York: Basic, 1992.
Appian. *Roman History*. Translated by Brian McGing. Vol. 4, *Civil Wars, Books 1–2*. Loeb Classical Library. Cambridge: Harvard University Press, 2020.
Averbeck, Richard. E. "Sacrifices and Offerings." In *Dictionary of the Old Testament: Pentateuch*, edited by T. Desmond Alexander and David W. Baker, 706–33. Downers Grove, IL: InterVarsity, 2003.
Avi-Yonah, Michael, and Moshe Dothan. "Ashdod: Ancient Ashdod." In *Encyclopedia Judaica*, edited by Fred Skolnik and Michael Berenbaum, vol. 2, 557. Detroit: Macmillan Reference, 2007.
Avi-Yonah, Michael. "Caesarea: From Ancient Times to the Mamluks." In *Encyclopedia Judaica*, edited by Fred Skolnik and Michael Berenbaum, vol. 4, 333–34. Detroit: Macmillan Reference USA, 2007.
Awabdy, Mark A. *Immigrants and Innovative Law: Deuteronomy's Theological and Social Version for the גר*. Forschungen zum Alten Testament 2. Reihe 67. Tübingen: Mohr Siebeck, 2014.
Baban, Octavian. *On the Road Encounters in Luke-Acts: Hellenistic Mimesis and Luke's Theology of the Way*. Paternoster Biblical Monographs. Milton Keynes: Paternoster, 2006.
Baldick, Chris. *The Oxford Dictionary of Literary Terms*. 4th ed. Oxford Quick Reference. Oxford: Oxford University Press, 2015.
Barber, Michael P. "Jesus as the Davidic Temple Builder and Peter's Priestly Role in Matthew 16:16–19." *Journal of Biblical Literature* 132.4 (2013) 935–53.
Barrett, C. K. "Attitudes to the Temple in the Acts of the Apostles." In *Templum Amicitiae: Essays on the Second Temple Presented to Ernst Bammel*, edited by William Horbury, vol. 48, 345–67. Journal for the Study of the New Testament Supplement Series. Sheffield: Sheffield Academic, 1991.
———. *A Critical and Exegetical Commentary on the Acts of the Apostles*. Vol. 1, *Acts 1–14*. International Critical Commentary. Edinburgh: T&T Clark, 1994.
Bauer, David R. *The Book of Acts as Story: A Narrative-Critical Study*. Grand Rapids: Baker Academic, 2021.

Bibliography

Baumgarten, Joseph M. *Studies in Qumran Law.* Studies in Judaism in Late Antiquity. Leiden: Brill, 1977.

Beale, G. K. "The Descent of the Eschatological Temple in the Form of the Spirit Part 2: Corroborating Evidence." *Tyndale Bulletin* 56.2 (2005) 63–90.

Blasing, Craig A., and Darrell L. Bock. *Progressive Dispensationalism.* Wheaton, IL: BridgePoint, 1993.

Becking, Bob. *Israel's Past Seen from the Present: Studies on History and Religion in Ancient Israel and Judah.* Beihefte zur Zeitschrift für die alttestamentliche Wissenschaft 535. Berlin: de Gruyter, 2021.

———. "The Identity of the People at Elephantine." In *Elephantine Revisited: New Insights in the Judean Community and Its Neighbors,* edited by Margaretha Folmer, 106–23. University Park: Eisenbrauns, 2022.

Berlin, Adele. *Zephaniah: A New Translation with Introduction and Commentary.* Anchor Bible 25A. New York: Doubleday, 1994.

Blenkinsopp, Joseph. *Isaiah 56–66: A New Translation with Introduction and Commentary.* Anchor Bible 19B. New York: Doubleday, 2003.

———. "Second Isaiah, Prophet of Universalism?" In *Essays on the Book of Isaiah,* 50–62. Forschungen zum Alten Testament 128. Tübingen: Mohr Siebeck, 2019.

Bock, Darrell L. *Acts.* Baker Exegetical Commentary on the New Testament. Grand Rapids: Baker Academic, 2007.

———. *Blasphemy and Exaltation in Judaism: The Charge against Jesus in Mark 14:53–65.* Eugene, OR: Wipf & Stock, 1998.

———. "The Book of Acts and Jewish Evangelism: Three Approaches and One Common Thread." In *To the Jew First: The Case for Jewish Evangelism in Scripture and History,* edited by Darrell L. Bock and Mitch Glaser, 53–65. Grand Rapids: Kregel, 2008.

———. "Isaiah 53 in Acts 8." In *The Gospel According to Isaiah 53: Encountering the Suffering Servant in Jewish and Christian Theology,* edited by Darrell L. Bock and Mitch Glaser, 133–44. Grand Rapids: Kregel, 2012.

———. Vol. 1, *Luke 1:1–9:50.* Baker Exegetical Commentary on the New Testament 3A. Grand Rapids: Baker Academic, 1994.

———. Vol. 2, *Luke 9:51–24:53.* Baker Exegetical Commentary on the New Testament 3B. Grand Rapids: Baker Academic, 1996.

Booth, Susan M. *The Tabernacling Presence of God: Mission and Gospel Witness.* Eugene, OR: Wipf & Stock, 2015.

Breneman, Mervin. *Ezra, Nehemiah, Esther.* New American Commentary 10. Nashville: Broadman & Holman, 1993.

Brower, Gary Robert. "Ambivalent Bodies: Making Christian Eunuchs." PhD diss., Duke University, 1996.

Brown, Francis, S. R. Driver, and Charles A. Briggs. *A Hebrew and English Lexicon of the Old Testament: With an Appendix Containing the Biblical Aramaic.* Oxford: Clarendon, 1906.

Brown, Jeannine K. "Narrative Criticism." In *Dictionary of Jesus and the Gospels,* edited by Joel B. Green, Jeannine K. Brown, and Nicholas Perrin, 619–24. Downers Grove, IL: InterVarsity, 2013.

Bruce, F. F. "Philip and the Ethiopian." *Journal of Semitic Studies* 34.2 (Autumn 1989) 377–86.

Bullough, Vern L. "Eunuchs in History and Society." In *Eunuchs in Antiquity and Beyond*, edited by Shaun Tougher, 1–17. London: The Classical Press of Wales; Duckworth, 2002.

Burke, Sean D. *Queering the Ethiopian Eunuch: Strategies of Ambiguity in Acts*. Minneapolis: Augsburg Fortress, 2013.

Burrell, Kevin. *Cushites in the Hebrew Bible: Negotiating Ethnic Identity in the Past and Present*. Biblical Interpretation Series 181. Leiden: Brill, 2020.

Caird, G. B. *The Language and Imagery of the Bible*. London: Duckworth, 1980.

Cairns, Ian. *Word and Presence: A Commentary on the Book of Deuteronomy*. International Theological Commentary. Grand Rapids: Eerdmans, 1992.

Calvin, John. *Commentary on the Book of the Prophet Isaiah*. Translated by William Pringle. Vol. 4. Grand Rapids: Eerdmans, 1948.

Carpenter, Eugene. *Exodus*. Vol. 1, *Exodus 1–18*. Evangelical Exegetical Commentary. Bellingham, WA: Lexham, 2016.

Carson, Cottrel R. "Do You Understand What You Are Reading? A Reading of the Ethiopian Eunuch Story (Acts 8.26–40) from a Site of Cultural Marronage." PhD diss., Union Theological Seminary, 1999.

Chatman, Seymour. *Story and Discourse: Narrative Structure in Fiction and Film*. Ithaca, NY: Cornell University Press, 1978.

Cheney, Victor T. *A Brief History of Castration*. 2nd ed. Bloomington: AuthorHouse, 2006.

Childs, Brevard S. *Isaiah*. Old Testament Library. Louisville: Westminster John Knox, 2001.

Chisholm, Robert B., Jr. *From Exegesis to Exposition: A Practical Guide to Using Biblical Hebrew*. Grand Rapids: Baker, 1998.

———. *Interpreting the Historical Books: An Exegetical Handbook*. Handbooks for Old Testament Exegesis. Grand Rapids: Kregel, 2006.

Christensen, Duane L. *Deuteronomy 21:10–34:12*. Word Biblical Commentary 6B. Nashville: Nelson, 2002.

Cicero. *Cicero in Twenty-Eight Volumes*. Vol. 10, *In Catilinam I–IV, Pro Murena, Pro Sulla, Pro Flacco*. Translated by C. Macdonald. Loeb Classical Library. Cambridge: Harvard University Press, 1977.

Clifford, Hywel. "From Exclusion to Inclusion? Deuteronomy 23:1–8 in Philo and Beyond." In *The Exegetical and the Ethical: The Bible and the Academy in the Public Square: Essays for the Occasion of Professor John Barton's 70th Birthday*, edited by Hywel Clifford and Megan Daffern, 175–99. Biblical Interpretation Series 197. Leiden: Brill, 2022.

Clouston, Eric. *How Ancient Narratives Persuade: Acts in Its Literary Context*. Lanham, MD: Rowman & Littlefield, 2020.

Cogan, Mordechai, and Hayim Tadmor. *II Kings: A New Translation with Introduction and Commentary*. Anchor Bible 11. Garden City, NY: Doubleday, 1988.

Cohen, Shaye J. D. "Crossing the Boundary and Becoming a Jew." *Harvard Theological Review* 82.1 (1989) 13–33.

Conzelmann, Hans. *Acts of the Apostles: A Commentary on the Acts of the Apostles*. Edited by Eldon Jay Epp and Christopher R. Matthews. Translated by James Limburg, A. Thomas Kraabel, and Donald H. Juel. Hermeneia–A Critical and Historical Commentary on the Bible. Philadelphia: Fortress, 1987.

———. *A Commentary on the Jewish Roots of Acts.* Vol. 2. Jerusalem: Academon, 2003.
Curtius, Quintus. *History of Alexander.* Translated by John C. Rolfe. Vol. 2, *Books VI–X.* Loeb Classical Library. 1946. Reprint. Cambridge: Harvard University Press, 1976.
Danker, Frederick W., Walter Bauer, William F. Arndt, and F. Wilbur Gingrich. *Greek-English Lexicon of the New Testament and Other Early Christian Literature.* 3rd ed. Chicago: University of Chicago Press, 2000.
Das, A. Andrew. "Acts 8: Water, Baptism, and the Spirit." *Concordia Journal* 19.2 (1993) 108–34.
Davies, Graham I. *A Critical and Exegetical Commentary on Exodus 1–18.* Vol. 2, *Exodus 11–18.* International Critical Commentary. London: T&T Clark, 2020.
Delitzsch, Franz. *Biblical Commentary on the Prophecies of Isaiah: Translated from the Fourth Edition with an Introduction by Professor S. R. Driver.* Translated by S. R. Driver. Vol. 2. Clark's Foreign Theological Library 44. Edinburgh: T&T Clark, 1890.
Dimant, Devorah. *History, Ideology and Bible Interpretation in the Dead Sea Scrolls.* Forschungen zum Alten Testament 90. Tübingen: Mohr Siebeck, 2014.
———. "The Vocabulary of the Qumran Sectarian Texts." In *Qumran und die Archäologie: Texte und Kontexte*, 347–95. Wissenschaftliche Untersuchungen zum Neuen Testament 278. Tübingen: Mohr Siebeck, 2011.
Douglas, Mary. *Mary Douglas: Collected Works.* Vol. 2, *Purity and Danger: An Analysis of Concepts of Pollution and Taboo.* London: Routledge, 2003.
Dozeman, Thomas B. *Commentary on Exodus.* Eerdmans Critical Commentary. Grand Rapids: Eerdmans, 2009.
Duckworth, George Eckel. *Foreshadowing and Suspense in the Epics of Homer, Apollonius, and Vergil.* New York: Haskell House, 1966.
Duguid, Iain M., and Matthew P. Harmon. *Zephaniah, Haggai, Malachi.* Reformed Expository Commentary. Phillipsburg, NJ: P&R, 2018.
Dunn, James D. G. *The Acts of the Apostles.* Grand Rapids: Eerdmans, 1996.
Edwards, James R. *The Gospel According to Luke.* Pillar New Testament Commentary. Grand Rapids: Eerdmans, 2015.
Ellis, E. Earle. "'The End of the Earth' (Acts 1:8)." *Bulletin for Biblical Research* 1 (1991) 123–32.
Evans, Craig A. *Ancient Texts for New Testament Studies: A Guide to the Background Literature.* Peabody, MA: Hendrickson, 2005.
Fantin, Joseph D. "Background Studies: Grounding the Text in Reality." In *Interpreting the New Testament Text: Introduction to the Art and Science of Exegesis*, edited by Darrell L. Bock and Buist M. Fanning, 167–96. Wheaton, IL: Crossway, 2006.
Fiorello, Michael D. *The Physically Disabled in Ancient Israel According to the Old Testament and Ancient Near Eastern Sources.* Paternoster Biblical Monographs. Bucks, UK: Paternoster, 2014.
Fishbane, Michael. *Biblical Interpretation in Ancient Israel.* Oxford: Clarendon, 1985.
Fisher, Marjorie M. "The History of Nubia." In *Ancient Nubia: African Kingdoms on the Nile*, edited by Marjorie M. Fisher, et al., 10–44. Cairo: The American University in Cairo Press, 2012.
Fitzgerald, Curtis W. "A Rhetorical Analysis of Isaiah 56–66." PhD diss., Dallas Theological Seminary, 2003.
Fitzmyer, Joseph A. *The Acts of the Apostles: A New Translation with Introduction and Commentary.* Anchor Bible 31. New York: Doubleday, 1998.

———. "The Ascension of Christ and Pentecost." *Theological Studies* 45, no. 3 (1984) 409–40.
Fox, Nickolas A. *The Hermeneutics of Social Identity in Luke-Acts*. Eugene, OR: Pickwick, 2021.
Friedl, Johanna. *Ein brüderliches Volk: Das ‚Bruder'-Konzept im Heiligkeitsgesetz und deuteronomischen Gesetz*. Österreichische biblische Studien 52. Berlin: Peter Lang, 2021.
Gangel, Kenneth O. *Acts*. Holman New Testament Commentary. Nashville: Broadman & Holman, 1998.
Garland, David E. *Acts*. Teach the Text Commentary. Grand Rapids: Baker, 2017.
Gillihan, Yonder Moynihan. "The גר Who Wasn't There: Fictional Aliens in the Damascus Rule." *Revue de Qumran* 25.2 (2011) 257–305.
Goldingay, John. *A Critical and Exegetical Commentary on Isaiah 56–66*. International Critical Commentary. London: Bloomsbury, 2014.
Goldingay, John, and David Payne. *A Critical and Exegetical Commentary on Isaiah 40–55*. Vol. 1. International Critical Commentary. London: T&T Clark, 2006.
Goldwurm, Rabbi Hersh. "Tractate Shekalim." In *Seder Moed Vol. II: Pesachim/Shekalim*, edited by Nosson Scherman and Meir Zlotowitz, 1–162. Artscroll Mishnah Series: A Rabbinic Commentary to the Six Orders of the Mishnah. New York: Mesorah, 1985.
Green, Joel B. "Acts of the Apostles." In *Dictionary of the Later New Testament and its Developments*, edited by Ralph P. Martin and Peter H. Davids, 7–24. Downers Grove, IL: InterVarsity, 1997.
———. "Narrative Criticism." In *Methods for Luke*, edited by Joel B. Green, 74–112. Methods in Biblical Interpretation. Cambridge: Cambridge University Press, 2010.
Grogan, Geoffrey W. "Isaiah." In *Proverbs-Isaiah*. Rev. ed. *The Expositor's Bible Commentary* 6. 435–863. Grand Rapids: Zondervan, 2008.
Guggenheimer, Heinrich W. *The Jerusalem Talmud Third Order: Našim. Tractate Yebamot*. Studia Judaica 29. Berlin: de Gruyter, 2004.
Gunn, David M., and Danna Nolan Fewell. *Narrative in the Hebrew Bible*. Oxford Bible Series. New York: Oxford University Press, 1993.
Guyot, Peter. *Eunuchen als Sklaven und Freigelassene in der griechisch-römischen Antike*. Stuttgarter Beiträge zur Geschichte und Politik 14. Stuttgart: Klett-Cotta, 1980.
———. "Eunuchs." In *Brill's New Pauly: Encyclopaedia of the Ancient World*, edited by Hubert Cancik, vol. 5, 172–74. Leiden: Brill, 2004.
Hackett, Horatio B. *A Commentary on the Original Text of the Acts of the Apostles*. 2nd ed. Boston: Gould and Lincoln, 1859.
Haenchen, Ernst. *The Acts of the Apostles: A Commentary*. Philadelphia: Westminster, 1971.
Hamilton, Victor P. *Exodus: An Exegetical Commentary*. Grand Rapids: Baker Academic, 2011.
Hamm, Dennis. "The Healing of the Temple Beggar as Lucan Theology." *Biblica* 67.3 (1986) 305–19
Harrington, Hannah K. *The Books of Ezra and Nehemiah*. New International Commentary on the Old Testament. Grand Rapids: Eerdmans, 2022.
Hayes, Christine E. *Gentile Impurities and Jewish Identities: Intermarriage and Conversion from the Bible to the Talmud*. Oxford: Oxford University Press, 2002.

Hayes, Joyce, and Mimi Santini-Ritt. "Women in Ancient Nubia." In *Ancient Nubia: African Kingdoms on the Nile*, edited by Marjorie M. Fisher, et al., 170–85. Cairo: The American University in Cairo Press, 2012.
Haywood, John. *The Penguin Historical Atlas of Ancient Civilizations*. London: Penguin, 2005.
Hengel, Martin. *Acts and the History of Earliest Christianity*. Translated by John Bowden. Philadelphia: Fortress, 1980.
———. *Between Jesus and Paul: Studies in the Earliest History of Christianity*. Waco, TX: Baylor University Press, 2013.
———. "The Geography of Palestine in Acts." In *The Book of Acts in Its Palestinian Setting*, edited by Richard Bauckham, 27–78. The Book of Acts in Its First Century Setting 4. Grand Rapids: Eerdmans, 1995.
Hensel, Benedikt. "Ethnic Fiction and Identity-Formation: A New Explanation for the Background of the Question of Intermarriage in Ezra-Nehemiah." In *The Bible, Qumran, and the Samaritans*, edited by Magnar Kartveit and Gary N. Knoppers, 133–48. Studia Judaica 104, Studia Samaritana 10. Berlin: de Gruyter, 2018.
Herodotus. *Herodotus*. Translated by A. D. Godley. Vol. 1, *Books I–II*. Loeb Classical Library. 1920. Reprint, Cambridge: Harvard University Press, 1960.
———. *Herodotus*. Translated by A. D. Godley. Vol. 2, *Books III–IV*. Loeb Classical Library. 1921. Reprint, Cambridge: Harvard University Press, 1957.
———. *Herodotus*. Translated by A. D. Godley. Vol. 3, *Books V–VII*. Loeb Classical Library. 1922. Reprint, Cambridge: Harvard University Press, 1963.
———. *Herodotus*. Translated by A. D. Godley. Vol. 4, *Books VIII–IV*. Loeb Classical Library. 1925. Reprint. Cambridge: Harvard University Press, 1961.
Hess, Richard S. "Leviticus." In *Genesis-Leviticus*. Rev. ed. *The Expositor's Bible Commentary* 1. 565–826. Grand Rapids: Zondervan, 2008.
Holladay, Carl R. *Acts: A Commentary*. New Testament Library. Louisville: Westminster John Knox, 2016.
Homer. *The Odyssey*. Translated by A. T. Murray. Vol. 1, *Books I–XII*. Loeb Classical Library. 1919. Reprint, Cambridge: Harvard University Press, 1946.
Hoop, Raymond de. "The Interpretation of Isaiah 56:1–9: Comfort or Criticism?" *Journal of Biblical Literature* 127.4 (2008) 671–95.
Horrell, David G. *Ethnicity and Inclusion: Religion, Race, and Whiteness in Constructions of Jewish and Christian Identities*. Grand Rapids: Eerdmans, 2020.
Ikram, Salima, and Christian Knoblauch. "Elephantine and Aswan." In *Ancient Nubia: African Kingdoms on the Nile*, edited by Marjorie M. Fisher, et al., 406–10. Cairo: The American University in Cairo Press, 2012.
Irwin, William. "What Is an Allusion?" *Journal of Aesthetics and Art Criticism* 59.3 (2001) 287–97.
Iser, Wolfgang. *The Implied Reader: Patterns of Communication in Prose Fiction from Bunyan to Beckett*. Baltimore: Johns Hopkins University Press, 1974.
Jackson, Robert B. *At Empire's Edge: Exploring Rome's Egyptian Frontier*. New Haven; London: Yale University Press, 2002.
Jeremias, Joachim. *The Parables of Jesus*. 3rd ed. London: SCM, 1972.
Jervell, Jacob. *Die Apostelgeschichte: Übersetzt und erklärt*. Kritisch-exegetischer Kommentar über das Neue Testament 3. Göttingen: Vandenhoeck & Ruprecht, 1998.

Johnson, Luke Timothy. *The Acts of the Apostles*. Sacra Pagina 5. Collegeville, MN: Liturgical, 1992.
Johnston, Gordon H. "The Nature of the Davidic Covenant in the Light of Intertextual Analysis." Paper presented at the Annual Meeting of the Evangelical Theological Society, San Francisco, CA, 2011.
———. "סִיר." In *New International Dictionary of Old Testament Theology and Exegesis*, edited by Willem A. VanGemeren, vol. 3, 288–95. Grand Rapids: Zondervan, 1997.
Josephus. *Jewish Antiquities*. Vol. 1, *Books 1–3*. Translated by H. St. J. Thackeray. Loeb Classical Library. Cambridge: Harvard University Press, 1930.
———. *Jewish Antiquities*. Vol. 2, *Books 4–6*. Translated by H. St. J. Thackeray and Ralph Marcus. Loeb Classical Library. Cambridge: Harvard University Press, 1930.
———. *Josephus: The Complete Works*. Translated by William Whiston. Nelson's Super Value Series. Nashville: Nelson, 1998.
———. *The Life. Against Apion*. Translated by H. St. J. Thackeray. Loeb Classical Library. Cambridge: Harvard University Press, 1926.
Jost, Franklyn L. "Abimelech." In *Dictionary of the Old Testament: Pentateuch*, edited by T. Desmond Alexander and David W. Baker, 6–8. Downers Grove, IL: InterVarsity, 2003.
Keener, Craig S. *Acts: An Exegetical Commentary*. Vol. 2, *Acts 3:1–14:28*. Grand Rapids: Baker Academic, 2013.
Kern, Philip H. "Paul's Conversion and Luke's Portrayal of Characters in Acts 8–10." *Tyndale Bulletin* 54.2 (2003) 63–80.
Kimbell, John. *The Atonement in Lukan Theology*. Newcastle upon Tyne, UK: Cambridge Scholars, 2014.
Kistemaker, Simon J. *Exposition of the Acts of the Apostles*. New Testament Commentary. Grand Rapids: Baker Book House, 1990.
Klingler, David R. *Validity in the Identification and Interpretation of Literary Allusions in the Hebrew Bible*. Eugene, OR: Pickwick, 2021.
Knauth, R. J. D. "Alien, Foreign Resident." In *Dictionary of the Old Testament: Pentateuch*, edited by T. Desmond Alexander and David W. Baker, 26–33. Downers Grove, IL: InterVarsity, 2003.
Koehler, Ludwig, Walter Baumgartner, and Johann J. Stamm. *The Hebrew and Aramaic Lexion of the Old Testament*. Translated and edited under the supervisions of Mervyn E. J. Richardson. 4 vols. Leiden: Brill, 1994–1999.
Kollmann, Bernd. "Philippus der Evangelist und die Anfänge der Heidenmission." *Biblica* 81.4 (2000) 551–65.
Korner, Ralph J. *The Origin and Meaning of Ekklēsia in the Early Jesus Movement*. Arbeiten zur Geschichte des antiken Judentums und des Urchristentums 98. Leiden: Brill, 2017.
Kuecker, Aaron. *The Spirit and the "Other": Social Identity, Ethnicity and Intergroup Reconciliation in Luke-Acts*. The Library of New Testament Studies 444. London: T&T Clark, 2011.
Kwon, JiSeong James. "Re-Examining the Torah in the Book of Isaiah." *Revue Biblique* 126.4 (2019) 547–64.
Kyrychenko, Oleksandr. "The Role of the Centurion in Luke-Acts." PhD diss., Laney Graduate School of Emory University, 2013.

Lacovara, Peter. "The Land of Nubia." In *Ancient Nubia: African Kingdoms on the Nile*, edited by Marjorie M. Fisher, et al., 5–9. Cairo: The American University in Cairo Press, 2012.

Lawrence, William F., Jr. "The History of the Interpretation of Acts 8:26–40 by the Church Fathers Prior to the Fall of Rome." PhD diss., Union Theological Seminary, 1984.

Le Cornu, Hilary, and Joseph Shulam. *A Commentary on the Jewish Roots of Acts*. Vol. 1. Jerusalem: Academon, 2003.

Leith, Mary Joan Winn. "Esther (The Greek Version Containing Additional Chapters)," in *The New Oxford Annotated Apocrypha: New Revised Standard Version*, edited by Michael D. Coogan, 53–68. New York: Oxford University Press, 2010.

Lenski, R. C. H. *The Interpretation of the Acts of the Apostles*. Columbus: Wartburg, 1944.

Lessing, R. Reed. *Isaiah 56–66*. Concordia Commentary. St. Louis: Concordia, 2014.

Lev, Sarra Leah. "Genital Trouble: On the Innovations of Tannaitic Thought Regarding Damaged Genitals and Eunuchs." PhD diss., New York University, 2004.

Levine, Amy-Jill. "Tobit." In *The New Oxford Annotated Apocrypha: New Revised Standard Version*, edited by Michael D. Coogan, 11–30. New York: Oxford University Press, 2010.

Levinsohn, Stephen H. *Discourse Features of New Testament Greek: A Coursebook on the Information Structure of New Testament Greek*. 2nd ed. Dallas: SIL International, 2000.

Lightfoot, J. B. *The Acts of the Apostles: A Newly Discovered Commentary*. Lightfoot Legacy Set 1. Downers Grove, IL: InterVarsity, 2014.

Liver, J. "The Half-Shekel Offering in Biblical and Post-Biblical Literature." *Harvard Theological Review* 56.3 (July 1963) 173–98.

Loader, William. *The Dead Sea Scrolls on Sexuality: Attitudes towards Sexuality in Sectarian and Related Literature at Qumran*. Grand Rapids: Eerdmans, 2009.

Longenecker, Bruce W. *Rhetoric at the Boundaries: The Art and Theology of the New Testament Chain-Link Transitions*. Waco, TX: Baylor University Press, 2005.

Longenecker, Richard N. *Luke-Acts*. Rev. ed. The Expositor's Bible Commentary 10. Grand Rapids: Zondervan, 2007.

Lüdemann, Gerd. *Early Christianity According to the Traditions in Acts: A Commentary*. Minneapolis: Fortress, 1989.

———. *The Acts of the Apostles: What Really Happened in the Earliest Days of the Church*. New York: Prometheus, 2005.

Marguerat, Daniel. "Saul's Conversion (Acts 9, 22, 26) and the Multiplication of Narrative in Acts." In *Luke's Literary Achievement: Collected Essays*, edited by C. M. Tuckett, 127–55. Journal for the Study of the New Testament Supplement Series 116. Sheffield: Sheffield Academic, 1995.

Marshall, I. Howard. *Luke: Historian & Theologian*. 3rd ed. Downers Grove, IL: InterVarsity, 1988.

Martin, Jannette Clarice. "The Function of Acts 8:26–40 within the Narrative Structure of the Book of Acts: The Significance of the Eunuch's Provenance for Acts 1:8c." PhD diss., Duke University, 1985.

Marshall, Anthony J. "Flaccus and the Jews of Asia: Cicero 'Pro Flacco' 28.67–69." *Phoenix* 29.2 (1975) 139–54.

Maxwell, John C. *Deuteronomy*. Communicator's Commentary Series Old Testament 5. Waco, TX: Word, 1987.

McConville, J. G. *Deuteronomy*. Apollos Old Testament Commentary 5. Downers Grove, IL: InterVarsity, 2002.

Merrill, Eugene H. *Deuteronomy*. New American Commentary 4. Nashville: Broadman & Holman, 1994.

Metzger, Bruce M. *A Textual Commentary on the Greek New Testament*. 2nd ed. New York: United Bible Societies, 1994.

Moffitt, David M. "Atonement at the Right Hand: The Sacrificial Significance of Jesus' Exaltation in Acts." *New Testament Studies* 62.4 (2016) 549–68.

Muraoka, T. *A Greek-English Lexicon of the Septuagint*. Leuven: Peeters, 2009.

Nakman, David. "Josephus and Halacha." In *A Companion to Josephus*, edited by Honora Howell Chapman and Zuleika Rodgers, 282–92. Blackwell Companions to the Ancient World. Malden, MA: Wiley-Blackwell, 2016.

Neill, Stephen, and Tom Wright. *The Interpretation of the New Testament 1861–1986*. 2nd ed. Oxford: Oxford University Press, 2003.

Neusner, Jacob. *The Mishnah: A New Translation*. New Haven; London: Yale University Press, 1988.

Niccum, Curt. "One Ethiopian Eunuch Is Not the End of the World: The Narrative Function of Acts 8:26–40." In *A Teacher for All Generations: Essays in Honor of James C. VanderKam*, edited by Eric F. Mason, vol. 2, 883–900. Supplements to the Journal for the Study of Judaism 153. Leiden: Brill, 2012.

Nolland, John. *Luke 9:21–18:34*. Word Biblical Commentary 35B. Dallas: Word, 1993.

Novakovic, Lidija. "Jews and Samaritans." In *The World of the New Testament: Cultural, Social, and Historical Contexts*, edited by Joel B. Green and Lee Martin McDonald, 207–16. Grand Rapids: Baker Academic, 2013.

Nutkowicz, Hélène. "Some Aspects of Family Bonds in the Judean Community of Elephantine." In *Elephantine Revisited: New Insights in the Judean Community and Its Neighbors*, edited by Margaretha Folmer, 24–35. University Park: Eisenbrauns, 2022.

O'Connor, David. *Ancient Nubia: Egypt's Rival in Africa*. Philadelphia: University of Pennsylvania Museum of Archaeology and Anthropology, 1993.

Orian, Matan. "The Purpose of the Balustrade in the Herodian Temple." *Journal for the Study of Judaism* 51, no. 4–5 (2020) 487–524.

Oswalt, John N. *The Book of Isaiah: Chapters 40–66*. New International Commentary on the Old Testament. Grand Rapids: Eerdmans, 1998.

Pao, David W. *Acts and the Isaianic New Exodus*. Wissenschaftliche Untersuchungen zum Alten und Neuen Testament 2. Reihe 130. Tübingen: Mohr Siebeck, 2000.

Parsons, Mikeal C. *Body and Character in Luke and Acts: The Subversion of Physiognomy in Early Christianity*. Waco, TX: Baylor University Press, 2011.

———. *Luke: Storyteller, Interpreter, Evangelist*. Peabody, MA: Hendrickson, 2007.

Pervo, Richard I. *Acts: A Commentary*. Hermeneia–A Critical and Historical Commentary on the Bible. Minneapolis: Augsburg Fortress, 2009.

Peterson, David G. *The Acts of the Apostles*. Pillar New Testament Commentary. Grand Rapids: Eerdmans, 2009.

Philo. *On the Creation. Allegorical Interpretation of Genesis 2 and 3*. Translated by F. H. Colson and G. H. Whitaker. Loeb Classical Library. Cambridge: Harvard University Press, 1929.

———. *On the Decalogue. On the Special Laws, Books 1–3*. Translated by F. H. Colson. Loeb Classical Library. Cambridge: Harvard University Press, 1937.

———. *On the Special Laws, Book 4. On the Virtues. On Rewards and Punishments*. Translated by F. H. Colson. Loeb Classical Library. Cambridge: Harvard University Press, 1939.

———. *The Works of Philo: Complete and Unabridged*. Translated by C. D. Yonge. New updated ed. Peabody, MA: Hendrickson, 1993.

Pietersma, Albert, and Benjamin G. Wright, eds. *A New English Translation of the Septuagint*. New York: Oxford University Press, 2007.

Polhill, John B. *Acts*. New American Commentary 26. Nashville: Broadman & Holman, 1992.

Price, Jonathan J. "Greek Warning Sign on Temple Mount, 23 BCE–70 CE." In *Corpus Inscriptionum Iudaeae/Palaestinae: A Multi-Lingual Corpus of the Inscriptions from Alexander to Muhammad*, edited by Hannah M. Cotton, et al., vol. 1, *Jerusalem, Part 1:1–704*, 42–45. Berlin: de Gruyter, 2010.

Propp, William H. C. *Exodus 1–18: A New Translation with Introduction and Commentary*. Anchor Bible 2. New York: Doubleday, 1998.

Pucci, Joseph. *The Full-Knowing Reader: Allusion and the Power of the Reader in the Western Literary Tradition*. New Haven, CT: Yale University Press, 1998.

Puskas, Charles B., and David Crump. *An Introduction to the Gospels and Acts*. Grand Rapids: Eerdmans, 2008.

Rabinowitz, Yoseif, trans. *Seder Nashim Vol. I(a)*: מסכת יבמות *Tractate Yevamos*. Edited by Rabbi Yehezkel Danziger. Artscroll Mishnah Series: A Rabbinic Commentary to the Six Orders of the Mishnah. New York: Mesorah, 1984.

Read-Heimerdinger, Jenny. "Acts." In *Discourse Analysis of the New Testament Writings*, edited by Todd A. Scacewater, 159–92. Dallas: Fontes, 2020.

Rebell, Walter. "χειροποίητος." In *Exegetical Dictionary of the New Testament*, edited by Horst Balz and Gerhard Schneider, vol. 3, 464. Grand Rapids: Eerdmans, 1993.

Regev, Eyal. *The Temple in Early Christianity: Experiencing the Sacred*. Anchor Yale Bible Reference Library. New Haven; London: Yale University Press, 2019.

Reich, Keith A. *Figuring Jesus: The Power of Rhetorical Figures of Speech in the Gospel of Luke*. Biblical Interpretation Series 107. Leiden: Brill, 2011.

Renz, Thomas. *The Books of Nahum, Habakkuk, and Zephaniah*. New International Commentary on the Old Testament. Grand Rapids: Eerdmans, 2021.

Resseguie, James L. "The Woman Who Crashed Simon's Party: A Reader-Response Approach to Luke 7:36–50." In *Characters and Characterization in Luke-Acts*, edited by Frank Dicken and Julia Snyder, 7–22. The Library of New Testament Studies 548. London: Bloomsbury, 2016.

———. *Narrative Criticism of the New Testament: An Introduction*. Grand Rapids: Baker Academic, 2005.

Rhamie, Gifford Charles Alphaeus. "Whiteness, Conviviality and Agency: The Ethiopian Eunuch (Acts 8:26–40) and Conceptuality in the Imperial Imagination of Biblical Studies." PhD diss., Canterbury Christ Church University, 2019.

Rhodes, James N. "Tabernacle and Temple: Rethinking the Rhetorical Function of Acts 7:44–50." In *Contemporary Studies in Acts*, edited by Thomas E. Phillips, 119–37: Mercer University Press, 2009.

Roloff, Jürgen. *Die Apostelgeschichte*. Das Neue Testament Deutsch 5. Göttingen: Vandenhoeck & Ruprecht, 1981.

Rom-Shiloni, Dalit. *Exclusive Inclusivity: Identity Conflicts between the Exiles and the People Who Remained (6th–5th Centuries BCE)*. Library of Hebrew Bible/Old Testament Studies 543. London: Bloomsbury, 2013.

Ross, Allen P. *Creation and Blessing: A Guide to the Study and Exposition of Genesis*. Grand Rapids: Baker, 1998.

Safrai, S. "Relations between the Diaspora and the Land of Israel." In *The Jewish People in the First Century: Historical Geography, Political History, Social, Cultural and Religious Life and Institutions*, edited by S. Safrai, et al., vol. 1, 184–215. Compendia Rerum Iudaicarum ad Novum Testamentum. Assen: Van Gorcum, 1974.

Sailhamer, John H. "Genesis." In *Genesis-Leviticus*. Rev. ed., 21–331. The Expositor's Bible Commentary 1. Grand Rapids: Zondervan, 2008.

Schnabel, Eckhard J. *Acts*. Zondervan Exegetical Commentary on the New Testament. Grand Rapids: Zondervan, 2012.

Schmidt, Karl Matthias. "Bekehrung zur Zerstreuung: Paulus und der äthiopische Eunuch im Kontext der lukanischen Diasporatheologie." *Biblica* 88.2 (2007) 191–213.

Schneider, Johannes. "εὐνοῦχος, εὐνουχίζω." In *Theological Dictionary of the New Testament*, edited by Gerhard Kittel and Gerhard Friedrich, translated by Geoffrey W. Bromiley, vol. 2, 765–68. Grand Rapids: Eerdmans, 1964.

Schnittjer, Gary E. "The Bad Ending of Ezra-Nehemiah." *Bibliotheca Sacra* 173 (Jan–Mar 2016) 32–56.

———. *Old Testament Use of Old Testament: A Book-by-Book Guide*. Grand Rapids: Zondervan, 2021.

Scholz, Piotr O. *Eunuchs and Castrati: A Cultural History*. Translated by John A. Broadwin and Shelley L. Frisch. Princeton, NJ: Markus Wiener, 2001.

Schramm, Brooks. *The Opponents of Third Isaiah: Reconstructing the Cultic History of the Restoration*. Journal for the Study of the Old Testament Supplement Series 193. Sheffield: Sheffield Academic, 1995.

Schüle, Andreas. "Eine Tora für Fremde und Eunuchen: Jesaja 56,1–8 als prophetische Gesetzgebung." In *Nachstenliebe und Gottesfurcht: Beitrage aus alttestamentlicher, semitistischer und altorientalistischer Wissenschaft für Hans-Peter Mathys zum 65. Geburtstag*, edited by Hanna Jenni and Markus Saur, 435–50. Alter Orient und Altes Testament 439. Münster: Ugarit-Verlag, 2016.

Schwartz, Daniel R. "2 Maccabees." In *The New Oxford Annotated Apocrypha: New Revised Standard Version*, edited by Michael D. Coogan, 241–75. New York: Oxford University Press, 2010.

Shepherd, William H., Jr. *The Narrative Function of the Holy Spirit as a Character in Luke-Acts*. Atlanta: Scholars, 1994.

Sleeman, Matthew. *Geography and the Ascension Narrative in Acts*. Society for New Testament Studies Monograph Series 146. Cambridge: Cambridge University Press, 2009.

Smith, Cooper. *Allusive and Elusive: Allusion and the Elihu Speeches of Job 32–37*. Biblical Interpretation 198. Leiden: Brill, 2022.

Smith, Gary. *Isaiah 40–66*. New American Commentary 15B. Nashville: Broadman & Holman, 2009.

Smith, Steve. *The Fate of the Jerusalem Temple in Luke–Acts: An Intertextual Approach to Jesus' Laments Over Jerusalem and Stephen's Speech*. The Library of New Testament Studies 553. London: Bloomsbury T&T Clark, 2017.

Snowden, Frank M., Jr. *Blacks in Antiquity: Ethiopians in the Greco-Roman Experience*. Cambridge, MA: Harvard University Press, 1970.

Southwood, Katherine E. "The 'Foreigner' and the Eunuch: The Politics of Belonging in Isaiah 56:1–8." *Biblical Interpretation* 30.4 (2022) 437–59.

Spencer, F. Scott. *Journeying through Acts: A Literary-Cultural Reading*. Peabody, MA: Hendrickson, 2004.

Sperber, Dan, and Deirdre Wilson. *Relevance: Communication and Cognition*. 2nd ed. Malden, MA: Blackwell, 1995.

Stachow, Mary Ann. "'Do You Understand What You Are Reading?' (Acts 8:30): A Historical-Critical Reexamination of the Pericope of Philip and the Ethiopian (Acts 8:26–40)." PhD diss., Catholic University of America, 1998.

Stein, Robert H. *Luke*. New American Commentary 24. Nashville: Broadman, 1992.

Sternberg, Meir. *The Poetics of Biblical Narrative: Ideological Literature and the Drama of Reading*. Indiana Studies in Biblical Literature. Bloomington: Indiana University Press, 1985.

Strabo. *The Geography of Strabo*. Translated by Horace Leonard Jones. Vol. 1, *Books I–II*. Loeb Classical Library. 1917. Reprint. Cambridge: Harvard University Press, 1960.

Stromberg, Jacob. *Isaiah after Exile: The Author of Third Isaiah as Reader and Redactor of the Book*. Oxford Theological Monographs. Oxford: Oxford University Press, 2011.

Suetonius. *Suetonius*. Translated by J. C. Rolfe. Vol. 2. Loeb Classical Library. 1914. Reprint. Cambridge: Harvard University Press, 1992.

Sweeney, James P. "Stephen's Speech (Acts 7:2–53): Is It as 'Anti-Temple' as Is Frequently Alleged?" *Trinity Journal* 23.2 (2002) 185–210.

Sweeney, Marvin A. *Zephaniah*. Hermeneia–A Critical and Historical Commentary on the Bible. Minneapolis: Augsburg Fortress, 2003.

Sweet, J. P. M. "A House Not Made with Hands." In *Templum Amicitiae: Essays on the Second Temple Presented to Ernst Bammel*, edited by William Horbury, 368–90. Journal for the Study of the New Testament Supplement Series 48. Sheffield: Sheffield Academic, 1991.

Tacitus. *Annals*. Translated by John Jackson. Vol. 3, *Books IV–VI, XI–XII*. Loeb Classical Library. Cambridge: Harvard University Press, 1937.

Talbert, Charles H. *Reading Acts: A Literary and Theological Commentary on the Acts of the Apostles*. Macon, GA: Smyth & Helwys, 2005.

Tannehill, Robert C. *The Narrative Unity of Luke-Acts: A Literary Interpretation*. Vol. 1, *The Gospel According to Luke*. Philadephia: Fortress, 1986.

———. *The Narrative Unity of Luke-Acts: A Literary Interpretation*. Vol. 2, *The Acts of the Apostles*. Minneapolis: Augsburg Fortress, 1990.

Thiessen, Matthew. "Geneology, Circumcision and Conversion in Early Judaism and Christianity." PhD diss., Duke University, 2010.

———. "Revisiting the προσήλυτος in 'the LXX.'" *Journal of Biblical Literature* 132.2 (2013) 333–50.

Thompson, Alan J. *The Acts of the Risen Lord Jesus: Luke's Account of God's Unfolding Plan*. New Studies in Biblical Theology 27. Downers Grove, IL: InterVarsity, 2011.

Thompson, John A. *Deuteronomy: An Introduction and Commentary*. Tyndale Old Testament Commentaries. London: InterVarsity, 1974.

Tigay, Jeffrey H. *Deuteronomy* דברים: *The Traditional Hebrew Text with the New JPS Translation*. JPS Torah Commentary. Philadelphia: Jewish Publication Society of America, 1996.
Trevaskis, Leigh M. *Holiness, Ethics and Ritual in Leviticus*. Hebrew Bible Monographs 29. Sheffield: Sheffield Phoenix, 2011.
Vargon, Shmuel. "The Blind and the Lame." *Vetus Testamentum* 46.4 (1996) 498–514.
Vlaardingerbroek, Johannes. *Zephaniah*. Historical Commentary on the Old Testament. Leuven: Peeters, 1999.
van der Toorn, Karel. *Becoming Diaspora Jews: Behind the Story of Elephantine*. Anchor Yale Bible Reference Library. New Haven; London: Yale University Press, 2019.
Van Tine, R. Jarrett. "Castration for the Kingdom and Avoiding the αἰτία of Adultery (Matthew 19:10–12)." *Journal of Biblical Literature* 137.2 (2018) 399–418.
von Dobbeler, Axel. *Der Evangelist Philippus in der Geschichte des Urchristentums: Eine prosopographische Skizze*. Texte und Arbeiten zum neutestamentlichen Zeitalter 30. Tübingen; Basel: Francke, 2000.
von Rad, Gerhard. *Deuteronomy: A Commentary*. Old Testament Library. Philadelphia: Westminster, 1966.
von Weissenberg, Hanne. "Deuteronomy at Qumran and in MMT." In *Houses Full of All Good Things: Essays in Memory of Timo Veijola*, edited by Juha Pakkala and Martti Nissinen, 520–37. Publications of the Finnish Exegetical Society 95. Göttingen: Vandenhoeck & Ruprecht, 2008.
Walker, Peter W. L. *Jesus and the Holy City: New Testament Perspectives on Jerusalem*. Grand Rapids: Eerdmans, 1996.
Wallace, Daniel B. *Greek Grammar Beyond the Basics*. Grand Rapids: Zondervan, 1996.
Waltke, Bruce K., and Michael O'Connor. *An Introduction to Biblical Hebrew Syntax*. Winona Lake, IN: Eisenbrauns, 1990.
Walton, Steve. "A Tale of Two Perspectives? The Place of the Temple in Acts." In *Heaven on Earth*, edited by T. Desmond Alexander and Simon Gathercole, 135–49. Carlisle, Cumbria: Paternoster, 2004.
Wearne, Gareth. "Linguistic Remarks on the Unity of 4QMMT and Its Implications for Hebrew in the Last Second Temple Period." *Revue de Qumran* 33.1 (2021) 61–91.
Widengren, Geo. "Yahweh's Gathering of the Dispersed." In *In the Shelter of Elyon: Essays on Ancient Palestinian Life and Literature in Honour of G. W. Ahlström*, edited by W. Boyd Barrick, Gösta W. Ahlström, and John R. Spencer, 227–45. Journal for the Study of the Old Testament Supplement Series 31. Sheffield: JSOT, 1984.
Williams, Margaret H. "Palestinian Jewish Personal Names in Acts." In *The Book of Acts in Its Palestinian Setting*, edited by Richard Bauckham, 79–113. The Book of Acts in Its First Century Setting 4. Grand Rapids: Eerdmans, 1995.
Williamson, H. G. M. *A Critical and Exegetical Commentary on Isaiah 1–27*. Vol. 2. International Critical Commentary. London; New York: Bloomsbury T&T Clark, 2018.
Wills, Lawrence M. "Judith." In *The New Oxford Annotated Apocrypha: New Revised Standard Version*, edited by Michael D. Coogan, 31–51. New York: Oxford University Press, 2010.
Wilson, Deirdre, and Dan Sperber. *Meaning and Relevance*. Cambridge: Cambridge University Press, 2012.

Wilson, Walter T., ed. and trans. *Philo of Alexandria: On Virtues: Introduction, Translation, and Commentary*. Philo of Alexandria Commentary Series 3. Leiden: Brill, 2011.

Wise, Michael, Martin Abegg Jr., and Edward Cook, trans. *The Dead Sea Scrolls: A New Translation*. San Francisco: HarperOne, 2005.

Witherington, Ben, III. *The Acts of the Apostles: Socio-Rhetorical Commentary*. Grand Rapids: Eerdmans, 1998.

Won, Young-Sam. *Remembering the Covenants in Song: An Intertextual Study of the Abrahamic and Mosaic Covenants in Psalm 105*. Eugene, OR: Wipf & Stock, 2019.

Woods, Edward J. *Deuteronomy: An Introduction and Commentary*. Tyndale Old Testament Commentaries 5. Downers Grove, IL: InterVarsity, 2011.

Wright, N. T. *Acts for Everyone, Vol. 1, Chapters 1–12*. New Testament for Everyone. Louisville: Westminster John Knox, 2008.

——— . *Luke for Everyone*. New Testament for Everyone. London: SPCK, 2001.

Xenophon. *Cyropaedia*. Translated by Walter Miller. Vol. 2. Loeb Classical Library. 1914. Reprint. Cambridge: Harvard University Press, 1961.

Yamauchi, Edwin M. *Africa and the Bible*. Grand Rapids: Baker Academic, 2004.

——— . "Ezra and Nehemiah." In *1 Chronicles-Job*. Rev. ed. *The Expositor's Bible Commentary* 4. 337–568. Grand Rapids: Zondervan, 2010.

Yellin, Janice W. "Naqa." In *Ancient Nubia: African Kingdoms on the Nile*, edited by Marjorie M. Fisher, et al., 230–37. Cairo: The American University in Cairo Press, 2012.

Zerwick, Max, and Mary Grosvenor. *A Grammatical Analysis of the Greek New Testament*. 5th ed. Rome: Editrice Pontificio Istituto Biblico, 1996.

www.ingramcontent.com/pod-product-compliance
Lightning Source LLC
Chambersburg PA
CBHW062043220426
43662CB00010B/1636